moving toward a new society

Susanne Gowan
George Lakey
William Moyer
Richard Taylor

NEW SOCIETY PRESS
PHILADELPHIA

Library of Congress
Catalog Card Number: 75-30449

Published by New Society Press

Copies available from:

Movement for a New Society
4722 Baltimore Avenue
Philadelphia, PA 19143

First Printing, January, 1976 - 5,000
Second Printing, May, 1976 - 5,000
Third Printing, November, 1976 - 5,000
Fourth Printing, May, 1979 - 5,000

Because this book is
about what it takes to
create a new society –
courage, gentleness, vision,
struggle, hope– we
remember our friends
Eli Hochstedler
 & Tom Coats
through whose lives shone
the vitality & joy of
revolution. We celebrate
the knowing of them.

Acknowledgments

Sue Carroll, who as one of the original authors of this project, contributed significantly to its content and direction until her interests and political thought took her to other work.

Wendell Hendricks who generously donated his services as typesetter and gave his support and enthusiasm.

Robert Irwin who began work with this book as a proofreader and whose editorial advice and attention to detail greatly enriched the project.

Tom Brown who patiently worked with suggestions and proposals in designing the cover of the book.

The many people who read the various drafts of this book and took the time to make comments that helped in shaping the final version.

Members of the Philadelphia Life Center who have worked with the book since its beginning offering valuable thinking, advice, and encouragement.

TABLE OF CONTENTS

1

Introduction

This book is about the ills of today's society and how we might move toward a new one.

In its original draft, *Revolution: Quaker Prescription for a Sick Society,* this book dealt with the sickness that the authors see in American society and with proposals for how it might be made well. We have retained the medical metaphor. It is an adequate image for how we have come to think and talk about how things are and what must be done.

The authors grew up supposing that our country was in fairly good shape, although it needed changes here and there. We now believe that our society is desperately ill; it needs a sound program of treatment if it is to avoid collapse.

No live individual is so completely sick that there are no areas of good health remaining. So, also, a society may be extremely ill but still retain some aspects of health until its ultimate death. We know that there is some good health still in America, and we hope that recovery can be built on that.

As there is no such thing as a completely healthy individual, there too, are potential illnesses in any society, no matter how apparently healthy. Our prescription, therefore, for the U.S. is no more a remedy for complete social health than a doctor's medicine is a promise of total individual well-being.

The wise worker for social change recognizes that "revolution" is a continuing process rather than a once-and-for-all transformation. The freshness of the new beginning, brought by fundamental structural change, can go sour for any number of reasons. But accepting that humans do not live in a world of absolutes—total sickness, perfect prescriptions, complete healthiness—we are nevertheless determined to join the many people who, both in this country and outside it, are struggling for basic change.

Struggling in the sixties

The authors of this book come from different backgrounds, but have at least one thing strongly in common: as young people we caught a glimpse of the potential of American democracy. Whether from high school teachers, family influences, or religious training we were convinced that the American experiment was brave and could be beautiful.

In the 1960's we found the United States in deep distress over moral, political, and economic issues. Black leadership, with a new sense of urgency, was calling citizens to awareness of injustices of racial discrimination and repression. The first of the American combat troops were introduced into Southeast Asia, making it possible for massive escalation of the Indochina War in 1965. National tensions rose and polarization became more prevalent. Democracy depends on citizens acting, and we did. We, along with hundreds of others, attempted to focus in on places where our work might make effective changes. Some of us worked with Martin Luther King, Jr., and other leaders of the civil rights movement. Some of us gave energies and time to anti-war efforts. We did community organizing in the city and suburbs. We came to know, in a variety of settings, the struggle for change in the nineteen-sixties and early nineteen-seventies.

"The Movement," as we used to call it (and sometimes still do) reflected America itself. The bravery was

there when people faced the helicopters and guns of
police and army. The music and symbols of affection
expressed the "soul" of the struggle. Innovation—both
organizational and analytic—was the character of the New
Left; even after some of that freshness wore off, many
activists were still daring to find new ways to cope with
new situations rather than falling back on the formulas of
the past.

Conflict of citizens with their government often
brings about a predictable response. Thousands of U.S.
citizens went to jail for protesting the Viet Nam war.
Peace groups were increasingly hampered by the infiltration of government agent provocateurs. The federal government put thousands of tax dollars into the harassment
and prosecution of well-known citizens such as Benjamin
Spock and William Sloan Coffin. Senator Sam Ervin
publicly chaffed at the increased military-intelligence
investigation of citizens. Even under the tension of
repression, when it was hard to do anything but maneuv-
er and manipulate, movement people could be found who
were honest and direct.

Also like America in general, movement people were
usually impatient and without a sense of history. Activists expected the instant remedies of consumer culture
to be found in political struggle as well. Anti-war people
usually failed to connect their moral outrage to the very
real grounds of their own oppression, and so came across
as strident and self-righteous.

Also reflecting life in the United States, struggle for
change involved people from clashing sub-cultures. Earn-
est black college students, white hippies, Wall Street
brokers, industrial workers, feminists, atheists, priests—
these and many more, made up the pluralist stew of
movement life. There was little coherence. Seeking was
often deafened by derision, flexible rationality over-
whelmed by rigid posturing. Like America, the thrust and
character of the movement kept changing in spite of
itself; reaction was more typical than planned initiative.

The accent was on protest; a saying "no" to powers
that take away our right of moral choice. But this saying

"no", however powerful, however necessary, or however good, might have played into the growing nihilism of Western culture. Everywhere there was a falling back, a "dropping-out" of those institutions previously held unimpeachable. Church attendance dropped, students increasingly became disenchanted with college, clergy became demoralized. In addition, alcoholism and drug addictions were on the rise and tranquilizer sales increased. Our plays, our poetry, our music often reflected emptiness and despair. Barely beneath the superficial glitter of our culture lay the evidences of a loss of hope in the person's ability to make a difference. Protest alone cannot support our need for affirmation and life. People are searching for some faith to live by, and yet traditional symbols are becoming empty and bereft of meaning for most persons. With our energies being poured into the protest that was necessary to focus attention on critical issues, little time or vigor was left for alternatives. Until quite recently few movement people worked on alternatives, either for the massive structures which need to be replaced, or even in their lives right now.

Working for positive change: an American tradition

Historians picture the United States as a dynamic country for good reason: it has been moving and changing and growing throughout its life. Much of that is negative, of course—stealing land from Indians, Mexicans, and others; exhausting resources; building an agricultural system on the backs of slaves; and exploiting the cheap work force provided by women. But that dynamism is also in the tradition of dissent and social change.

The campaign to abolish slavery is still an inspiration to many Americans who believe that evil institutions *can* be done away with. Sojourner Truth, Frederick Douglass, and the other abolitionists were not impressed by the argument that slavery is part of human nature, any more than we should be impressed by the variations on the argument which are still around today. One of the heroes of that campaign, William Lloyd Garrison, publically burned the American flag to demonstrate his conviction that the flag should represent freedom, not the brutality and suppression of slavery.

In the period after the civil war, working people discovered the boycott. After the bloodiness of the 1860's, they found it exhilarating to use means of struggle which did not require weapons. Socialism was in the air since the terrible poverty and exploitation produced by expanding industry could be seen everywhere; but these new ideas of social order were matched by innovation in protest. Not only were workers using the boycott, but blacks were conducting freedom rides on St. Louis streetcars and Susan B. Anthony was committing civil disobedience for the right to vote.

The White House was first picketed by the woman suffrage movement. These feminists of the early 1900's suffered beatings at the hands of men and frequent jailings. (The anti-suffrage men argued that women were too tender to endure the rough and tumble of politics; it is not clear why they thought women were tough enough to be beaten on the street and made wage-slaves in the sweatshops of industry.) Today, woman's right to vote seems obvious, and the dispute has shifted to other aspects of her fight to assert full personhood.

Of course, all those campaigns and books and study groups were limited by their times. It was not possible then to achieve freedom and dignity for people, to abolish slums, poverty, war, and discrimination. Economic and political inequality had not then been allowed to become public issues. Helen Keller and many other great Americans argued that the profit motive of capitalism was in contradiction with the needs of people. The wisdom of visionaries like Helen Keller did not have a chance to be understood at that time. Our chance now is to continue that tradition of questioning, of seeking, and of understanding our own experience while working in the dynamism that is America.

Analysis out of action

One of the characteristics of humans is the ability to learn from experience. The child learns that something cannot be done by one way but by another. Based on this information, s/he tries yet another way. Soon the reasoning process opens up more and more possibilities. One of the ways social change happens is by persons focusing on an issue that is important to them, acting on it, evaluating what happened, analyzing the meaning and significance of the events in relation to other events, and then moving on to more action.

The authors started to write this book as a study group of AQAG (*A Quaker Action Group*), and our motivation stems partly from the experience of AQAG in its work for peace and justice.

AQAG began in 1966 to use nonviolent direct action for confronting violence and injustice, both in America and abroad. In the voyages of the sailing ship *Phoenix* which carried medical supplies to North and South Viet Nam, in the reading of the names of the Viet Nam war dead on the Capitol steps, in the commitment to the Poor People's Campaign in 1968, in supporting the struggle of the Puerto Rican people against the target practice of the U.S. Navy on Culebra, AQAG tried to develop a long-term commitment and a willingness to suffer in the struggle for truth.

Like other organizations working in the 1960's, AQAG found it remarkably difficult to advance peace and justice in the American system. With each movement victory, the system strongly resisted further change. Movement set-backs were frequent.

Each evil which we saw could be superficially interpreted as the result of an irrationality or of a vested interest within a basically good system. Consequently, our campaigns were shallow and failed to get to the roots of the problems. Our perspective was limited and we became aware that we were not in a position to wage the kind of campaign which was necessary to confront the underlying disease of our society. We had to find a way to delve deeper to the roots of those problems of society against which we and others were struggling. Our work had been good, but we were now ready to move on.

We had come to the place where we had to question the presuppositions upon which our political-economic system is built. Our concrete experience in moving into the arena of social change with our whole lives required a commitment to analysis. We needed to see more clearly where those critical ills of society were and how we might further act on them.

Action out of analysis

When *A Quaker Action Group* was laid down in 1971, many of its members joined with others to form a decentralized network of social change groups called the *Movement for a New Society*. The groups, which represent a variety of religious and humanist convictions, agree that a one-dimensional approach to change is not enough. An authentically radical movement should combine struggle with personal sharing and support for the participants; should link analysis with development of alternative institutions. Social change activists should integrate vision with a strategy for getting to that vision, and training in skills with living the new values now.

In the summer of 1971, while the Movement for a New Society network was beginning, three of the authors were in a study group called a *Macroanalysis Seminar*. We were studying the relationship of the U.S. economy and government to the Third World. Hearing about the massacres in East Pakistan we did further research and discovered that Pakistan was one of the many military dictatorships supported by the United States. The West Pakistani government was at that very time relying on U.S. shipments of arms and massive economic support in pursuing its policy of suppressing the people of East Pakistan.

The Macroanalysis Seminar grew and became an action group, launching a canoe blockade of ships carrying supplies to West Pakistan. The group talked with

members of the International Longshoremen's Association to enlist their support. The result was the complete
closing of the Port of Philadelphia to West Pakistani ships
and the refusal of Longshoremen to load arms for West
Pakistan anywhere in the United States.

Continued thinking about the United States political
economy led the authors to see the web which relates the
industrial giants to the Pentagon, and both to the depletion of Earth's resources. As we learned more about the
distribution of wealth in this country we began to
connect the boondoggles for military corporations with
the poverty of millions of Americans.

That study led to another Movement for a New
Society group which raises fundamental questions
through focus on the proposed B-1 bomber. The B-1 is an
ecological threat, a terror-weapon for the Third World,
and an example of the power and wealth of the military-
industrial complex. While opposing the B-1 we can
increase awareness of the sickness of American society
and also propose a better way: peace conversion. Having
learned from the nineteen-sixties that piecemeal change is
not enough, we go beyond economic conversion to
include change of the lines of power, change of foreign
policy, and an end to exploiting the Earth.

The Movement for a New Society network, then, is
closely connected with some of the ideas in this book.
One of those ideas is that there will be no radical change
without radical consciousness. Intellectual work is one
dimension of that consciousness. This book is one of the
pieces of thought and analysis that MNS people are
doing. Many thousands of copies of this book in various
mimeographed drafts have already been used by individuals, study groups, and colleges; the feedback has been
part of the revision process which resulted in the present
book.

We are well aware of the limitations of this book; we
have left out important areas of human life and change
because we had little new to say or were unclear without
doing much more research. We are also limited by our
own background: although two of us are working class in

origin, we are, after all, white Americans. Because this book was orginally a limited edition draft, we were not concerned that four authors, with other contributors, might not have as smooth an approach as a single author. Our main concern then, as it is now, was to say what we felt was important and to get this into the hands of those concerned individuals who are already working in social change or are asking how they might begin to make a difference. Some things are said several times. Some things are mentioned but given short shift. We accept these shortcomings and encourage others to take up the work and continue reflecting, sharing, writing, and exploring new ideas. During the five long years of work, a number of people have been co-workers with us, and we have benefited from the lively dialogue in response to previous drafts.

The dialogue, the sharing, the common struggle remind each of us that we are not alone. History tells us that we come from a rich tradition of critics and visionaries whose contributions serve as a model for us all. Over two thousand years ago wandering Hebrew prophets expressed in fiery words the fullness of a just society. Jesus, born of the same people, showed in his simple and courageous life style what a truly liberated person is like. He was angry with hypocrisy and injustice not because he was neurotically driven but because he loved freely; he rebelled not because he was willful but because he was psychologically free to respond to the social situation of his time. Jesus asked his followers to struggle for a kingdom in which the oppressed are liberated and human needs are met.

From diagnosis to prescription

For those with a commitment to fundamental social change, then, caring is not enough. Knowing the problem is not enough. Action alone is not enough. A strategy without resolve is not enough. We must be able to move from the diagnosis to the prescription for the patient to have a chance at good health.

In order to make a diagnosis of the illness, medical workers examine the patient for symptoms; they can notice the symptoms because they have some clarity about what good health looks like. In Chapter Two we share our picture of good social health. We then document, in Chapter Three, some of the symptoms of America's sickness. Each symptom would require a book in itself; in fact, several have been written, some referred to in our footnotes.

Part II, the diagnosis, is in three chapters. In Chapter Four, "Environmental Crisis", we describe a major new awareness which should influence the tradition of radical thought. Chapter Five focuses on the intimate relationship of the functions of the American economy to those of the Third World. We hardly stretch a point to call that chapter "The Exported Plague". In "Anatomy of the Political Economy" we reach behind the headlines to sketch the underlying framework of wealth and economic power.

What is our vision of a new society? Blueprinting is not appropriate at this point, but we know that clarity about our goals helps to clarify the work we should be doing now. We hope that all the groups working for change will put forward their visions of an egalitarian, just society, out of their own experience and research. A healthy radical movement will involve dialogue among various segments on particular visions, and in time some consensus may emerge.

Part III, Prescription, states some of our vision: what a just economic system might look like; how an America which learned how to live without its disease could contribute to the health of the world; what a sensitive body politic would look like; and how global conflict will be dealt with.

Finally, having examined, diagnosed, and prescribed for these ailing institutions, we suggest a program of treatment. Treatment begins, in Part IV, with a scenario describing in narrative form how forces might mobilize for change. Since the scenario is full of conflict, the question naturally arises, "Why not armed struggle?"

After that discussion, we state the organizing principles behind our strategy. A separate chapter is devoted to the old controversy of "reform versus revolution." In the last chapter we become more personal again, bringing change back to the center of our own lives. The authors share some of their own experiences and point out other models which provide exciting alternatives of effecting social change. We attempt to point out those areas which need attention—our own weaknesses as well as society's. The easiest thing in social change is to become arrogant; an antidote to that poison is to challenge ourselves to change.

Think and act; act and think

If there is one thing in our own experience that we most want to share, it is the combination of action and analysis. The "paralysis of analysis" which frequently afflicts intellectuals is as unfortunate as the knee-jerk response of mindless activism. A living revolution provides a third way—the erosion of old divisions of labor and function; a work style of integrity, of oneness, which releases energy and makes us grow.

We wish for every reader a loving, non-competitive atmosphere in which you can break down your own dependencies on the decaying Old Order and take up the intellectual and action challenges of creation—the struggle for a new society.

Part I: Examination

2

Aspects of a Healthy Society

Many Americans look upon the United States as the world's healthiest nation. Observers point to its large GNP, broad program of higher education, low death rate, and democratic institutions as measures of its success. Also noted are its eradication of many diseases, high per capita income, freedom of expression, large foreign aid program, and application of technology. Even America's poor have high levels of consumption compared with the majority of people in the poor nations.

But *is* the United States really well? Or is it deathly ill? Here are some criteria we would consider basic to a healthy society; in the following chapters we will compare the United States, and the U.S. roles in the world, with these standards in making an assessment of the need for change.

- *Physical security:* Everyone has adequate food, clothing, shelter, and health care. Each person's basic physical needs are met, and there is adequate production to meet these needs.
- *Equality:* There are no rich as well as no poor; social benefits, social services, and social costs are spread as evenly as possible to everyone, without distinctions based on race, sex, or religion.
- *Non-exploitation:* Personal income is based on an individual's work and needs, rather than on passive ownership.

- *Work:* There is opportunity to develop and express one's own skills, talents, thought, and creativity. People are not alienated from their work, but take pride in it as a contribution to mutual social well-being.
- *Democracy:* People have the opportunity to participate in making the decisions that affect them, whether in the community, the workplace, the larger society, or the world. An important measure of new social and economic structures is whether those structures facilitate participation or inhibit it. Even in large structures consensus, rather than slim majorities, is sought.
- *Wholeness:* Spiritual well-being, personal growth, and loving relationships are valued more than material possessions.
- *Community:* A desire for mutual well-being replaces the driving motive of profit maximization. Interpersonal and community cooperation take precedence over individualism and competition. People are valued as people, rather than being categorized and put into hierarchies according to race, sex, class, and age.
- *Freedom:* Freedom is defined as the right, not to exploit or oppress others, but to develop and communicate ideas, to change occupations, to worship, and to organize for social purposes—including fundamental change.
- *Conflict:* Conflict is accepted as a natural part of life. The prevailing style of dealing with conflict involves openness and direct communication between opposing points of view, in the spirit of seeking the truth in the situation. Participants may practice non-cooperation or accept self-suffering as a means of pressing for a just resolution. The intent is to win people over, not to win over them.
- *Ecological harmony:* Humankind lives in balance with the natural environment and conserves natural resources. There is a deep concern for the survival of future generations. Planned use of resources to serve

human needs, not aggregate growth of output, is sought. The different cultures of the world share techniques for minimizing waste.

- *World community:* The needs and desires of the world community take precedence over national or local interests. People consider themselves world citizens rather than national citizens. There is no political or economic domination of one area of the world by another; instead all people enjoy equally the highest quality of life possible within the limitations of resources and environment.

We realize that the reader may differ with us on one or another of these values. We have tried to make them explicit in order to examine today's America from a clear value perspective.

The values—or criteria of societal health—outlined in this chapter, are intended to be in some sense realizable. While they are perhaps a long way off for most societies today, they seem to us to be approachable. That is, we do not intend a mere exercise in the following chapters, comparing the U.S. society with pie-in-the-sky ideals that are hopeless of achievement. We will mention in the course of the book societies that begin to embody some of these values today, and we will attempt to sketch a vision of a more healthy society that could be built out of our own.

3

Symptoms of
a Diseased Society

If we look at the U.S. today in light of the criteria of health spelled out in the previous chapter, it is clear that we live in a sick society. In this chapter we will mention a few of the most obvious symptoms of ill health.

Item: In spite of the New Frontier, the Great Society, and the War on Poverty, the U.S. Census Bureau reported 25.5 million Americans living in "official" *poverty* in 1970.[1] One in every ten Americans (one in every 3 blacks) lives in official poverty—the same as was estimated at the turn of the century. However, the official poverty line has probably been set too low; certainly many families with incomes above the poverty line cannot afford necessities. Even the average factory production worker earns less than the Labor Department's "low" urban budget for a family of four, $7,214.[2]

Item: Good *medical care* is beyond the reach of millions of Americans. Medicare covers less than half of the medical bills of the elderly.[3] Those under 65 who have medical insurance find that it meets only 22% of their medical expenses.[4] Because of gaps in insurance coverage and the high cost of hospitalization and treatment, many families are wiped out financially by sickness. In many health indices, the U.S. is far worse than other nations: we rank 18th in the risk of infant mortality (just above Hong Kong),[5] 18th in male life expectancy, and 11th in female life expectancy.[6]

Item: Millions of our *aged* are left destitute and lonely as they come to their later years; nursing home care is a national disgrace. One of every four elderly Americans lives in poverty![7]

Item: Within the U.S., the top 2% of the population own as much *wealth* as the bottom 94%, and the top 10% of the population have as much *income* as the bottom 50%.[8]

Item: *Taxation* does not significantly alter the imbalance of income distribution. Federal income taxes only slightly reduce the percentage of income received by the richest 20% of the population—from 45.5% to 43.7%[9]—while state and local taxes are clearly regressive. 1,338 persons with adjusted gross incomes in excess of $50,000 a year paid no federal income tax in 1970.[10] A whopping 40% of U.S. corporations pay *no federal income tax.*[11]

Item: Economic *discrimination* against blacks and women continues. In 1970 the median income for full-time year-round workers was $9,615 for white men, $6,435 for black men, $5,536 for white women, and $4,447 for black women.[12] This represented a decrease in women's income as a proportion of men's from 64% in 1955 to 59% in 1970.[13]

Item: Tax "expenditures" made by the federal government through *tax loopholes,* or preferences (e.g., capital gains, tax-free state and local bonds, preferences to home-owners, etc.), are a form of "welfare" distributed disproportionately to the rich. The three thousand American families with incomes over $1 million got an estimated $2.2 billion in 1972 from tax preferences, while the six million families with incomes under $3,000 got only $92 million. For families with incomes over $1 million the tax "welfare" amounted to $14,000 a week additional income, as compared to 30¢ a week for families with incomes under $3,000.[14]

Item: The private profit system enables some Americans to earn tremendous incomes based not on their own work but on their already acquired wealth. David Packard, during his three years as Deputy Secretary of Defense, earned $23 million in *profits and dividends* from his stock in the Hewlett-Packard Company (which, in accordance with conflict of interest requirements, he donated to charity).[15]

Item: The ability to defend one's *legal rights* depends on money. According to former Attorney General Ramsey Clark, "civil justice" exists only for the 10% who can afford lawyers.[16] Programs such as public defenders and legal aid are generally under-staffed and under-financed. Half the people in America's prisons have not been convicted and are there primarily because they cannot afford bail or advice.[17]

Item: The United States has a *hereditary* propertied class not unlike the aristocratic Europe which Americans so often disdain. At least 70% of American fortunes are inherited, rather than amassed during a single lifetime.[18]

Item: Over 5 million persons were officially *unemployed* at the end of 1971—not including those who had given up looking for work or were forced to work part time. Moreover, unemployment compensation is unavailable to many who are disqualified by state eligibility rules. For example, in 1967, only 42% of the unemployed received any benefits.[19]

Item: *Compensation* for work varies considerably, and has little relationship to the usefulness of the work to society. Housework and child-care are generally not compensated at all, and such occupations as banker and physician garner tens of times as much income as other occupations requiring as much education or as many hours of work. Also, money is valued to such an extent that people doing valuable work at little or no salary are made to feel that their work is less important than higher-paid work.

Item: Private business and government are linked so as to make *democracy* scarcely meaningful.[20] Former Secretary of Health, Education, and Welfare John Gardner described our nation as no longer one "in which any man can run for office and hope to win. In most states and districts he has to be wealthy or put himself under obligation to sources of wealth."[21]

Item: Major political decisions such as the Vietnamese War and its escalation, invasions of the Dominican Republic and Cuba, the Nixon economic plan, and increased unemployment, are executed *without public debate* or effective recourse.

Item: *Secrecy* pervades the political economy. Decisions are made in secret by business and government, often in contrast to public statements. The disclosure of the Pentagon Papers by Daniel Ellsberg revealed the extent to which we are deceived about public policies.

Item: Private corporations *control* the economic life of communities as well as the nation. These corporations, without consultation with workers or consumers, produce products and control consumption through massive advertising.

Item: Our society is plagued by *perverted values* of consumerism and competition. Self-respect is widely defined in terms of financial status, owning a late-model car, dressing stylishly, etc. Controlled by private profits for a few, the economy spews out products of affluence, waste, and military and environmental destruction while basic needs for food, clothing, health, housing, transportation, and aesthetics go unmet.

Item: People are *alienated* from their communities. A National Urban Coalition commission assessing the situation in the cities in 1971 reported that: "Few of these people with whom we spoke believed that America's dominant institutions, public or private, either would or could respond meaningfully to their immediate grievances, their long-range needs, or, especially, their tastes, preferences and desires."[22]

Item: *Middle-class* Americans have to put up with inflation, immense consumer debt, and poorly-made products—such as automobile bumpers which cannot withstand a six-mile-per-hour impact.[23] At the same time they live with medical insecurity and poor services.

Item: There is increasing awareness that *racism, sexism,* and other forms of dehumanization pervade our personal relationships and institutions. Attempts to change these basic social patterns strike at the foundations of our political economy.

Item: *Surveillance* of U.S. citizens and officials is extensive. Even members of Congress, Senators, and state governors are the subjects of intelligence gathering.[24]

Item: Two-thirds of the federal tax dollar goes to past, present, and future *wars.* Seventy billion dollars or more per year is spent on the military.

Item: *Pollution* poses a threat to human survival. Lead introduced into the environment has increased 400% in the past 25 years. Pollution of waterways has already led to the outbreak of one new disease in 1965 due to the growth of soil bacteria in artificially-enriched waters, threatening us with epidemics of other new, serious diseases. Plasticizers, used in plastic packaging, automobile seat covers, toys, and many other common items, present a potential health hazard due to their recently-discovered effects on cell growth.[25]

Item: *New production technologies,* particularly since the Second World War, have greatly increased the impact of our economy on the environment. In agriculture, textiles, automobile production, packaging, and many other spheres of enterprise, new nondegradable synthetic fibers replace natural ones, non-renewable resources are used in place of renewable ones, and power-consumptive processes replace power-conserving ones.[26] Most of our presently key *non-renewable resources* will have been virtually used up and will be prohibitively expensive within 100 years.[27]

Item: The U.S. restricts travel, refuses to take key issues to the United Nations, exploits other nations, supports military dictatorships, and in other ways *inhibits the growth of world community.*

[1] U.S. Department of Commerce, "Consumer Income," Current Population Reports Series P-60, No. 77, May 7, 1971.

[2] Labor Research Association, *Economic Notes,* June, 1972, p. 4.

[3] AFL-CIO Legislative Department, *National Health Security,* (1971, Fact Sheet No. 1).

[4] Report of the Carnegie Commission on Higher Education, quoted in the *New York Times,* Oct. 30, 1970.

[5] Heilbroner, Robert, "Benign Neglect in the United States," *Transaction* magazine, (Vol. 7, No. 12), Oct. 1970, p. 16.

[6] AFL-CIO, *op. cit.*

[7] Senate Special Committee on Aging "Economics of Aging, " cited in the *New York Times,* Jan. 18, 1971.

[8] Herman P. Miller, *Rich Man, Poor Man* (N.Y.: Crowell, 1971), pp. 147-157.

[9] Edward C. Budd, *Inequality and Poverty* (1967), pp. xiii, xvi.

[10] Rep. Henry S. Reuss, "Wealthy Have Better Chance of Escaping All Taxes than Most Others, Rep. Reuss Says," newsrelease, Mar. 1972.

[11] Robert Dietsch, "40% of U.S. Firms Do Not Pay Taxes," *American Report* (vol. II, No. 37), June 23, 1972, p. 5.

[12] U.S. Dept. of Commerce, "Consumer Income," Current Population Reports, Series P-60, No. 78, May 20, 1971.

[13] *New York Times,* Feb. 11, 1972.

[14] Philip M. Stern, testimony, hearings before the Subcommittee on Priorities and Economy in Government of the Joint Economic Committee, U.S. Congress, Jan. 14, 1972, p. 76.

[15] *New York Times,* Dec. 21, 1971, p. 1.

[16] Ramsey Clark, *Crime in America* (1970).

[17] *Statistical Abstract of the U.S.: 1971,* p. 157.

[18] Ferdinand Lundberg, *The Rich and the Super-Rich* (N.Y.: Lyle Stuart, 1968), pp. 189, 195.

[19] Sar A. Levitan, *Programs in Aid of the Poor for the 1970s* (Baltimore: The Johns Hopkins Press, 1969), p. 39.

[20] G. William Domhoff, *The Higher Circles* (N.Y.: Random House, 1970).

[21] *New York Times,* July 4, 1971, op. ed. page.

[22] National Urban Coalition Commission on the 70's, "The State of the Cities." Washington, Sept. 1971, p. 8.

[23] Figure cited by an official of the Goodyear Tire and Rubber Company in Vance Packard, *The Waste Makers* (N.Y.: David McKay, 1960).

[24] *New York Times,* Feb. 29, 1972, p. 1.

[25] Barry Commoner, *The Closing Circle* (N.Y.: Knopf, 1971), pp. 167, 221-229.

[26] Barry Commoner, *ibid.*

[27] Donella H. Meadows et al., *The Limits to Growth* (N.Y.: Universe Books, 1972), pp. 66-67.

Part II: Diagnosis

4

Environmental Crisis

Perhaps the most awesome symptom of an ailing America is its contribution to the rapid deterioration of the Earth's environment. The Earth is a spaceship with finite resources and environment. Even though there is now a heightened public consciousness about this ecological spaceship, the programs supported by almost everyone—radicals, conservatives, Russians, Americans, rich and poor—imply a maximum-growth economy which assumes a world of inexhaustible resources, unlimited waste and pollution reservoirs and indestructible ecosystems. America, as the most consumptive and wasteful nation, consequently has the most detrimental impact on the world's ecosystems. Environmental conservation efforts are failing because they are being tried within this frontierlike limitless view of resources. Consequently, spaceship Earth is faltering, and humanity, its crew, is in danger. We need a spaceship political-economy and culture.[1]

ECOLOGICAL DANGER SYMPTOMS—EVERYONE KNOWS, BUT FEW WORRY

Most Americans believe there is an environmental crisis. This belief was reflected by President Nixon: "We face the prospect of ecological disaster requiring total mobilization by all of us."[2] However, there is consider-

21

able disagreement regarding the outcome. Conventional wisdom assumes we will be saved before disaster strikes, while a vocal minority, especially many scientists and ecology-minded citizens, remain skeptical. The disagreement is not whether there's a crisis, but whether widely-held solutions are really adequate. The ecological debate, therefore, should focus not so much on the specific threats to our environment, but on the validity of popularized solutions. Consequently, we will only briefly describe some of the more salient environmental problems, and then focus more fully on solutions. The major problems we will mention are: depletion of resources, environmental deterioration, and the population explosion.

Depleting Resources

One of the ecological danger symptoms particularly threatening to Western civilization is the rapid depletion of non-renewable resources. "Mines bear no second fruit." Yet, since World War II, more metal has been consumed than in all previous history, and its consumption is expected to increase at an exponential rate into the foreseeable future.[3] If present trends continue, many experts believe most key mineral resources will be exhausted within the next 50 years. For example, according to Preston Cloud, professor of biogeology at the University of California, extrapolations from the U.S. Bureau of Mines data show the world's reserves of platinum, silver, gold, tin, zinc, lead, copper, tungsten, uranium 235, natural gas and crude oil will be exhausted by the year 2000.[4] Equally alarming conclusions have been reached by an increasing number of scientific sources, including *The Limits to Growth,* (the M.I.T.-Club of Rome study), *Blueprint for Survival,* and the Menton Statement, which has been signed by thousands of scientists. As the world's top energy consumer, the United States is particularly threatened by the impending energy crisis: traditional sources are either running out or are ecologically disastrous. Here we are referring to the actual, long-term energy crisis—not the energy "scare" precipitated in 1973-4. New safe energy sources are needed for even the present production and consumption levels to be continued, and it is projected there will be a tripling of these levels by the year 2000.[5]

The crisis of depleted resources is already a living reality for about half the people in the world, particularly for the majorities in the Third World. Their deprivations are getting worse each year. Food, for example, is one of our most indispensable resources. Yet, late in the Twentieth Century, (food-scientist Georg Borgstrom reports) more than half the children alive will die of malnutrition.[6] The United Nations reports that 10,000 people died daily from malnutrition during the 1960's and that the situation will get worse during the present decade.[7] ✳ Third World populations also consume proportionately much less of other key world resources, such as minerals and fossil fuels.

Deteriorating Environment

The life-sustaining environment of living beings is complicated, limited, delicate, and, to a frightening extent, unknown. Yet deliberate human activity is destroying it. Air pollution, for example, which contributes to such serious illnesses as emphysema, bronchitis, cancer and heart disease, is increasing exponentially.[8] Air pollution in towns of under 100,000 population has become about as severe as that in big cities.[9] It is said that the air we breathe is not fit to eat—our annual consumption of air pollutants exceeds the modest standards allowed by the Food and Drug Administration. The U.S. Surgeon General estimates that 400,000 children have dangerously high levels of lead in their blood and 33 per cent of black children tested in 27 cities have "excessive" amounts.[10] Modern humans already have 25 to 50 times as much lead in them as primitive humans, and tests of the polar ice cap layers show an exponential increase in lead air pollution since 1750.[11] Some of the many other dangerous air pollutants include carbon monoxide, sulphur oxides, nitrogen oxides, hydrocarbons, particulate mat-

✳ 1990 - 50,000 deaths/day.

ter, mercury, heat and dirt. Anne and Paul Ehrlich also list other forms of pollution which have reached critical levels: unpotable water, solid wastes, pesticides and related compounds, radiation and chemical mutagens, noise, and world-wide epidemics. Apocalyptic consequences could be precipitated by climatic changes due to increased energy production and use.[12] The Ehrlichs and Barry Commoner have described the immediate possibilities of breakdowns in the complicated ecological life-support systems such as the nitrogen, carbon, oxygen, mineral and energy cycles.[13] For updated information about the depressing, deteriorating state of our human habitat, the reader should see the scientific monthly magazine, *Environment*.

People, People, People . . . .

The last danger symptom we'll mention is ourselves, you the reader and we the writers. We're exploding. We're a population bomb. The doubling time for the world's population has become increasingly shortened: 10 million years, to 1600, to 200, to 60, to now 35 years for doubling. Every three years the Earth has an additional population the size of the United States'. By the year 2000, China and India probably will each have over a billion people, Mexico 140 million (it's now 51 million), and the United States, despite the recent reduction in its birth rate, will probably be 270 million—an increase of "only" 60 million in 30 years.[14] Barring disaster, the world's population will probably be about 7 billion by the year 2000, and no let-up is in sight. Poverty and hunger are expected to increase proportionately, and it's questionable whether the environment can take the increased strain. The influential Committee on Resources and Man of the National Academy of Sciences reports, " . . . a human population less than the present one would offer the best hope."[15] But Sir Peter Medawar warns that the Earth can only hold 500 million people at the U.S. level, and Paul Ehrlich sets the figure at 200 million.

Prophets or Doomsdayers?

An increasingly impressive array of scientists and organizations warn of impending ecological calamity. The Ehrlichs report that a "1968 UNESCO conference concluded that man had only about 20 more years before the planet started to become uninhabitable because of air pollution alone."[16] Barry Commoner estimates the "point of no return" at about 20 to 50 years away.[17] And the "Blueprint For Survival", signed by thousands of scientists around the world, says "If current trends are allowed to persist, the breakdown of society and the irreversible disruption of the life-support systems on this planet, possibly by the end of the century, certainly within the lifetimes of our children, are inevitable."[18]

These dire warnings have been received by the American citizenry with both alarm and aplomb. After the initial shock wears off, with an almost blind faith that problems will always be taken care of in the future as they are believed to have been in the past, such warnings are shrugged off. But can we rely on popular solutions?

THE FAILURE OF POPULAR SOLUTIONS

Myth 1: Technology will solve our environmental problems

Western Civilization has an almost blind faith that science and technology can solve almost any problem.

We are frequently reminded of the successes of modern technology, but its failures are usually overlooked. In *The Closing Circle,* Barry Commoner shows that "our most celebrated technological achievements—the automobile, the jet plane, the power plant, industry in general, and indeed the modern city itself—are, in the environment, failures."[19] He reminds us that the automobile "has rendered urban air pathogenic, burdened human bodies with nearly toxic levels of carbon monoxide and lead, embedded carcinogenic particles of asbestos in human lungs and killed and maimed many thousands annually." Pesticides are making their way through the food chain into human beings and killing off other animals. According to the Ehrlichs, American mothers' milk contains so much DDT that it would be banned if sold on the interstate market.[20]

Detergents require three times as much energy to produce as does soap, release much mercury into the environment, and release twenty times the amount of phosphate into the environment as does the soap they have replaced. That is, the detergent technology has caused twenty times the environmental deterioration. The production of synthetic materials also requires enormous energy and releases vast amounts of mercury.[21]

As Commoner and others point out, these problems are brought about primarily by the kind of technology and affluence we have in the West, and not so much by population increases:

> Nearly all of the stresses that have generated the environmental crisis in the U.S.—smog, detergents, insecticides, heavy use of fertilizers, radiation—began about 20-25 years ago. In that period there has been a sharp rise in the *per capita* production of pollutants. For example, total utilization of fertilizer has increased about 1400 percent. In that period the U.S. population increased by 43 percent. This means that the major factor which has increased pollution in the U.S. since 1945 is not the number of people, but the intensified effects of ecologically faulty technology on the environment.[22]

The negative environmental side effects of modern technologies are also not caused by minor flaws in their application. All of these polluting technologies succeeded in their goals—increased yield per acre, synthetic fabrics, atomic blasts, and electric power. Their problem, however, is that they're narrow-minded and out of step with natural cycles. Their purpose is to solve particularized problems in narrow contexts, but ecology requires just the opposite—relationships among broad, world-wide ranges of complicated natural systems about which we still know precious little. Consequently, modern technology of the kind to date will probably continue to speed up ecological Armageddon.

Myth 2: Atomic energy will solve our environmental problems [23]

Over one thousand atomic fission plants are expected to provide almost all of the nation's expected three-fold energy increase during the next thirty years, producing 60 percent of the electric power by the turn of the century.[24] Other potential new sources, such as solar and fusion, are not expected to produce much energy before then, and new dangers are associated with them. Advocates argue that all energy production methods are harmful to humans and the environment, but that nuclear fission is the safest, cheapest and cleanest of available alternatives to meet our energy growth needs. On the other hand, opponents, made up mainly of a sizeable portion of the scientific community and an increasing number of informed citizens, are worried about the safety and survival of humanity.

A major concern is the fear of devastating accidents. An accidental release of only 1 percent of the radio-activity at the fuel processing plant in South Carolina, for example, would probably require the evacuation of the entire East Coast. The Atomic Energy Commission estimated that a core-meltdown accident in a power plant one-fifth the size of the ones being built today would kill 3,400 people (not counting long-range radio-activity deaths), injure 45,000 people up to a radius of 45 miles, and contaminate an area equivalent to Pennsylvania, New Jersey, New York, Maryland and Virginia.[25] Yet the Emergency Core Cooling System, the ultimate safety system to prevent meltdowns, has never been tested under operating conditions and has failed its simulated model tests.[26]

Even in the most-controlled high technology projects, there is a possibility of unforeseen major accidents. There have already been many serious and potentially serious accidents as well as other flaws. After the 1966 accident in the Fermi atomic plant, for example, officials considered evacuating Detroit.[27] The plant has since switched from atomic to fossil fuel. Another problem recently detected is the damaged fuel rods which control the reactions in the new, big reactors.[28] An AEC report dated October 1973, entitled "Study of the Reactor Licensing Process," stated that in a 17 month period "approximately 850 abnormal occurrences" happened in the operations of atomic plants and that "The large number of reactor incidents coupled with the fact that many of them had real safety significance, were generic in nature, and were not identified during the normal design, fabrication, erection, and pre-operational testing phases, raises a serious question regarding the reliability of the licensing process."[29]

On May 29, 1974, the *New York Times* reported that the AEC had admitted to 861 "abnormal" events occurring at the nation's 42 nuclear power plants last year. More than half of the problems were considered insignificant, while 371 had some potential of being hazardous. Eighteen events were considered directly significant and 12 of them involved the release of radioactivity at rates above permissible limits beyond the plant site. Rather than strengthening the licensing procedure, the Administration relaxed safey precautions for nuclear licensing in 1974 to speed up atomic electricity production.

Some types of accidents are particularly difficult to prevent. Atomic plants cannot withstand direct crashes by today's largest airliners, as was threatened, for example, by skyjackers against the Oak Ridge reactor on November 11, 1972. Former Navy demolition officer Bruce Welch, testified in March, 1974 before the Joint Congressional Committee on Atomic Energy, "I could pick three to five ex-underwater demolition, Marine Reconnaissance or Green Beret men at random and sabotage virtually any nuclear reactor in the country . . . . There is no way to stop such activity other than to maintain a system of civil surveillance more strict than that maintained during the last world war . . ." Another danger is earthquakes. It is frightening enough that several atomic plants are built on or near geological faults, but the additional fact exists that earthquakes can also occur where no present fault exists.[30]

The transportation and storage of the waste-products is another serious problem. Because of their extreme radioactivity, some wastes must be kept under perpetual care for a half-million years, much longer than the life-time of any civilization. Within thirty years the projected annual wastage will be equal to about 11,500 megatons of nuclear fission bombs. Even a very small loss rate would have serious effects on the human population.[31] Over 80 million gallons of atomic wastes are now temporarily stored in tanks which must be replaced about every 25 years while waiting for a safe, permanent storage. And another 60 million gallons will be produced within the next several decades.

Extreme caution must be taken in selecting a storage place—the continuation of life as we know it may be in the balance. Yet in February of 1972, the Atomic Energy Commission selected the Lyons, Kansas salt mines as the permanent storage site and requested $3.5 million from Congress to buy 2,000 acres. The Kansas State Geological Survey, however, subsequently charged that the AEC exhibited incompetence in selecting the site, and revealed in *Technology Review* that the salt beds were "a bit like a piece of Swiss cheese" in that 180,000 gallons of water disappeared in a test there proving the mines extremely dangerous for nuclear storage.[32] The AEC then dropped the plan. Consequently, athough the atomic energy program is going forward, there is presently no reliable storage place for the most dangerous substances known to humans.

Another problem with nuclear fission, particularly the breeder reactors, the main type of reactor being promoted, is that they produce plutonium—lots of plutonium—one of the most lethal substances to humans. If spread evenly around the world, for example, an estimated 10 pounds would soon cause every human being to die from cancer.[33] Yet a March 21, 1974 AEC report states that by the year 2020, there would be 5,000 tons of the

previously scarce plutonium in the atomic power program, with 100,000 shipments taking place per year. This
is a depressing thought considering highway, rail and air
accident rates. However, the AEC would have us believe
that lethal doses of plutonium are to be transported
without accidents. AEC Commissioner Larson has said
that a 1 or 2% loss rate (stolen, lost or misplaced) of
plutonium is normal and unavoidable. By 1980 that will
be 900 pounds annually![34]

Small-scale nuclear warfare would become more
likely. A Nagasaki-type bomb can be made relatively
easily with 11 pounds of plutonium, and as the high-
priced plutonium becomes plentiful, widely dispersed and
frequently transported, even the AEC has expressed
concern that a blackmarket might well come into existence.[35]

It should be always kept in mind that the by-prod-
ucts of the atomic energy plants are of immense danger
themselves. India's atomic blast in the Spring of 1974,
which proliferated atomic weaponry capability to the
first poor Third World nation, was fueled by waste from
Indian atomic energy plants. In the U.S. as in other
countries, it would be possible for political groups or
even unaffiliated or mentally deranged individuals to use
nuclear weapons or release raw wastage or threaten
sabotage to nuclear plants or to transport vehicles.

Extremely dangerous hazards are also associated
with nuclear power even in "normal" operations, such as
low-level radiation and thermal pollution, and we urge
people to read about these elsewhere.[36] However, Nobel
Physics Laureate Hannes Alfven points out that the rule
of thumb of all complicated technology is, "If anything
can go wrong, it will", and he says of atomic plants that
the normal operations depend on a great many things
which can go wrong:

> Fission energy is safe only if a number of critical devices
> work as they should, if a number of people in key positions
> follow all their instructions, if there is no sabotage, no hijacking
> of the transports, if no reactor fuel processing plant or repro-
> cessing plant or repository anywhere in the world is situated in a

region of riots or guerrilla activity, and no revolution or war—even a 'conventional' one—takes place in these regions. The enormous quantities of extremely dangerous material must not get into the hands of ignorant people or desperados. No acts of God can be permitted.[37]

The problems associated with splitting the atom are a difference in kind from others humans have historically faced:

> Leading nuclear experts like Dr. Alvin Weinberg, director of Oak Ridge Nuclear Laboratory, Dr. Albert Crewe, former director of Argonne Laboratory, and Dr. Hannes Alfven, 1970 Nobel Laureate in Physics at the University of California at San Diego, acknowledge that unsuspected or uncorrected deficiencies in nuclear power technology could create "catastrophe for the human race", "serious danger for the entire population of the world", or "a total poisoning of the planet." Obviously, nuclear electricity is one of the most profound moral issues of our time.[38]

Since the risks associated with it are extreme, nuclear energy should obviously be approached slowly, and with utmost caution. However, exactly the opposite is happening. The atomic age is being thrust upon us—not because it has been proved safe, but to meet our economic growth requirements for electricity. This is despite strong opposition from a formidable portion of the scientific community, and also despite historical experience that technological innovations have often brought unanticipated, hazardous secondary effects. As Barry Commoner points out, this has been particularly true for atom splitting:

> Massive nuclear testing which began with the development of the hydrogen bomb in 1953 was well under way before most of its biological consequences were appreciated. The unanticipated tendency for world-wide fallout to deposit preferentially in the North Temperate Zone was unknown until 1956; the hazard from iodine and carbon-14 was not brought to light until 1957; the special ecological factors which amplify the fallout hazard in the Arctic were elucidated for the first time in 1960;

experiments which suggest that strontium-90 may cause hereditary damage by becoming concentrated in the chromosomes
were first reported in 1963.[39]

Another frightening aspect of atomic energy is that
the main institution responsible for guarding us against its
hazards, the Atomic Energy Commission, is also charged
with *promoting* atomic energy production—and it clearly
is pursuing the latter more vigorously. In fact, the AEC
resembles an atomic energy public relations department
in charge of sales rather than a protector of the public. As
the head of the AEC stated in 1971, "From its inception
the AEC has fostered and protected the nuclear industry."[40] For example, it often refuses official testimonies
of bona fide opponents of atomic energy at its public
hearings, has put off its testing of the Emergency Core
Cooling System and suppresses information detrimental
to the atomic energy program. Virtually all of the
negative information has either come from unofficial
sources or has been forced from the AEC by citizens'
actions. However, many people previously associated
with the AEC now make public testimonies. Even the
AEC's first chairman, David Lilienthal, has now written,
"Once a bright hope shared by all mankind, including
myself, the vast proliferation of atomic power plants has
become one of the ugliest clouds overhanging
America."[41]

In conclusion, we fear that rather than saving us
from our exponentially-increasing energy requirements,
atomic energy may kill us. We favor a moratorium on the
production of electricity by atomic energy (except possibly for one or two extremely small test units) until
there has been sufficient data and open public debate to
guarantee their safety level. Until such time we favor the
reduction of America's energy production, if that is the
alternative.[42]

Myth 3: The government will solve our environmental problems

Many people's fears about the environment are

allayed by their irrational belief that the government will protect them from any serious ecological dangers. The president's bold rhetoric about reclaiming the purity of the air, water, and environment, along with the continual barrage of governmental policy, laws and programs, give the public the impression that the government not only has the will to act, but is taking strong measures. However, in our view, governmental activity, on the balance, has significantly contributed to environmental deterioration. The government's numerous, highly publicized environmental programs are similar to new balls tossed into the air by a juggler, but after the initial fanfare, rather than being caught, most of the balls fall to the ground out of the public spotlight, failing to achieve their original stated goals.[43]

Many government activities, rather than just failing to help, have been ecologically damaging in themselves. For example, the government has given extensive support to the automobile, perhaps America's number one polluter, over mass transportation: gasoline taxes are disbursed almost exclusively to highways rather than mass transit, model changes (which help sell more and bigger cars) have been underwritten by large capital depreciation allowances, and enormous depletion allowances have made oil cheaper. The government also has built dams which flood valuable land, supported the SST, contributed money to off-shore drillings, helped distribute pesticides, opposed the moratorium on whale-killing, and supported the ecologically dangerous Alaskan pipe line!

Many environmental organizations have learned during the past few years that the legal approach is frustrating: not only are meaningful laws difficult to get passed, but once passed, are poorly enforced. One of the strongest laws to protect American waterways from pollution, the Refuse Act, was passed in 1899. That strong law empowered the Army Corps of Engineers to control water pollution by requiring companies issuing large amounts of pollutants into navigable waterways to apply for a license from the Corps. However, in 72 years the Corps has never issued one license—even though there are an estimated 40,000 companies in violation of the law.[44]

Clean air has met the same fate. In a formal agreement between the Anaconda Copper Mining Company and the United States Attorney General:

> The defendant, Anaconda Copper Mining Company, agrees that it will at all times use its best efforts to prevent, minimize, and ultimately to completely eliminate the emission and distribution from its smelting works at Anaconda, Montana, of all deleterious fumes, particularly those containing sulphur dioxide.[45]

That was in 1911! In 1971, that plant was spewing about 21,000 tons of sulphur dioxide into the air each month, and asking the State Board of Health to abandon its strict emission standards.[46] That same year the chairman of the President's Council on Environmental Quality called sulphur oxides "the most serious pollutant in the atmosphere today.[47] However, rather than enforcing its previous agreements or utilizing existing laws, President Nixon put the blame on Congress for failing to act on all the ecology legislation he proposed and recommended a new tax on sulphur oxides.[48] The juggler-administration preferred to toss new balls into the air rather than to deal responsibly with existing vehicles for environmental health.

Another stumbling block to effective governmental action is that major polluters, big corporations, often control environmental programs. For example, the President's advisory council on environmental programs affecting industry, the National Industrial Pollution Control Council, is composed of 63 top executives of major corporations and industry associations. In violation of the law, they hold closed meetings with no public records.[49] On the state level, a *New York Times* investigation concluded "most of the state boards primarily responsible for cleaning up the nation's air and water are markedly weighted with representatives of the principal sources of pollution."[50] A former head of an Anaconda subsidiary, for example, is chairman of Montana's Water Pollution Control Council.[51] The study also notes rapid increases in water and air pollution by corporations breaking laws and going unpenalized by the states. Meanwhile, the federal government does little about air pollution, claiming that the states are primarily responsible.

Even the two federal agencies specifically responsible for protecting the environment cannot be counted on. In its first annual report, the President's Council on Environmental Quality concluded its energy section: "All in all, the short-range energy situation seems tolerable with the exception of the environmental ill effects. The longer run outlook causes more concern . . ."[52] What is critical for an environmental agency if it isn't the environment? It sounds strangely like an oil company rather than an environmental safety agency. Perhaps the explanation is that the chairman of the Citizens' Advisory Committee on Environmental Quality, which "advises the President and the Council on Environmental Quality on all aspects of environmental quality and recommends actions by the Federal, State, and local governments and by the private sector", is Laurance Rockefeller.[53]

The other key environmental Federal agency, the Environmental Protection Agency (EPA), was established in 1970 to consolidate all pollution control programs in a new, independent agency. The EPA's record, however, has been disastrous for the environment. True, it has held press conferences in which it has thrown new balls in the air—new standards, new methods of enforcement, demands for new laws, new threats to industry—but after the first news coverage, the balls have mostly fallen unnoticed. Since its inception, the EPA has been responsible for enforcing the strong anti-water-pollution law, the Refuse Act of 1899, already mentioned. But a House Government Operations Committee found that the EPA not only failed to effectively enforce the act, but that it used the act to give license to corporations to pollute.[54] In 1972 the EPA violated Federal anti-water-pollution policy by allowing metropolitan New York City to dump sewage sludge in the ocean.[55] In another case, the Federal court declared that the EPA illegally gave a two-year extension to 17 states to comply with air pollution standards.[56] The EPA even opposed the recycling of cans and bottles (thereby supporting the Aluminum Association's position), basing their opposition on a soon-to-be-completed study they were supposed to be undertaking. After numerous claims that the study was forthcoming, the EPA admitted that it had never existed.[57] The *Economic Report of the President* admits that voluntary economic controls don't work because they ask "people to acquiesce in conduct that they find contrary to their own interests but also to their view of fairness, propriety, and efficiency".[58] Still the EPA head urged voluntary control of pollution by industry.[59]

The government's overriding commitment to economic growth is probably the chief reason why it cannot effectively protect the environment. The government must cater to the powerful corporations, workers and consumers who consider growth in their best interest. Consequently, the EPA supported the SST, and the AEC is advocating fission energy—both potential ecological disasters—because economic growth requires them. Also, in 1970 President Nixon said that we must reclaim our air and water, and headlines read, "President Orders Curbs on Dumping in Waterways".[60] However, a few months later he opposed the clean water bill (unanimously passed in the Senate), claiming that it would be too expensive, have too big an impact on selected industries, and might drive some industries from the country, causing adverse effects on employment, foreign trade and the balance of payments.[61] The government's attitude towards the environment was depicted when President Nixon said that in addition to clean water and air "we are also committed to a strong economy and we are not going to allow the environmental issue to destroy the industrial system that made this the great country it is".[62]

Finally, the government's lack of environmental priority was revealed when it was forced to act during the crunch of the 1973-74 energy scare. It sided overwhelmingly with the oil companies and economic growth in initiating programs under the banner of Operation

Independence. It used the "crisis" to act against environmental safeguards regarding the Alaskan Pipelines, nuclear reactors, coal, offshore drilling, strip mining, shale oil, partial renewal of DDT for forests, water pollution, air pollution, and against rationing of oil consumption.

Myth 4: Economists will solve our ecological problems

Economists traditionally have not considered the environment in their calculations. Their chief goal has been maximum growth in goods and services (GNP). In fact, Paul Samuelson has proclaimed economics as "the science of economic growth". Second, they have only a short-run outlook: "In the long run", Keynes said, "we're all dead." Also, the economists' key economic indicators, such as GNP, employment, inflation, income, and profits, measure neither deterioration nor improvement in the quality of the air, water or land. Consequently, economists have contributed to both the depletion of natural resources and the destruction of the environment.

In recent years, however, economists have realized the seriousness of environmental problems and put forth their solution: internalize environmental costs. That is, environmental costs should be added to production costs, and, thereby, to the prices of products and services.[63] Since high-polluting products will have higher prices, their demand will be reduced and so will pollution. In addition, as particular resources become scarce, market forces will further increase their prices, thereby reduce their consumption; higher prices will also encourage the use of synthetic or more plentiful natural substitutes.

The economists' solutions for the environmental problem, however, are both ineffective and unacceptable for a number of reasons. First, the environmental burden would fall mostly on the poor; many products would be priced beyond the poor's ability to pay, but the more affluent could continue to consume and pollute. The poor simply couldn't afford many basic necessities if their prices included their total costs to the environment.

For example, if the ecological costs of pesticides, inorganic fertilizers, feedlot organic wastes, and farm machinery were added to food prices, the poor would be much hungrier.[64] Moreover, there would be a general increase in the disparity between the rich and poor through increased prices and decreased wage income.[65] In surveying economists' proposals about the environment, the Dorfmans concluded that "the questions of equity and distribution are scarcely mentioned," in fact, their importance is sometimes clearly denied.[66] In our view, however, the inequity is already far too great and any efforts toward a better world need to reduce it.

Second, the economists' solution is particularly inadequate regarding depleting resources. Some resources have no substitute for key uses, and for some others, the substitutes themselves are becoming scarce. For example, hundreds of much-used synthetics are produced from oil which is running out. What price is to be put on resources which have been completely depleted? Another problem is that many of the synthetic substitutes are extremely harmful to the environment. Their production often consumes enormous quantities of electric energy and many are non-biodegradable, which causes environmental deterioration and hazards to human health. If their prices included their true environmental costs, few people could afford them.

Another difficulty with the economists' solution is that environmental problems are so intertwined that the contribution of any one pollutant is difficult to measure. In addition, the substitute for one problem may cause another problem that's bigger. Also, since many environmental problems are not detected for years after the original activity and much damage is done, it's too late to add the pollution tax.

It is difficult to know some of the costs to people. What price should be put on terminal cancer, lead poisoning, rarely seeing the sun, noise, bronchitis, congenital deformity or environmental ugliness? What price should be added for the untold damage to future generations? And who would demand that the costs to future generations or Third World peoples be added to the costs of present-day American costs of production: Industry? The U.S. government? Consumers?

Finally, the economists' solutions are impractical because they rely on the federal government to impose ecological taxes that would directly contradict its economic priority of maximum production, employment and purchasing power.[67] John Hardesty points out that pollution taxes would curtail growth or even reduce GNP because they would (1) reduce real disposable incomes, (2) "fall most heavily on such mainstays of the economy as automobiles, petroleum and defense"—which have no adequate substitute, and (3) also, "be imposed on capital goods, basic material imputs (for example steel and paper), and fossil fuels due to their high degree of complicity in environmental destruction."[68] Hardesty calls the idea of pollution taxes "pseudo events" because they have not and cannot happen to any meaningful extent because they too directly conflict with the government's first priority of maximum GNP growth.

Consequently, as already shown, even the Federal environmental agencies give priority of economics over ecology. And, rather than taxing dwindling scarce minerals, the government subsidizes their depletion because the economy needs them. Even the gargantua of polluters, the automobile, is greatly subsidized rather than curbed despite damning evidence. Not only has the government subsidized highways, oil, gas, Detroit capital equipment, and removed auto excise taxes, but the Government Technical Committee's Office of Science and Technology has recommended easing auto exhaust emissions standards rather than tightening them because the rules would add $755 to the retail price of the average car and strict enforcement of rules will cost $63 billion more than the benefits they would bring in the decade from 1976 to 1985.[69] A year later the EPA postponed enforcing its standards on automobile emissions, declaring this postponement was in the public interest because the auto industry couldn't produce enough properly equipped new automobiles to meet the demand to purchase them.[70] The government's rejection of the economists' solutions, however, is most evident by its complete omission of the environment in the *Presidents Economic Report of 1973,* as we have noted, while calling for the economy to "expand substantially in 1973."[71]

Not only does the government's priority on economic growth prohibit the economists' pollution-tax solutions, but, as pointed out by Hardesty,

> Given present technical knowledge and its application, environmental destruction is primarily a function of the level of GNP, and the faster it grows the faster the environment is destroyed. While certain types of products contribute relatively more to environmental destruction, most components of GNP are in some way environmental-destruction linked.[72]

The government's dilemma, therefore, is either to bring about economic collapse now or bring about both economic *and* ecological collapse later—it has chosen the latter.

THE THIRD WORLD: AN ECOLOGICAL PERSPECTIVE

Another myth is that economic growth, modern technology and population control programs will solve the problems of the Third World poor. The political-economic reasons why economic growth cannot much help the world's poor are spelled out in the Exported Plague chapter of this book. There, we deal with the fact that within the non-socialist world, even "successful" economic growth in the poor countries does not reach the poor.

From an ecological perspective, world-wide industrialization through American-style economic growth is not only impossible, but the attempt will probably bring about ecological Armageddon. Even the dire forecasts of resource depletion and environmental breakdowns mentioned earlier assume that the consumption rates of the world's poor do not increase. Anne and Paul Ehrlich, however, have made the following calculation assuming that the Third World nations reach their goals of industrialization:

> ... to raise all of the 3.6 billion people of the world of 1970 to the American standard of living would mean ... the extraction of some 75 times as much iron as is now extracted annually, 100 times as much copper, 200 times as much lead, 75 times as much zinc, and 250 times as much tin. The needed iron is theoretically available, and might be extracted by tremendous efforts over a long period of time, but a serious limit could be imposed by a shortage of molybdenum, which is needed to convert iron to steel. Needed quantities of the other materials far exceed all known or inferred reserves. Of course, to raise the standard of living of the projected world population of the year 2000 to today's American standard would require doubling all of the above figures. But, far from concentrating on ways to help UDCs (Under Developed Countries) while making a maximum effort to husband limited resources, economists in the DCs (Developed Countries) want to *increase* the rate of domestic consumption of nonrenewable resources far above that of 1970, while population growth continues. Our environment cannot stand 'world industrialization', partly because of the thermal limits mentioned earlier; but even if it could, the problem of supplying the raw materials alone staggers the imagination. [73]

Even if the Ehrlichs' scenario were achieved many poor would not be reached without considerable redistribution. It has been said that raising the world to American levels of production, consumption and pollution would be like giving everyone first class accommodations on the *Titanic*.

Like economic growth, modern *technology* has not been very beneficial to the world's poor. On balance, it probably has had a negative effect. First, perhaps the most successful has been modern medicine which has been responsible for lowering the death rate, especially among infants. However, a secondary effect has been a population bomb which is growing faster than people's needs are being met.

Second, most technologies exported to the Third World have related to economic growth through industrialization: manufacturing processes and techniques, super-highways, modern ports, skyscrapers. All have contributed to successful economic growth rates, but, as already mentioned, the majority of people have not been helped much. Moreover, modern farming combined with the attraction of industrial employment are contributing to massive migrations into cities in Africa, Asia, and Latin America, adding to their enormous slums, poverty, unemployment, disease and crime.[74] One *New York Times* report cites Jakarta as not atypical of dozens of other Asian cities: "The city government says nearly three-fourths of the citizens live in dwellings considered inadequate and unsafe—in conditions that most Americans would not see, let alone experience, in a lifetime."[75] Another report, "Technological Age Adds to Asians' Plight," states:

> The Asian poor do not yet have the cars and television sets produced by an industrialized society. But they do have the new problems of an affluent society: air and water pollution, traffic jams, chaotic flows of population from the countryside into the cities, mushrooming slums, technological unemployment and breakdown of government services.[76]

Many of the most-heralded miracle technologies which have been applied to the Third World may be long-run disasters. One example is the modern dams used for electric power and irrigation. Garrett Hardin condemns the Aswan Dam in Egypt because it is depriving the land of fertilization, salinating the soil, reducing the Mediterranean fish catch by 97%, contributing to the eroding of the Nile delta by storms and increasing the dreaded disease schistosomiasis. The hydro-power dams are causing a rapid rise in the number of its victims.[77]

In the drought-stricken Sahel, one in every seven Sahelian babies dies before it is a year old, half die before they are ten, and few live to see forty. This is in an area that is crisscrossed with thousands of deep boreholes, drilled at a cost of between $20,000 to $200,000 each. In an effort to meet the basic needs of the peoples of the West African states, livestock herds were increased and boreholes were drilled to find water for the stock and people. Unfortunately the land could not support the trampling of the herds and the sparse vegetation was soon gone. Cattle and humans died within sight of water. Modern technology has added to the plight of an already desperate people.[78]

Our final example is the green revolution. Just a few years ago the fight against world hunger was declared won by the green revolution's new technologies: a variety of modern agricultural methods including irrigation, insecticides, and fertilizers, and large-scale, one-crop farming. Most accounts now agree with that of *The Limits to Growth* as it refers to the green revolution:

> The ultimate effects of this socio-economic positive feedback loop are agricultural unemployment, increased migration to the city and perhaps even increased malnutrition since the poor and unemployed do not have the means to buy the newly produced food. [79]

Some of its first and biggest successes, however, are being reversed. Even the Philippines, the land where the green revolution began and which achieved rice self-sufficiency in 1970, is now experiencing increasingly massive rice shortages, according to the National Food and Agricultural Council.[80]

There are a number of serious secondary effects: The green revolution has helped increase the gap between the rich and poor farmers and regions because the richer ones can afford the expensive irrigation, pesticides, storage, transportation, seeds and fertilizers. The green revolution's single-crop farming is extremely unstable because of its susceptibility to pestilence. Also, its extensive irrigation requirements are increasing human diseases such as malaria and those caused by snails. For example, an estimated one-quarter of malaria incidence in India today is a result of irrigation and dams.[81]

In the long run, the modern, green revolution-type food production cannot succeed in feeding the world because it is too energy-intensive. Every calorie of input using traditional farming methods produces five to fifty calories of food, but industrialized food methods require five to ten calories of energy input to get one in food. That's over 25 times more energy required by modern methods. In a recent *Science* article, Professors John and Carol Steinhart conclude that the choice seems to be "either less-intensive food production or famine for many areas of the world."[82]

The green revolution also is making the Third World more dependent on the United States, particularly on the already powerful American corporations such as those controlled by Ford and Rockefeller interests. These corporations produce and control much of the new seeds, fertilizers, pesticides, research and training. The control over food and hunger is a new form of imperialism. As Hubert Humphrey, one of the key men responsible for the green revolution and the Food For Peace Program, put it:

> I have heard . . . that people may become dependent on us for food. I know that was not supposed to be good news. To me that was good news, because before people can do anything they have got to eat. And if you are looking for a way to get people to lean on you and to be dependent on you, in terms of their cooperation with you, it seems to me that food dependence would be terrific . . .[83]

One reason why the green revolution is not winning its battle against hunger is that its focus is food *production* when the real problem is food *demand.* That is, the capitalist world's hungry are also its poor who cannot afford to purchase food on the market, and the green revolution does not increase their ability to buy food, it reduces it.[84] Food is not grown to feed people who need it, but to feed people who have *demand* for food in the *economic* sense; that is, food is grown to feed people who have the money to buy it on the open market. If you are hungry, but don't have money to buy food you are not counted in the calculations of world food demand.[85] The green revolution grows along with world hunger.

In summary, the application of technology to the

Third World has not much helped the poor majority
there. In fact, there have been many harmful secondary
effects. Most of the successes have occurred to the
affluent, increasing political and economic inequalities
and stabilizing social systems which help cause the majorities' problems. It is unlikely, therefore, that more technology (within the present social system) will be helpful.

A third effort to solve the world poor's problems is
birth control programs. The population boom in poor
nations is considered the major cause of their poverty.[86]
However, although we consider population growth a
major problem in the world today, and agree that family
planning is important in the ultimate fight against population size, *we oppose birth control as the major and
primary approach to either curbing population growth or
alleviating poverty.*

First, it doesn't work. The effectiveness of birth
control devices requires the motivation to use them;
people must first desire them and this desire is found
lacking in the majority of people in the poor nations.
Some of the barriers to motivation include religious
objections as well as a general lack of planning of most
anything in the lives of the poor. When life defies
planning, all planning—including family planning—is ir-
relevant. Moreover, many poor people consider children
an economic asset.[87] Consequently, even families who
want sterilization in India postpone it until after achieving an average of 4.5 children.[88] The Ford Foundation's
specialist on Asian population concluded, "Motivation is
the major factor and motivation for family planning is
basically lacking in most Asian societies."[89]

Second, the major focus on the conception control
approach diverts attention from the chief cause of population growth and blames the nonwhite poor population.
In our view, the major cause of population growth is not
individual, but determined by historical forces in the
society at large. Therefore, population control efforts
must first attack these society-level forces. The following
historical analysis might help clarify our position.

The nature of the whole society has historically

been the main determiner of population size and growth.[90] Pre-industrialized societies had extremely low population size and growth. Their high birth rate was about matched by their high death rate. Although they had a high "normal" death rate (mostly from high incidence of infant mortality), their populations had a tendency to rise until a calamity of war, famine, or pestilence reduced it back to near the starting point, only to repeat the cycle again. The industrial revolution, however, changed this pattern. The application of new medical knowledge reduced both the normal death rates as well as those from calamities, without reducing the birth rates. Consequently, the industrial revolution, with its medical advances, *caused* a population explosion in the newly industrialized nations. This explosion was furthered by the increased capacity for meeting basic needs of food, clothing and shelter. Therefore, since the industrialized nations were populated by whites, there was a subsequent white population explosion. Between 1800 and 1930 the caucasian world population increased from about 22 per cent of the human species to about 35 per cent.[91] During this time the world's nonwhite population increased very slightly. Then, another phenomenon of the industrial revolution occurred; the population growth rate of the industrialized nations decreased. This time-delayed decrease was caused by new cultural, economic and institutional forces including high standards of living, lower infant death rates, the beginning emancipation of women, and economic and social security. It is also important to know that birth rates in industrialized nations began falling rapidly before there was much application of modern birth-control techniques. (The annual population growth rates in the white, industrialized nations today, however, are about 1%, still much higher than the pre-industrial-revolution rate.)[92]

With this historical perspective, let us again consider the Third World today. The Third World's population explosion is only two or three decades old. Like the white population explosion which preceded it, it has been caused by the industrial revolution. However, unlike the predominantly white nations, the majority of people in the Third World countries are not receiving the economic benefits of the industrial revolution. Consequently, until that happens, their population bomb will not be diminished. If present trends continue, their rapid population increase will be stemmed only by a return of calamities, probably famine.[93]

What implications does all this have for population control in the Third World? We believe that population control programs are completely inadequate without simultaneously meeting the basic needs of the Third World people. This cannot happen within their present political-economic and social systems— which to a great extent are supported and maintained by the United States and other industrialized nations.[94] Americans who are interested in curbing population growth in poor nations should concentrate on trying to stop American support of oppressive social systems in the Third World.[95] Population control projects, however, have not been able to take this approach because they are mostly financed by the Ford Foundation or Rockefeller interests and therefore are prevented from opposing the present political-economic-social systems of the Third World.[96]

There is another problem often associated with that of population: many people believe that the increase in Third World population is the major threat to the depletion of the world's resources and the deterioration of its environment. We disagree. In our view, these problems are caused mainly by the affluent, white populations in the industrialized nations. Between 1800 and 1960, the population of the Third World increased about two and one-half times, but the world production of coal increased from about 15 million tons in 1800, to 1,809 million tons in 1960.[97] Petroleum/natural gas consumption grew from 1 million tons in 1870 to 1,073 million in 1960. These resources were consumed almost entirely by the industrialized white nations. In the United States, "the mileage of surfaced roads increased 97 per cent between 1930 and 1940".[98] Since World War II, the U.S. production of synthetic fibers is up 5,980 per cent, mercury up 3,930 per cent, air conditioners up 2,850 per cent, plastics up 1,960 per cent and fertilizer nitrogen up 1,050.[99] The world consumption of electricity is doubling every 17 years—two times the rate of world population increase—and the American electrical consumption is doubling every 10 years! Energy consumption is a good indicator of resource depletion and environmental pollution.

Each American consumes about seven times the amount of the average world citizen.[100] Paul Ehrlich points out that, "Each American has roughly 50 times the negative impact on the Earth's life-support systems as the average citizen of India. Therefore, in terms of eco-system destruction, adding 75 million more Americans will be the equivalent of adding 3.7 billion Indians to the world population."[101] Ehrlich further estimates that the United States population growth is about 25 times more serious than that of the Third World.[102] He estimates that a world consisting of just 50 million Americans would eventually destroy the planet.[103] *The Limits to Growth* concluded that even if the world's population was stabilized by 1975, economic growth would soon be stopped by depletion of non-renewable resources.[104]

The focus of population control on the Third World poor, therefore, is obviously misplaced. They consume and pollute relatively little. Our concern about population, resources and environment should first be placed on the white populations of the United States and the other industrialized nations—they must be curbed first.

In summary, from an ecological perspective, economic growth, technology, and conception control are inadequate solutions for the problems of the Third World's poor. Concerned Americans should first reduce the United States' consumption and pollution. To alleviate population growth and poverty we should stop American economic exploitation and support of political oppression in the Third World.

Some additional barriers to popular solutions of ecological problems

In addition to these specific limitations of the popular solutions just mentioned, there are some *general conditions* which tend to undermine all attempts at solving environmental problems. First, *time-delays in nature*.[105] The biological chain reactions take time; therefore, the ultimate ecological impact of human actions often may not be known for decades. Consequently, this causes a tendency in, humans to overshoot the environment's capacity. Second, *the exponential rates of increase* in pollution and resource depletion also create in us a tendency towards environmental overshoot and "sudden" breakdowns. The illustration of the lilies in the pond best dramatizes this problem. If a lily is put in a pond on the first day of the month and grows exponentially so that by the 30th day the pond is completely filled, on what day is the pond half-filled? On what day is the pond one-quarter filled? Because the pond is only one-quarter filled on the 28th day (and still only half filled on the 29th day) the problem does not seem very serious even several days before the pond is covered. This seems to be, in a very general way, similar to our environmental trends. Third, the interrelatedness of everything in nature means you can't do one solitary thing that affects nature without having many other effects.

Fourth, many solution attempts make environmental problems worse by *treating symptoms* rather than causes. For example, the world's oil supply is dwindling, but rather than reducing the amount of oil consumption, the government has increased its subsidies to oil companies so they can increase their hunt for more obscure oil fields. This has succeeded in reducing the symptom oil shortages, but has speeded up the problem of oil depletion.[106] A final barrier is the *unknown*. The studies and reports of nearly every environmental problem state that little is known about the long-run effects on humans and more research is needed. We'll just mention several that were in the First Annual Report of the Council on

Environmental Quality regarding energy:

> The combined effect of carbon dioxide pollution and heat pollution is strongly in the direction of warming the earth's atmosphere. Particle pollution tends to lower the earth's temperature. Which pollution effect will ultimately dominate? Will we indeed drown or will we freeze? Despite firm predictions by some ecologists, we do not know the answers. Careful monitoring and extended research are required if we are to manage our global climate wisely. These questions may become critical in the future.[107]

It is not known to what extent oil films on oceans alter evaporation, radiation emission, or turbulence. Yet 5 to 10 million tons of oil are put into the ocean each year by humans—not counting disasters.[108]

Conclusions: Failures of popular solutions to environmental problems

Because of the tremendous danger involved, we believe that the present path is reckless to the extent of being immoral. We need to take a path in the opposite direction; the risks are so great we need to err on the side of caution. We believe, therefore, that safety, world justice and responsibility to future generations requires tremendous *reductions* in American production, consumption and modern technologies.

POLITICAL-ECONOMY AND CULTURE VS THE ENVIRONMENT

America's behavior, at first glance, appears to be illogical and unreasonable. However, our race towards Armageddon is a logical outcome of some of the fundamental foundations and principles of our society which are at the heart of our political-economic system and culture.

The *private enterprise system* is an ecological anachronism.[109] The pursuit of maximim individual gain through competition and the marketplace contradicts the

requirements of a spaceship which necessitates consideration of the entire crew, careful planning, cooperation,
thrift, small-is-good, minimum accumulation and equal
portions. The quest for the most profits by corporations,
for example, has spurred the ecologically harmful modern
technologies. Barry Commoner points out that the soap
companies' switch to detergents increased profits from
31% of sales to 47%,[110] and the replacement of steel and
lumber by aluminum, cement, plastics, and resins increased profits by about 40 to 300 per cent.[111] American
utility companies are making choices on the basis of their
maximum profit as their overriding concern, and their
choice of fission energy as the major method of meeting America's future electricity needs doesn't make sense
from a safety viewpoint, but it does from a maximum
profits viewpoint.[112]

> It is not technology but our gross misuse of technology
> that lies at the root of the ecological crisis. If we use our
> technology to make a profit, to accumulate wealth and power
> for a small privileged sector of society, then of course technol-
> ogy will be destructive.[113]

The American *culture* of maximum production and
consumption is also an ecological anachronism. Perhaps
the most widely-used measure of success in our society is
the annual growth in the real Gross National Product.
However, GNP is not a measure of either happiness or
even the economic welfare of the nation. The GNP
includes military spending, advertising, excessive packaging, built-in obsolescence, unnecessary model changes,
and excessive baubles of affluence such as electric carving
knives. On the other hand, it does not subtract the
negatives of resource depletion, environmental deterioration and damage to human health which increase with
economic growth.

Moreover, the GNP does not even measure the
material well-being of people, but it is a measure of what
goes through the economy ("throughput"). The *more*
resources and products which go through the economy
each year the better off we are, according to the GNP

indicator. However, in a spaceship, this is exactly the reverse of the way a good indicator should work. From an ecological perspective, the *less* we consume the better off we are. The GNP would drop if Americans were content with an ecologically-sound, simple lifestyle. Within the present economy and culture, therefore, we have a choice of depression and unemployment or ecological disaster.

The need for a maximum GNP is also related to our private enterprise economy: maximum profits are related to maximum production and consumption. Using the example of automobiles, larger cars are more environmentally destructive: they use more materials and energy in production, use more gas and oil when operated, and pollute more in both their use and disposal. However, the automobile industry has foisted large cars onto the American public because, according to Henry Ford, "minicars make miniprofits."[114]

Another limitation of the private enterprise system is that it cannot meet the needs of the world's poor, and, in fact, increases the gap between rich and poor. Food and other limited resources in the capitalist world, for example, go mostly to the "haves" who can afford to purchase them, while the poor majority have no economic "demand" in the market place and, therefore, do not get their needs met. While over a billion people are hungry, therefore, much of the world's richest agricultural land is withdrawn from production through government subsidies, cash crops are grown in the hungry nations for the over-fed, and the hungry nations are net exporters of protein. In the capitalist world, the problem is not so much how to increase production capability as it is how to increase the purchasing power of the poor and hungry. This is what the capitalist system cannot do. This is also what the green revolution or increased technology can't do. In fact, they do the opposite.

In the American political-economy and culture of growth, acceptable solutions to social problems must be generally consistent with economic growth, more business, bigger profits, more complicated technology, and more government subsidies to the big corporations. It is not surprising, therefore, that one major "solution" to environmental problems in America has been the creation of an Environmental Industrial Complex (EIC) which will parallel the Military Industrial Complex.[115] (Many corporations are in both.) This solution proclaims an all-out direct attack on pollution by the use of antipollution technology and equipment. Accordingly, pollution-control is expected to be one of the biggest economic-growth sectors in the 1970's. Studies estimate that over one-quarter of a trillion dollars will be spent on "cleaning up" the environment in the next ten years.[116] Some of America's largest corporations (who are also its largest polluters) will produce the new anti-pollution control technology and equipment, and the government will pay for most of it. For example, Gallen points out that the chemical industry, the second biggest water polluter, "is in the enviable position of reaping sizable profits by attempting to clean up rivers and lakes (at public expense) which they have profitably polluted in the first place."[117] Weisberg describes the EIC scenario:

> . . . The business of pollution control will in fact make a profit out of pollution while at the same time generating more pollution: more growth will be the remedy applied to the perils of growth.[118]

This is demonstrated in a recent massive study of the steel industry by the independent Council on Economic Priorities (CEP) which found, according to the *Philadelphia Inquirer,* that big steel plants continue to "ravage" the environment despite heavy spending on anti-pollution devices.[119] Weisberg shows that although the anti-pollution approach seems illogical as far as the whole society is concerned, there is a clear private rationality to it. That is, within the context of rapid GNP growth, increasing pollution will call for increased production of pollution-control devices and technology, which in turn generates more profits and meets the growth needs of big corporations—all at the expense of the society at large and future generations. EIC will tend to stifle meaningful ecology actions by giving the impression that something positive is already being done. Meanwhile, industry and environmental agencies will try to make pollution a problem of the individual rather than the political-economic system and the culture of growth by blaming the victims and calling for their rehabilitation. That is, the citizenry are asked to drive at more ecological speeds on the highway, stop littering, recycle their cans and bottles, and keep the lights out in empty rooms.

The American political-economy and growth culture harm the environment, contribute to injustice regarding the world's poor and future generations, and risk ecological disaster.

SOME CONDITIONS FOR A HUMANE SOCIETY FROM AN ECOLOGICAL PERSPECTIVE

The first condition of an ecologically humane society is the *ending of the political-economic system of private enterprise:* it cannot provide an ecologically safe environment or meet the needs of the poor; it can't justly redistribute the world's limited resources between or within nations. Moreover, the private enterprise system gives increasing proportions of economic and political power to those in whose interest the environment is now threatened.

A second condition for achieving a new society is the *de-development* of the now over-developed countries: the U.S. and other industrialized societies must reduce their inordinate consumption of limited resources and halt the deterioration of the environment. While this will require a wide variety of approaches, including simpler technology, recycling, greatly reduced waste, etc., the most important is a drastic reduction in the Gross National Product. Hardesty, Clement, and Jencks believe that the United States should reduce its GNP by 60 to 70 per cent.[120] To be reasonably just and ecologically safe, however, the U.S. probably should reduce its consumption of resources by 80 to 90 percent. Ivan Illich in his book, *Energy and Equity,* argues that democracy, freedom and equity, in either a specific nation or the whole world, require that the level of per capita energy consumption be above that of the poor nations, but extremely below the present consumption in the United States.[121] Although the private enterprise system is a primary cause of ecological deterioration, so is the culture of conspicuous affluence. Consequently, for industrialized nations, just switching to a socialistic or egalitarian order is not enough—de-development is still required.

A third condition of the new society is *re-development:* a simple, economically-secure lifestyle which is more compatible with nature and has a primary emphasis on people. The present-day values of individualism, competition, maximum production, maximum consumption, bigness, complicated and unnatural technology, short-range perspective, equal opportunity and elitism would be replaced by collectivism, cooperation, minimum production, minimum consumption, smallness, simple and natural technology, long-range view, equal conditions for people and democracy. (These will be discussed in more detail in the Prescription section.) The Quality of Life for people in a de-developed/re-developed America would be greatly improved.

ECOLOGICAL CONSERVATISM AS POLITICAL RADICALISM

The ecology movement has been adopted by the whole gamut of the political spectrum, including some who are apolitical, elitist, and anti-poor. Many of the world's birth control programs are staffed by America's middle class and paid for by the super-rich who fear the growing Third World masses will consume the world's limited resources and spread revolution.[122] *Limits to Growth* fills a book trying to estimate when the world will run out of resources, and have famines and pestilence, but it reveals its elitism by ignoring that these are already realities for over half the capitalist-world's population today and by not discussing the causal role of the political-economic system (which paid for the report).

The ecology movement has been criticized for being politically conservative and anti-poor. One critic writes that it's anti-poor because "the hungry hordes are viewed as a hostile force and to be resisted at all costs", and it's anti-revolutionary because it's nonpartisan and apolitical when strong political struggle is required.[123] The ecology movement is also believed to be middle class and elitist in advocating a freeze on wealth and income levels and distribution, when, according to Passell and Ross' arguments for a $2-Trillion Economy, massive increases in the U.S. economy are required to meet the needs of the Third World poor.[124]

Despite the sometimes misuse of the ecological issue, we must incorporate its realities into our social change analysis, strategies, goals, and programs. This is particularly true because we agree with Herman Daly that "ecological conservatism breeds economic radicalism."

> In the past growth has been a solvent for sticky income problems. As long as everyone gets absolutely more the fight over relative shares will be less intense. But in the stationary state relative and absolute shares move together and the focus will shift to distribution of the stock of wealth, which is a far more radical issue than the distribution of income.[125]

The radicalism of zero growth is recognized by *Newsweek* economic columnists. Henry Wallich says, "Growth is a substitute for equality of income. So long as there is growth there is hope, and that makes large income differentials tolerable."[126] In our view, since capitalism cannot much redistribute wealth and income, and because its own internal logic requires growth, the end of growth will cause a public challenge to the system of private enterprise.

In conclusion, though conservatives have adopted the ecological issue, we not only believe that humanitarians must include the ecological realities in their change efforts, but that they should demand an end to the private enterprise economy, and the beginning of de-development and re-development, which are radical human necessities.

[1] Some of the basic concepts in the introduction appear in Kenneth Boulding's classic article, "The Economics of the Coming Spaceship Earth", in Warren A. Johnson and John Hardesty, (eds.), *Economic Growth vs. The Environment* (Belmont: Wadsworth, 1971).

[2] James Rathlesberger, ed., *Nixon and the Environment: The Politics of Devastation.* (NY: Village Voice, 1972), preface, p.vii.

[3] T.S. Lovering, "Non-Fuel Mineral Resources in the Next Century" in John Holdren and Paul Ehrlich, eds., *Global Ecology* (NY: Harcourt Brace Jovanovich, 1971).

[4] Preston Cloud, "Realities of Mineral Distribution", *The Texas Quarterly,* 1967; Also is in Philip Nobile and John Reedy, eds., *The Complete Ecology Fact Book* (Garden City: Anchor, 1972), p. 356; Also see Donella Meadows, et al, *The Limits To Growth* (NY: Signet, 1972) p. 54 ff; Richard Falk, *This Endangered Planet: Prospects and Proposals for Human Survival,* (NY: Vintage Books, 1972) p. 159 ff.

[5] U.S. Department of the Interior, "United States Energy: A Summary Review", January, 1972, p. v.

[6] *The San Francisco Chronicle,* December 14, 1969, p. 31.

[7] The United Nations, "Trends in the Social Situation".

[8] See Council on Environmental Quality, *Environmental Quality: The First Annual Report of the Council on Environmental Quality.* Government Printing Office, 1970, p. 16-17; Meadows, *op. cit.,* p. 71.

[9] Council on Environmental Quality, *Environmental Quality: The Second Annual Report of the Council on Environmental Quality.* Government Printing Office, 1971, p. 8.

[10] *The New York Times,* June 15, 1972, p. 33. Lead poisoning in children comes mostly from air pollution rather than lead-based paint, evidently, according to an Environmental Protection Agency report described in *The New York Times,* September 7, 1971, p. 17; similar conclusions were reported by a National Institute of Mental Health report, see the *Philadelphia Inquirer,* February 15, 1972, p. 1.

[11] Meadows, *op. cit.,* p. 80

[12] See Paul R. Ehrlich and Anne H. Ehrlich, *Population, Resources, Environment: Issues in Human Ecology.* (San Francisco: W.H. Freeman & Co., 1970), especially ch. 6.

[13] *Ibid., Chapter 7;* Barry Commoner, *The Closing Circle: Nature, Man & Technology,* (NY: Knopf, 1971)

[14] The United States Census Bureau report according to *The New York Times,* April 4, 1973, p. 24.

[15] Faulk, *op. cit.,* p. 134-5.

[16] Paul and Anne Ehrlich, *op. cit.,* p. 118 ff.

[17] Commoner, *op. cit.,* p. 232

[18] *The Ecologist,* Vol. 2, No. 1, January 1972, "A Blueprint for Survival", p. 1. Also available in paperback.

[19] Commoner, *op. cit.,* p. 80.

[20] Robert L. Heilbroner, *Between Capitalism and Socialism: Essays in Political Economics.* (NY: Vintage Books, 1970) p. 274.

[21] Commoner, *op. cit.,* p. 153-158.

[22] Barry Commoner, "The World's Largest Ecology Seminar" in J. D. Allen and Hanson, eds., *Recycle This Book! Ecology, Society, and Man.* (Belmont: Wadsworth, 1972) p. 11.

[23] We wish to credit the Environmental Coalition on Nuclear Power, A-400 Benson East, Jenkentown, PA, 19066, for much of the research in this section. Also, see issues of *Nuclear Opponents,* Citizen's Energy Council, Box 285, Allendale, N.J. 07401.

[24] U.S. Department of the Interior, *op. cit.*

[25] Wash-740 report, "Theoretical Possibilities and Consequences of Major Accidents in Large Nuclear Power Plants", U.S. Atomic Energy Commision, Washington, D.C., March, 1957.

[26] See Forbes, Ford, Kendell, and McKenzie, "Nuclear Reactor Safety: An Evaluation of New Evidence," *Nuclear News,* September, 1971, published by the American Nuclear Society; Also see *The New York Times,* December 11, 1971, p. 1.

[27] Richard Curtis & Elizabeth Hogan, *Perils of the Peaceful Atom* (NY: Doubleday & Company, Inc., Copyright 1970) p. 1 ff.

[28] *Science,* Vol 177, July 28, 1972, p. 330, "Nuclear Safety: Damaged Fuel Ignites A New Debate in AEC."

[29] See Richard Curtis & Elizabeth Hogan, *op. cit.,* p. 70 ff.

[30] See John W. Gofman, "Time for a Moratorium" in "The Case for a Nuclear Moratorium", (Washington, Environmental Action Foundation), p. 7.

[31] *Ibid.*

[32] See *Technology Review,* Spring, 1972; Also, *The New York Times,* February 17, 1971, p. 27, "Kansas Geologists Oppose a Nuclear Waste Dump."

[33] Gofman, *op. cit., p. 7.*

[34] *Environment,* May 1974, p. 21; Deborah Shapley, "Plutonium Reactor Proliferation Threatens a Nuclear Black Market," *Science,* Vol 172, April 9, 1971.

[35] *Ibid.*

[36] See, for example, Curtis & Hogan, *op. cit.;* "The Case for a Nuclear Moratorium", *op. cit.;* Ernest J. Sternglass, *Low-Level Radiation* (NY: Ballantine Books, 1972); John W. Gofman and Arthur R. Tamplin, *Poisoned Power: The Case Against Nuclear Power Plants,* (Emmaus, PA: Rodale Press, 1971); Roger Rapoport, *The Great American Bomb Machine* (NY: Ballantine Books, 1972).

[37] "Bulletin of the Atomic Scientists, May, 1972, as reported in "The Case For a Nuclear Moratorium, *op. cit., p. 1.*

[38] Senator Mike Gravel, "Finding The Critical Mass" in "The Case For A Nuclear Moratorium", *op. cit., p. 14.*

[39] Barry Commoner, "Test Fallout and Water Pollution" in *Scientist and Citizen,* December, 1964, as reported in Curtis & Hogan, *op. cit., p. 189 ff.*

[40] *The New York Times,* October 21, 1971, p. 1.

[41] As quoted by Egan O'Connor, "Radiation Forever, Men Playing God", *Engage,* August, 1970, published by the Board of Christian Social Concerns, The United Methodist Church.

[42] In addition to many "ecology" groups, many governmental bodies have supported an atomic production moratorium: In 1973 the Swedish government declared a moratorium on building atomic plants pending an independent investigation of their hazards. Also, in June, 1971, the AEC's own technical advisor, Dr. Morris Rosen, advised the AEC to declare a moratorium on new plants, increased power, and new designs until there was adequate experience and research. (Reported on the American Broadcasting Company's televised special on Atomic Energy, May 31, 1973.) Also, the New Jersey State Senate Ad Hoc Committee on Energy and the Environment recommended a state-wide moratorium on atomic plants, even if it required a reduction in the demand for energy, pending a long-range energy study. (*Philadelphia Inquirer,* April 6, 1973, p. 1-D.)

[43] Many critics have sarcastically compared the government's 1970's fight against pollution to its innocuous 1960's "War on Poverty" (with its innumerable programs which were highly publicized when each started), which failed to stem the tide of increasing American poverty. The head of the Environmental Protection Agency also agrees with this analogy. *(The New York Times,* December 13, 1971, p. 46.)

[44] *The New York Times,* December 28, 1970.

[45] *The New York Times,* December 17, 1971, p. 1.

[46] *Ibid.,* p. 1.

[47] *The New York Times,* February 9, 1971, p. 65.

[48] *Ibid.*

[49] *The New York Times,* October 15, 1970, "U.S. Pollution Control Panel Bars Environmental & Consumer Observers".

[50] *The New York Times,* December 7, 1970, p. 1.

[51] *Ibid.,* p. 50.

[52] The Council on Environmental Quality, *Environmental Quality: The First Annual Report of the Council on Environmental Quality.* Government Printing Office, 1970, p. 161.

[53] The Council on Environmental Quality, *Environmental Quality: The Third Annual Report of the Council on Environmental Quality,* Government Printing Office, 1972, p. 428.

[54] The U.S. Congress House Committee on Government Operations, *Enforcement of The Refuse Act of 1899,* 92d Congress, 2d session, (Government Printing Office, 1972).

[55] *The New York Times,* March 11, 1972, p. 46.

[56] *The New York Times,* February 2, 1973, p. 1.

[57] *The New York Times,* February 5, 1972, p. 14.

[58] The U.S. Government, *The Economic Report of the President,* Government Printing Office, February 1971, p. 79.

[59] *The New York Times,* January 13, 1971, p. 65.

[60] *The New York Times,* December 24, 1970.

[61] *Providence Evening Bulletin,* November 17, 1971, p. 32.

[62] *The New York Times,* February 1, 1971, p. 80.

[63] See, for example, Robert Dorfman and Nancy Dorfman, eds., *Economics of the Environment: Selected Readings,* (NY: Norton, 1972)

[64] See Commoner, *Closing Circle, op. cit., p. 148.*

[65] Commoner *op. cit.,* p. 271.

[66] Dorfman *op. cit.*

[67] The U.S. Government, *The Economic Report of the President,* Government Printing Office, February 1973, p. 71.

[68] John Hardesty, et al, "Political Economy and Environmental Destruction", in *The Review of Radical Political Economics,* Vol. 3, No. 4, Fall-Winter, 1971, p. 86.

[69] *The New York Times,* March 20, 1972, p. 1.

[70] *The New York Times,* April 12, 1973, p. 1.

[71] The U.S. Government, *The Economic Report of the President,* GPO, February, 1973, p. 82.

[72] Hardesty, *op. cit.,* p. 85.

[73] Paul Ehrlich and Anne Ehrlich, *op. cit., p. 61-62.*

[74] See, for example, *The New York Times,* March 20, 1973, "The Jobless and Their Problems Jam Asian Cities", p. 1; *The New York Times,* January 18, 1972, p. 41, "Technological Age adds to Plight of Asians"; *The New York Times,* April 30, 1972, "Black Africa's Cities Teem With Youths Seeking Jobs But Finding Poverty, p. 14.

[75] *The New York Times,* March 20, 1973, p. 12.

[76] *The New York Times,* January 18, 1972, p. 41.

[77] Garrett Hardin, *Exploring New Ethics For Survival: The Voyage of the Spaceship Beagle,* (Baltimore: Penguin Books, 1972), p. 40-41

[78] See "Drought" by Martin Walker, *The New York Times Magazine,* June 9, 1974; and "The Making of the Sub-Saharan Wasteland" by Claire Sterling, *The Atlantic Monthly,* May 1974.

[79] Meadows, *op. cit.,* p. 153 ff.; Also see *Environment,* July/August, 1972, p. 11; *Monthly Review,* June, 1972 Supplement; Anne and Paul Ehrlich, *Population, Resources, and Environment, op. cit.,* p. 96 ff.; *The New York Times,* April 15, 1973, "The Green Revolution Hasn't Ended Hunger"; *The New York Times,* October 12, 1972, p. 8, "Land Disputes Thwarting Green Revolution in India", *The New York Times,* April 19, 1973, "Protein Lack Is Vast, But Poor Lands Do Little", p. 10.

[80] *The New York Times,* February 14, 1972, p. 5.

[81] *Too Many,* Georg Borgstrom, copyright 1969, 1971 by Georg Borgstrom. Copyright 1969 by Macmillan Publishing Co., Inc. p. 201.

[82] See Anthony Lewis, *The New York Times,* April 22, 1974, Op. Ed.

[83] Hubert Humphrey, 84th Congress, First Session, Senate Committee on Agriculture and Forestry. Hearings: Policies and Operations of P.L. 480, p. 129, 1957; also see Harry M. Cleaver, Jr., "The Contradictions of the Green Revolution", in *Monthly Review.* June, 1972, p. 82 ff., on how food has been a political weapon of U.S. historically.

[84] See Cleaver, *Monthly Review, Ibid.; The New York Times,* April 19, 1973, p. 10.

[85] See *The New York Times,* 15 March, 1974, p. 28; and, *International Economic Report of the President, 1974;* Government Printing Office.

[86] See for example, Lester B. Pearson, *Partners in Development; Report of the Commission on International Development* (NY: Praeger Publishers, 1969), esp. p. 55; *The New York Times,* March 19, 1972, p. 18, "Each Birth

in Asia Makes the Poverty More Desperate ."

[87] See Mahmood Mamdani, *The Myth of Population Control: Family, Caste, and Class in an Indian Village,* (NY: Monthly Review Press, 1973).

[88] *The New York Times: Encyclopedia Almanac, 1970,* p. 364.

[89] *The New York Times,* March 19, 1973, p. 18.

[90] For a fuller description and documentation of this argument see Carlo M. Cipolla, *The Economic History of World Population* (Great Britain: Penguin Books, 1970).

[91] Cipolla, *op. cit.,* p. 105.

[92] See the "Exported Plague" chapter of this book.

[93] See *Environment,* July/August, 1972, p. 10; Meadows, *op. cit.,* chapter 3; Commoner, *The Closing Circle, op. cit.,* chapter 11; Cipolla, *op. cit.,* p. 93.

[94] See the "Exported Plague" chapter of this book.

[95] This is quite different from the popular assumptions that population growth must be stopped before economic benefits can be gained.

[96] See, for example, William Barclay, Joseph Enright, Reid T. Reynolds, "Population Control in the Third World" in *North American Congress on Latin America Newsletter,* Vol. IV, No. 8, December, 1970.

[97] Cipolla, *op. cit.,* p. 55.

[98] Paul Sweezy, "Cars and Cities", *Monthly Review,* April, 1973, p. 6-7.

[99] Commoner, *The Closing Circle,* p. 154.

[100] Meadows, *op. cit.,* p. 108

[101] *The New York Times,* November 4, 1970, p. 43.

[102] *Environment,* July/August, 1972, p. 10; Also see Falk, *Op. Cit.,* p. 138 ff; John McHale, *World Facts and Trends,* Second Ed. (NY: Collier Books, 1972). p. 86-87.

[103] *The New York Times,* November 4, 1970, p. 43.

[104] Meadows, *op. cit.,* p. 161

[105] Meadows, *op. cit.,* p. 81

[106] See *ibid.,* p. 156 ff., where this process, called "reducing the negative feedback loops", is described.

[107] *Environmental Quality* 1970, *op. cit.,* p. 100.

[108] *The National Geographic,* December 1970, "Our Ecological Crisis".

[109] This does not mean that a planned or socialist system is necessarily better. As will be argued later, all societies of massive economic growth and affluence are ecologically harmful. However, a planned economy may have much less waste.

[110] Commoner, *The Closing Circle,* p. 259.

[111] *Ibid.,* p. 264.

[112] See, for example, The Philadelphia Electric Company's booklet, *The PE Story;* their presentation before the New York Society of Security Analysts, June 17, 1970.

[113] Murray Bookchin, "Ecology and Society", in J. David Allan and Hanson, eds., *op. cit.,* p. 215.

[114] Commoner, *The Closing Circle, op. cit.,* p. 264.

[115] See Barry Weisberg, "The Politics of Ecology" in *Liberation,* January 1970; Martin Gallen, "The Making of a Pollution-Industrial Complex", *Ramparts,* May 1970.

[116] *Newsweek,* June 12, 1972, "The Big Cleanup"; Also see K. William Kapp, *The Social Costs of Private Enterprise* (NY: Schocken Books, 1971), p. xiii; Meadows, *op. cit.,* p. 86; Falk, *op. cit.,* p. 30.

[117] Gallen *op. cit.,* p. 2

[118] Weisberg, *op. cit.*

[119] *The Philadelphia Inquirer,* June 5, 1973, p. 3-C.

[120] Hardesty, *op. cit.,* p. 91.

[121] See Ivan Illich, *Energy and Equity,* (NY: Harper and Row, 1974)

[122] Barclay, *op. cit.*

[123] Richard Neuhaus, *In Defense of People* (NY: Macmillan Company, 1971)

[124] Peter Passell and Leonard Ross, "Don't Knock the $2-Trillion Economy" and their book: *The Retreat From Riches: The Gross National Product and Its Enemies* (NY: Viking, 1974).

[125] Herman E. Daly, "The Canary Has Fallen Silent", *The New York Times,* Op. Ed., October 14, 1970.

[126] *Newsweek,* January 24, 1972, p. 62; also see Brzezinski,"The Politics of Zero Growth" in *Newsweek,* March 27, 1972.

5

Exported Plague

INTRODUCTION

Struggling countries have dominated history, the stronger trying to dominate the weaker while battling other powers for supremacy. For the past several centuries, Western European nations and late-comer, the United States, had carved up virtually the entire world among themselves, each exploiting and oppressing the militarily inferior people in their respective spheres of domination. Beginning with Russia in 1917, however, an increasing number of underdeveloped nations have joined the counter-system of socialism, bringing vast benefits to about one-third of the world's previously poverty-stricken peoples. No one can look at China's egalitarianism, "serve the people" spirit, extensive health services, and general material progress without being deeply impressed, particularly when compared with its Asian neighbors or with the massive despair, starvation, corruption and inequality of China's non-socialist past. Similar gains in medical care, housing, education, social security, economic development, etc., have been made in Russia, Cuba, and North Korea. Even Eastern Europe can point to significant achievements for its citizens.[1]

Yet even modern powers which call themselves socialist often relate to their neighbors in an exploitative and dominating fashion:

(1) Outright military *invasion,* as when the USSR moved into Hungary and Czechoslovakia, or when China "ordered the Peoples' Liberation Army to march into Tibet."[2]

(2) Using *foreign aid* as a lever of economic sanctions, as when Khrushchev in 1960 removed nearly all Soviet technicians from China. This brought the Chinese charge that Moscow's "perfidious actions disrupted China's national economic plan and inflicted enormous losses upon China's socialist reconstruction."[3]

(3) Exerting direct and indirect *political control* as in the Stalinist period when Eastern European coutries' political, military and police apparatuses were heavily influenced by Soviet and Soviet-appointed personnel and advisors. Persons who deviated from the accepted path in politics or economics found themselves faced with possibility of arrest, torture, forced confession and execution.[4]

(4) Manipulating *trade relationships* to the advantage of the developed socialist nation, as exemplified by Russian trade with Eastern Europe after World War II, which, according to one estimate, allowed the USSR to extract $20 billion net (measured in U.S. dollars) from the area over an 11-year period.[5] Fidel Castro claimed that European Communist states sold Cuba industries with a backward technology, and China has charged that Soviet assistance has been mostly in the form of trade and that "prices of many of the goods we imported from the Soviet Union were much higher than those on the world market."[6]

(5) General *foreign policy.* China charged the USSR, "You bully those fraternal countries, whose economies are less advanced, oppose their policy of industrialization and try to force them to remain agricultural countries and serve as your sources of raw materials and as outlets for your goods."[7]

Despite these evidences of socialist "imperialism," the peoples of the previously poverty-stricken, now socialist nations have fared much better since their withdrawal from the capitalist sphere, especially in comparison to previous conditions and to those of the remaining under-developed capitalist nations.

This chapter, however, will focus on the American relationship to the Capitalist poor nations because (1) the United States is our chief concern, and (2) most of the poverty-stricken and hungry people in the world today (numbering over one billion) live in underdeveloped nations exploited by the American-led capitalist sphere.

The United States has emerged this century as the world's undisputed economic leader. Comprising only six percent of the world's population and land area, it consumes between 30 and 50 percent of the world's annual production. Its political economic system, consequently, is often exhaulted as a paragon to be imitated by others, particularly the now underdeveloped nations. However, such acclaim may be as unwarranted as emulation by the poor nations is impossible. The "free world" has almost 2½ billion people living in an integrated political-economic order, about 700 million of whom live in the rich developed nations. But the praise given the American-centered capitalist system is dubious because about 1.5 billion poverty-stricken people live within it, and their condition continues to deteriorate. Although environment and limited natural resources prevent imitation of American consumption patterns, so do political, economic, and military forces. Moreover, in seeking their own interests, American business and government play a major role in the increasing impoverishment and oppression of the masses in the never-to-be-developed nations whose only hope is economic and political independence.

UNITED STATES CORPORATIONS EXPLOIT THE THIRD WORLD [8]

The American people hold a common concern to help the world's poor masses overcome economic poverty and political oppression. While direct humanitarian efforts are considered temporary expedients, western-style economic development is believed to be the best road toward attaining political freedom and ending poverty. It is assumed that American private enterprise, which has so successfully served the American economy, can best propel the Third World into economic take-off. This view however, is increasingly being questioned. Although American business penetration does create some jobs, payroll, fixed machinery, taxes for governments, skills training and technology, it also exploits the poor nations, prevents full development, perpetuates political domination, and exacerbates the poverty and hunger of the majority of people.

Capital Appropriation

Capital investment is considered the touchstone of economic development,[9] and it is generally presumed that by expanding overseas, American firms provide much of the required developmental capital. However, only 15 percent of new American overseas investments between 1957 and 1965 was money sent from the U.S., 20 percent was obtained locally and 65 percent was reinvested overseas profits.[10] Consequently, rather than increasing the amount of investment capital available, American firms depleat it by repatriating huge profits. *Life* Magazine, for example, stated editorially on July 18, 1969, "The U.S. is taking more out of Latin American countries than we are putting in. Ever since 1962, U.S. investors have brought home more money than they have invested in the same year. In 1967, repatriated profits exceeded private investments by more than a billion dollars." And in 1970, U.S. firms repatriated $4.9 billion more in profits and other forms of return on investments than they invested in all underdeveloped nations.[11]

Not only have American firms drained poor nations of surplus capital throughout the "decade of development", but between 1950 and 1965, U.S. corporations appropriated profits ($25.8 billion) from the poor nations amounting to almost three times the inflow of U.S. investment dollars ($9.0 billion).[12] Moreover, the Western rich nations have similarly decapitalized the now underdeveloped nations for centuries.[13] One notorious example is the report from the Chilian government that the expropriated earnings from that poor country by four U.S. corporations over a 60-year period exceeded the entire gross national product of Chile during that time.[14]

Appropriated profits, however, are not the only means by which American firms decapitalize poor nations. Pierre Jalee reports that in 1965 U.S. corporations invested $1.5 billion in Third World nations while repatriating profits of $4.9 billion. That amount is three times as much repatriated in profits as invested.[15] However, if the drain of Third World payments for interest on loans and credits is added to the profits returned to the U.S. in that year, the total capital drain was over $6 billion. Additionally, if the capital loss of Third World nations due to deterioration of terms of trade is added, ($4.5 billion in 1965) the total drain of capital was over $10 billion in 1965.[16] (This does not include $1.5 billion net loss in shipping costs.)

The poor nations of the world, therefore, have been contributing capital for the development of the rich nations.

Ownership and Control of Means of Production

The developed capitalist nations have gained extensive ownership and control over the political economies of the poor nations (while simultaneously decapitalizing them). In 1970, for example, American firms increased their ownership (and control) of productive capital in the Third World by $6.8 billion, according to *Jeremiad*.[17] Frederick Donner, writing as chairman of the Board of General Motors, explains this process from the corporate perspective:

> Let me summarize our overseas record during the past fifteen years in terms of some objective measures of business accomplishment. At the end of 1950, the value of General Motors' net working capital and fixed assets overseas was about $180 million ... By the close of 1965, this investment had increased to about $1.1 billion or approximately six times the

amount in 1950. This expansion was accomplished almost entirely from financial resources generated through General Motors operations overseas and from local borrowings which could be repaid through local earnings. As a result . . . our overseas subsidiaries remitted about two-thirds of their earnings to the United States. [18]

Although European nations fear that American ownership threatened their independence, the poor nations, whose economies are much smaller, are even more threatened. [19] The amount of U.S. direct investment in the poor nations is almost equal to U.S. investment in Western Europe. [20] According to *Newsweek,* U.S. investors employ about two million South Americans, pay one-fifth of the taxes and produce one-third of the exports of South America. [21] Brazil, because of its enormous size, and is often cited as a model of developmental success, is a good example. After experiencing phenomenal growth during the 1960's, "foreign investors—mostly from the U.S.," reports *Newsweek* in 1970, "own 82% of the country's industry." [22] The following description of American economic control in Peru is not atypical of other poor nations:

> Anderson Clayton dominates the wool and cotton production market. The Grace Co., the Chase Manhatten Bank, the First National City Bank of N.Y., the Northern Peru Mines, Marcona Mines and Goodyear establish the prices for agricultural products and control 80% of the raw materials. The International Petroleum Co. (IPC), a subsidiary of Standard New Jersey, owns the oil that represents 80% of national production. The American Smelting & Refining Co. and Cero de Pasco Corp., which owns over 1.2 million acres, reign over copper and other mining production. The Bell Telephone Co. has taken over the telephone services . . . [23]

The extent of U.S. control over Third World economies was noted in the *New York Times'* "Economic Survey of the Americas": "Because the key industries or markets of Latin America were usually controlled by U.S. companies, policy tended to be made or influenced in the North rather than in the region involved." [24]

Excess Profits

Economic exploitation is also evident by the much higher rate of profit return on investments in the poor nations. The *Survey of Current Business* (an official government publication) reports that in 1970 " . . . the rate of return on investments in less developed countries was 21.0 percent, roughly twice the yield on investments in the developed areas."[25] Although Latin America, Asia, and Africa together have only one-third of U.S. private direct foreign investments, they account for two-thirds of profits from those investments.[26]

Trade Relations

Third World nations are increasingly exploited through trade relations with the developed nations. The powerful, giant corporations, with American government cooperation, control prices and markets for both raw materials coming from and finished goods shipped to underdeveloped nations.[27] Consequently, Third World nations' terms of trade have deteriorated. The 7% drop in average prices of raw commodities exported by poor nations was accompanied by skyrocketing prices of U.S. manufactured exports.[28] In one six-year period the trade value of a jeep went from fourteen bags of coffee to thirty-nine.[29] In 1965 alone, the United Nations estimated a terms-of-trade dollar loss of over $4 billion for underdeveloped nations. There is a corresponding equal dollar gain to the developed nations.[30]

Also resulting from their dependent trade position, the Third World's share of world exports declined from 30% in 1948, to 20% in 1965, to 17.6% in 1970.[31] The United States' "free trade" policies have often been one-way affairs. The *New York Times,* for example, reports " . . . United States tariff barriers and other devices . . . effectively bar more than 800 Latin products from the United States market," and that the "Latin American share of the U.S. market has dropped by one-third since the start of the Alliance for Progress."[32]

The effect of this cost-price-markets squeeze put on Latin (and other Third World) nations is summarized in the *Christian Century;*

> The price of raw materials tends to fall and the price of manufactured goods to rise. Thus copper, tin, oil, wool, meat, hides, nitrates, tropical fruit, coffee and cocoa—Latin America's major products—buy less and less manufactured goods per unit. How can a country develop when its population is increasing and its exports are bringing in fewer and fewer manufactured goods? And if the Latin Americans are getting even less manufactured goods for their raw materials, then the developed countries are getting even more raw materials for their manufactured goods. This kind of situation, together with interest on loans, shipping regulations, banking restrictions, etc., amounts to what is called economic imperialism. [33]

Third World Economies

Another consequence of foreign domination is that the main sectors of Third World economies (agriculture, extractive industries and manufacturing) serve corporate interests of the developed nations and the desires of the Third World's affluent minority while overlooking the needs of their poor majority.

The *agricultural sector* is the most notorious example because the poor nations are hungry nations. An estimated 10 to 20 million people die each year from starvation, and over 40% of them are children under five years old. [34] Moreover, the per capita protein available in hungry nations has declined about 6% since World War II. [35] This increasing hunger is not primarily caused by either population growth or stunted agricultural production, but from massive exports of agricultural products to the overfed nations. Much of the arable land, previously taken over by colonizers and now controlled by large corporate plantations, produce "cash crops"—in essence they grow money, rather than food to feed hungry people. Frances Moore Lappe writes, "The Food and Agricultural Organization of the U.N. reports that *non-edible* agricultural production is growing at a faster rate

than edible food production in the developing countries."[36] Between 1958 and 1964, for example, the
hungry nations, agricultural production for *export* (e.g.,
coffee, tobacco, cocoa, tea, bananas, natural rubber, etc.)
grew by 31%, 2.2 times faster than their total agricultural
production and faster than their population growth.[37]
Moreover, much of the *protein* produced is also exported
to the over-fed nations. The hungry nations are net
exporters of protein.[38]

If the poor nations consumed the protein they
already produce, their hunger would greatly diminish. Dr.
Georg Borstrom, an international food science authority,
reports that the fish meal now exported from Africa
would make up 50% of that continent's protein shortage,
and the Peruvian exports to the over-fed nations alone
would bring the protein level of all South America to
Southern European levels.[39]

> The food shortage and world hunger seem in some queer
> way to be overlooked in most plans for industrialization and
> investments . . . In a series of hungry countries around the world
> all these proposterous deliveries of food and feed to the Western
> world are recorded with considerable satisfaction and as a sign
> of a flourishing economy. It is certainly not indicative of a
> sound economy that Southern Rhodesia up to the present crisis
> furnished the luxury markets of London (Smithfield) and
> Madrid with meat that brought money into the pockets of a few
> white colonizers, while at the same time 95% of the Rhodesian
> population suffered various degrees of malnutrition and certain-
> ly could not afford meat in their diet . . . The United States is at
> present being provided with shrimp from more than sixty
> countries, among them Hong Kong, India, Surinam, Panama,
> and Mexico. In all these countries this shrimp would fill a crying
> need . . .
> . . . One-third of the world's population can simply not
> expect that it will be allowed to continue to gulp down
> two-thirds of the world's food . . . [40]

China and Cuba's virtual elimination of hunger and
poverty while still "undeveloped" (but after social revolution) are further evidence that political-economic systems
play a critical role in these maladies. Programs against

world hunger and poverty, therefore, should be *more* concerned (in the short-run) that Third World agriculture serve hungry people than with population control and food shipments.

The fastest-growing economic sectors of the Third World nations are *minerals* and *energy,* growing much faster than those sectors of the developed nations. Between 1958 and 1965 the production in extractive industries of Third World nations grew by 97%, while these industries grew by only 19% in the developed countries. [41] However, these industries also do not benefit the poor masses because they, too, are mostly exported to developed countries. The poor nations face, moreover, an even gloomier future as their non-renewable resources become depleted. Venezuela's oil is an example of a lucrative but dwindling resource which gives great benefit to a relatively few rich Venezuelan and American financiers, but the conditions of most citizens, who receive no benefits from the depletion of their nation's chief resource, deteriorate. [42]

In contrast to its "successful" exporting sectors, the Third World's *manufacturing sector* remains underdeveloped, producing only 6.5% of the world's manufactured goods and growing at a rate of 35% less than that of the advanced capitalist nations.[43] About 90% of the Third World's exports are raw or semi-finished materials and only 10% are manufactured goods, while 79% of the developed nations' exports to the poor nations are manufactured goods. [44] This international division of labor within the capitalist sphere benefits the developed nations' corporations which want the Third World's raw products for their own industries, Third World markets for their own manufactured goods, and don't want competition from less expensive finished products. Consequently, while 63% of American foreign investments in developed nations were in manufacturing, only 22% in the Third World were in manufacturing. Most of this manufacturing was in either assembly of parts made in the U.S. or in light industry, but not in heavy industries required for independent classical "economic take-off." [45]

THE UNITED STATES GOVERNMENT EXPLOITS THE THIRD WORLD

It is not by coincidence that the world's great economic powers also have been the world's political and military powers: overseas dominance by corporations requires overseas dominance of government. A chief purpose of American foreign policy has been to keep as many nations as possible available to the maximum free reign of its corporations by whatever means necessary: loans, grants, technical assistance, treaties, threats, penalties, subversion, military assistance, and as a last resort, direct military intervention.

Foreign Aid

Foreign aid deserves extensive consideration because (1) it is purportedly the government's most magnanimous effort; if *it* exploits and oppresses the poor nations, the remaining self-interested aspects of foreign policy must do so even more. (2) It is a chief method of control over Third World nations. That many people have benefited from foreign aid is not questioned here, surely millions have been helped and many lives saved. The question, however, is whether the harm from aid far outweighs its benefits to the poor peoples.

To the American public, foreign aid is altruistic to the extent of depriving ourselves:

> ... we have too much of a 'give-away' policy. I think we should take care of our own first.
>
> So many people are out of jobs here and the country is helping other countries ... Our own people should be helped before foreign countries.
>
> I don't want the taxpayers of the U.S. to feed the rest of the world forever. We could go broke. [46]

However, governmental documents and statements, including those of AID, hold a quite different view, as shown in this Foreign Relations Committee report:

> The U.S. government is not a charitable institution, nor is it an appropriate outlet for the charitable spirit of the American people . . . Technical assistance is only one of a number of instruments available to the U.S. to carry out its foreign policy and to promote its national interests abroad . . . these tools . . . include economic aid, military assistance, security treaties, surplus agricultural commodities-disposal policies . . . [47]

In practice, "national interests abroad" primarily means American business interests which already have been shown to be injurious to the Third World.

The Alliance for Progress, Food for Peace and other American "aid" programs do not constitute a neo-Marshall Plan for the Third World.

> The Marshall Plan consisted essentially of outright *grants* to industrialized and potentially rich European nations because it was a program to save Western capitalism, an objective so fundamental in importance to the United States that $13 billion appeared a small price to pay for the survival of world capitalism. The impoverished Third World receives tied American *loans*, not grants, because this is a major means to extend capitalism and economic control into that sphere . . .

> Then why does the United States loan funds to poor nations that in the long run will lose thereby? First, most of the loans go to build an internal infrastructure which is a vital prerequisite to the development of resources and direct United States private investments. Then, there is the fact that to repay loans in dollars requires the borrowing nations to export goods capable of earning them, which is to say, raw materials of every sort. Development in this form increases the Third World's dependence on Western capitalist nations, so that loans become integrating and binding liens. [48]

Loans to nations which are not industralizing causes a kind of "addiction" that requires increasingly larger borrowings to pay debts from earlier loans.

> . . . [debt] servicing aid was beginning to wipe out the advantages of loans to the developing nations, so that in 1964,

for example, the Export-Import Bank received $100 million more from Latin America than it lent to it. [49]

In 1967, 75% of the gross capital flow into Latin America was utilized to pay external public debts,[50] and the World Bank study of 80 less-developed countries showed their debt service increased twice as fast as their export earnings.[51] Through massive loans, therefore, the poor countries became increasingly controlled by the lending rich nations and the "international" lending institutions.[52] It is questionable whether even no-interest and un-tied loans to underdeveloped nations, whose economics serve their own and foreign rich, would much help the poor masses.

Life raises another important facet of aid: "The U.S. actually gives little direct aid, and hamstrings the loans it does make . . . the money must be spent on high-priced U.S. goods, half of which must be shipped in U.S. vessels at higher rates.[53] Probably even more damaging is the requirement that recipient nations solve social problems primarily through private enterprise, thereby hindering direct governmental efforts to meet social needs.

Even the most sacrosanct aid program, "Food for Peace," gives questionable benefits to Third World peoples. Like other aid programs, its purpose is not philanthropic, as indicated by its lawful title, "The Agricultural Trade Development and Assistance Act of 1954." Its purpose is not to feed the world's hungry, but "to increase the consumption of U.S. agricultural commodities in foreign countries, to improve the foreign relations of the U.S., and for other purposes." It is to feed American agricultural businesses' hunger for profits which have been burdened by over-production. Over half the food is *sold* to the hungry nations; the form of payment to the U.S. is credit called "counterpart funds", whose spending in the poor nations is controlled by the United States. Some of the credits are used to pay for extensive American military and other overseas operational costs (rents, salaries of foreign personnel, local purchases, etc.) thus enabling the U.S. to spend surplus food rather than scarce dollars in poor countries. Also, counterpart funds are loaned to U.S. corporations for their investment purposes and for market development of U.S. private food sales. These and other uses of counterpart funds aggravate the balance of payment problems of the poor nations while helping those of the U.S. The loan-like character of food aid also furthers recipients' dependency:

> PL 480 . . . has been achieved at *no* net cost to the U.S., while having indebted aid-recipient countries to the extend of some $22 billion, thereby tying them to the purse strings of the U.S. State Department and Treasury for nearly twenty years to come. [54]

In some instances, food shipments actually reduce the amount of home-grown food available in hungry nations because of its "dumping" effect. The increased supply of a particular product lowers prices, often forcing domestic farmers to switch to growing products for export to the U.S. As local farmers stop growing edible products for domestic consumption, the more the purpose of food aid to increase American food exports is accomplished. In this way hungry nations also become more dependent on the U.S. for edible foods. [55] Finally, Food for Peace has supplied oppressive military dictatorships with $1.5 billion in war materials and services from counterpart funds which the American government gives to recipient nations, but specifically earmarked for military purchases from the U.S. [56] In conclusion, the spectre of food aid is whether the hungry people of the world would be better off (and better fed) without it. Certainly, if Third World agriculture were geared to serve their hungry, there would hardly be need for food assistance, but that requires a political solution which is, in part, prevented by Food for Peace's economic and military support of oppressive regimes.

America also uses aid as an economic and political control device through continual threats, often carried out, of aid-withdrawal. U.S. aid to Brazil, for example, fell from $81.6 million to $15.1 million from 1962 to 1964 during liberal Goulart's presidency, which was much disliked by the U.S., but jumped back to $122.1 million in 1965 after a coup of "good" reactionary generals. [57]

As emphasized by Eugene Black, former president of the World Bank, direct benefits to American business and economy is another chief function of aid:

> (1) Foreign aid provides a substantial and immediate market for U.S. foods and services. (2) Foreign aid stimulates the development of new overseas markets for U.S. companies. (3) Foreign aid orients national economies toward a free enterprise system in which the U.S. firms can prosper. [58]

And an A. I. D. report explains:

> Our foreign economic assistance program as a whole has had by-products of substantial benefit to the U.S. economy. For example, Food for Peace has helped us manage our agricultural surpluses while making its important contribution to development. AID development loan dollars, now spent in large preponderance in the U.S., contribute substantially to employment in our export markets after U.S. assistance is phased out. (Indeed, in considering projects for development funding, AID now also takes into account any special potential for future trading relationships between the U.S. and recipient countries.) [59]

More specifically, another AID report shows its business and economy support in 1971:

> The Agency for International Development purchases $975,000,000 worth of commodities in fiscal year 1971, with 99% of it . . . being spent in the U.S. . . . Foreign aid provides important business for U.S. companies and manufacturers.
>
> In addition, there were $632 million in technical service contracts with U.S. companies, consulting firms, and institutions . . .
>
> Termination of foreign aid could cost about 70,000 U.S. jobs in the first year following termination (and over 50,000 in subsequent years).
>
> (Termination) would have an immediate adverse effect on

U.S. exports. AID financed in fiscal 1971: 16.4% of all U.S. exports of iron and steel mill products, 25% of all U.S. fertilizer exports, 15.7% of all U.S. exports of railroad equipment . . .

Elimination of AID financing would also have a significant effect on the U.S. shipping industry. Over the period of FY 1964-FY 1969, the cargo financed under Foreign Assistance Act programs has ranged from 22-30% of the total cargo moving on U.S.-flag shipping.

In FY 1971, the U.S. exported $300 million in agricultural commodities under Title II of PL 480 . . . The farmers of America have a direct stake in the extension of the aid program . . .

(AID has) contracts with 120 U.S. universities (with a) total cumulative value of $232,165,442. [60]

AID's most negative feature, however, is its reinforcing of oppressive dictatorial regimes which are friendly to U.S. business, but oppressive of their own people. President Nixon acknowledged the sizeable number of dictatorships supported by U.S. aid:

We presently provide military and/or economic aid to 91 countries around the world. I checked these various countries as far as their heads of government are concerned, and in only 30 of those countries do they have leaders who are there by any standard that we would consider fair. We would have to cut off aid to two-thirds of the nations of the world, in Africa, in Latin America, in Asia, to whom we are presently giving aid, if we apply the standards that some suggest we apply to South Vietnam. [61]

Since over half of the 30 "democratic" nations mentioned are developed nations, the overwhelming majority of poor nations given aid must have unfairly constituted governments. The necessity to support dictatorships throughout the Third World is explained by a congressional committee:

U.S. military assistance programs, which began as efforts to bolster counties on or near the periphery of what was then the Sino-Soviet Bloc has changed substantially in their approach. They are now more often used to bolster governments which face insurgencies of one sort or another. By the very nature of these activities, the U.S. has become closely identified with the existing governments, and oftimes its materials are used to suppress insurgents whether or not they are Communist . . . our role in meeting insurgencies is indivisible from those of the governments running those countries. [62]

As Robert McNamara, as Secretary of Defense stated in 1966:

Whether or not Communists are involved or not, violence anywhere in a taut world transmits sharp signals through the complex ganglia of international relations; and the security of the U.S. is related to the security and stability of nations half a globe away. [63]

It is understandable therefore, why over half of American foreign aid, about five billion dollars annually, is military assistance. [64] Part of military assistance for 1970 included $518 million to dictatorships in underdeveloped nations for Public Safety Programs, listed by the Comptroller General as "U.S. Economic Assistance Related to Internal Security," which, according to AID, " . . . can serve to prepare civil police forces to prevent the development of threats to internal order before they become explosive problems requiring military action." [65] However, since virtually all poor recipient nations are dictatorships, all aid to the Third World, even economic aid, serves to oppress the masses of people. American aid, therefore, defies the American Revolutionary spirit that all people are endowed with inalienable rights of life, liberty and the pursuit of happiness and "that to secure these Rights, Governments are instituted among men, deriving their just powers from the consent of the governed, that whenever any form of government becomes destructive of these ends, it is the right of the people to alter or abolish it, and to institute new government . . . as to them shall seem more likely to effect their safety and happiness." [66] The effect of foreign aid, however, has been to establish American interests and privileges over the rights of Third World peoples.

Senator Edward Kennedy cites some of the failures of aid to achieve results:

> ... their (Latin American countries) economic growth per capita is less than before the Alliance for Progress began; in the previous eight years U.S. business has repatriated $8.3 billion in private profits, more than three times the total of new investments; the land remains in the hands of a few; one-third of the rural labor force is unemployed and 13 constitutional governments have been overthrown since the Alliance was launched. [67]

And Paul Prebish, head of the UN's Latin American Institute for Economic and Social Planning reported to the Inter-American Development Bank on the 10 years of Alliance for Progress:

> New patterns of concentration of income have emerged. Those at the top of the social pyramid have conspiciously prospered, but the benefits of development have hardly touched the broad masses relegated to the low-income strata. [68]

Many ardent Congressional supporters of aid, such as Senator Church are "taking their leave":

> ... American economic aid is commonly used to promote industrialization programs which generate a high level of consumption for the privileged, with little, if any, trickle-down benefit for the dispossessed. At the same time, American military assistance, ... help[s] such regimes as those of Brazil, Greece and Pakistan to suppress reformist movements. In this way, American aid is being used not to promote development but for the quite opposite purpose of supporting the rule of corrupt and stagnant—but vociferously anti-communist-dictatorships ...
> ... However much we may have wanted reform and development, we wanted 'stability', anti-communism, and a favorable climate for more investment ...
> ... In addition to financing American exports, our foreign aid, both economic and military, has encouraged relationships of sustained dependency on the U.S. ... No less than military aid, our economic assistance creates and perpetuates relationships of dependency.
> ... Dependency on the U.S. grows steadily, too, with the

mounting burden of servicing past debts ... (which) keep the poor countries on a 'short leash.' As grace periods end on loans falling due in the 1970's, the poor countries find themselves paying out even greater amounts to finance past debts, new loans will be effectively neutralized ...

(U.S. corporations) decapitalize Latin America by withdrawal of profits, they plow back of their profits to gain increasing control of the mineral assets, industry and production of Latin American counties ...

... the conviction is taking increasing hold that the poverty of the poor counties is not the result of imperfections in the old 'models' of development but rather in the inevitable result of the policies and practices of the rich countries. ... I can no longer cast my vote to prolong the bilateral aid programs ... In far too many countries, as in the case of Brazil, we poured in our aid money for one overriding purpose, to furnish American capital with a 'favorable' climate for investment ...[69]

Military Force

Since military force is ultimately required to maintain world domination, the U.S. is the planet's military leader, spending over $1.1 trillion for military purposes since 1945. About 65% of its annual Federal budget is spent on past, present and future wars.[70]

American military intervention with Third World nations take direct and indirect forms. *Direct* intervention by U.S. military forces has occurred throughout American history. Senator Dirkson, for example, listed in the *Congressional Record* of June 23, 1969, 162 direct U.S. military interventions in foreign, mostly Third World, countries from 1795 to 1945 "to protect U.S. interests." This listing included only interventions unauthorized by Congress.[71] Since 1945, the U.S. has militarily intervened in Korea, Cambodia, Laos, Thailand, Lebanon, The Bay of Pigs, Formosa, Vietnam, and the Dominican Republic, while covertly intervening elsewhere, as in Guatamala, Iran, and Bolivia. Millions of American servicemen are still stationed in more than 30 foreign countries.[72]

The *indirect* method uses the carrot of military and economic support for "friendly" regimes and the stick of threats of its withdrawal, as well as support of military coups.[73] Many regimes are dependent on American military assistance, which is extensive. In 1970, for example, it included: military grants, $2.8 billion; government military sales, $842 million; commercial sales, $567 million; turnover of military property, $248 million; and internal security assistance, $515 million.[74] Many Third World dictatorships are included in the 53 different American defense commitments with foreign nations mentioned by Magdoff.[75] The United States' overseas military role will probably increase in coming years, as conditions in poor nations deteriorate further for most people and socialist alternatives become more viable.

Anti-Communism and Anti-Democracy

American foreign policy contradicts its democratic ideology. Recall President Nixon's acknowledgment that most Third World nations supported by the United States are essentially totalitarian states. The long list of American-supported dictatorships includes Pakistan, Greece, Taiwan, Brazil, Spain, Guatamala, South Vietnam, Rhodesia, South Africa, et al. The American war in Vietnam could have been entirely avoided had President Eisenhower been willing to accept the government about to be democratically elected there in 1954; he prevented the elections because he believed "80% of the population would have voted for the Communist Ho Chi Minh."[76] And more recently, in little more than one year, the U.S. supported the genocidal army of Pakistan's dictatorship against the democratically elected party and undefended masses of East Bengal, violated the U.N. trade sanctions against Rhodesia's oppressive white government, gave Spain $400 million in aid and a pledge to support the defense system of dictator Franco, praised Brazil's dictator-General Medici at a White House reception, blessed Greece's dictator-Generals with a celebrated Vice-presidential visit, eased the embargo against shipping military equipment to totalitarian Union of South Africa, and gave $435 million in economic credits to colonial Portugal. Simultaneously, the U.S. strongly opposed Chile's Allende government, the most democratically elected government in Latin America. The U.S., however, recognized the new government of Chili after a military coup overthrew Allende. This coup made another military dictatorship of Chili, which had been the Latin American nation with the best history of democracy. Seemingly few, if any, friendly "anti-communist" regimes are too totalitarian to receive American support, while no socialist effort seems too democratic to oppose.

The support of democracy and freedom is clearly not the basis of American foreign policy in the Third World. In practice, freedom in the underdeveloped nations seems to be the freedom of American Corporate privilege. The "ideal" poor nations, therefore, have an American-dependent economy and an oppressive, client-dictatorship dependent more on Washington than their own people. *Newsweek,* for example, reports, "The only nations in Latin America where U.S. businessmen and Washington policy-makers can be fairly sure they won't be unpleasantly surprised are those controlled by repressive regimes."[77]

Finally, American anti-communism policy led to a breakdown in democracy at home, causing President Johnson to say he would continue the Indochina War even if one person supported it, and President Nixon, also elected on an end-the-war platform, to say he would continue his present policies despite overwhelming (73%) public opposition:

> I am certain a Gallup Poll would show a great majority of the people would want to pull out of Vietnam. But a Gallup Poll would also show that a great majority of people would want to pull three or more divisions out of Europe. And it would also show that a great majority of the people would cut our defense budget. Polls are not the answer. You must look at the facts.[78]

Moreover, Washington's unpopular and unjust support of dictatorships has often required secrecy from both the public and Congress; thereby, undermining democratic institutions and traditions and bringing the U.S. itself closer to totalitarianism.

The Indochina War

The United States' government's most notorious overseas role is its Indochina War. Apologists, no longer claiming its purpose is peace and freedom, say the war is a mistake and benefits no one. However, this consistent 26-year policy was not a mistake. The American government underwrote much of France's Vietnam War costs, prevented the 1954 elections precipitating renewed fighting, imposed the Diem regime and bolstered its fighting capability, conspired to Diem's overthrow because he was about to make peace with the North,[79] and sent half-a-million American troops—all while it could have ended the "mistake" at any time by withdrawing its troops and support. The war has been costly to the Indochinese, American troops and the American public, but many war-related corporations have reaped great profits. The war serves as an important strategic benefit to all American multi-national corporations: (1) it helps preserve their privileges in nearby resource-rich nations such as Indonesia,[80] which might be threatened by a series of socialist victories (the domino theory), (2) serves as a lesson to other Third World peoples, (3) ideologically preserves the private enterprise system by its public indoctrination against the evils of Communism and (4) legitimizes American support of anti-communist dictatorships. The Indochina War is not an isolated, mistaken incident of minor importance, but a largescale repeat of wars past and a preview of "Vietnams" to come throughout the Third World resulting from a foreign policy of domination in support of exploitative economic relations. America's unswerving foreign policy was summarized in President Kennedy's resolve: "I am determined upon our system's survival and success, regardless of the cost and regardless of the peril."[81]

U.S. ECONOMIC SUCCESS DEPENDS ON THIRD WORLD BUSINESS, RESOURCES, UNDER-DEVELOPMENT AND POVERTY

Despite celebrated pronouncements of the American economy's self-sufficiency, the United States' high consumption living and galloping economic growth are extremely dependent on Third World business, resources, underdevelopment and poverty.

Third World Business

In support of the contention that the U.S. is economically independent, it is usually pointed out that American foreign trade is "only" 5% of the total GNP, and trade with the Third World is only 1.5%.[82] However, even these percentages might be considered significant since the all-important automobile industry's total production is also 5% of GNP and the military budget, which creates recessionary ripples with the slightest cutbacks, is not much bigger than 7%. But most American overseas business comes from American foreign subsidiaries, not from mainland trade. Therefore, adding the $160 billion of foreign affiliate sales to U.S. exports of $43 billion, over $200 billion total foreign business in 1970 was a significant 20% of the total U.S. GNP.[83]

The chief significance of Third World nations, however, is their contribution to American corporate profits, rate of return on investments, and economic expansion rate. About 20% of U.S. corporate profits are earned from foreign investments, and two-thirds of these profits come from the Third World; therefore, the now underdeveloped nations account for almost 13% of total U.S. corporate profits.[84] And recall that the return rate on foreign investments in the Third World is twice that in developed nations.[85] Finally, and not least important for the growth-dependency of the United States, American investments and profits are growing at a much faster rate overseas, including the Third World, than at home.[86] From government reports, Thomas Weisskopf shows that after-tax foreign profits of American business rose steadily from 6.8% of their total profits in 1950, to 17.6% in 1969.[87]

Third World Resources

In 1953, President Eisenhower said in his inaugural address:

> We know . . . that we are linked to all free peoples not merely by a noble ideal but by a simple need. No free people can for long cling to any privilege or enjoy any safety in economic solitude. For all our own material might, even we need markets in the world for the surpluses of our farms and our factories. Equally, we need for the same farms and factories vital materials and products of distant lands.[88]

The Third World consumes one-third of U.S. exports, absorbs one-third of U.S. foreign investments, provides cheap labor, contributes two-thirds of U.S. foreign profits and 12% of all U.S. corporate profits. The most critical dependency of the United States on the Third World, however, is the dependency on those resources which are vital to industrialization.

The United States' past status of relative resource-independence is rapidly deteriorating. Because minerals are the products of millions of years, mines bear no second crop. Instead, they become depleted with use—and much use already has been made of American resources. Consequently, the President's Commission on Foreign Economic Policy concluded in 1954:

> This transition of the United States from a position of relative self-sufficiency to one of increasing dependence upon foreign sources of supply constitutes one of the striking economic changes of our time. The outbreak of World War II marked the major turning point of this change.
>
> Both from the viewpoint of our long-term economic growth and the viewpoint of our national defense, the shift of the United States from the position of a net exporter of metals and minerals to that of a net importer is of overshadowing significance in shaping our foreign economic policies.

We have always been almost entirely dependent on imports for tin, nickel, and the platinum group of metals. In addition, our requirements for asbestos, chromite, graphite, manganese, mercury, mica, and tungsten have been generally covered by imports. Prior to World War II this was about the extent of our list of strategic materials, that is, mineral substances of which our requirements are wholly or substantially supplied by foreign sources. At present, by contrast, the United States is fully self-sufficient only in coal, sulfur, potash, molybdenum and magnesium. [89]

Furthermore, according to resources expert, Dr. Preston Cloud, if present trends continue for twenty years, the United States will be depleted of its reserves of crude oil, natural gas, uranium 235, maganese, chromium, nickel, tungsten, cobalt, copper, lead, zinc, tin, aluminum, gold, silver, and platinum. [90]

The Third World, which produced 37.5% of the capitalist sphere's mineral resources in 1965, is the primary source of many key resources required by the developed nations' industries. The Third World produced the following proportions of the world's production of these resources: 72% of the cobalt, 45% of the maganese, 59% of the bauxite, 95% of the chrome ore, 44% of the copper ore, 96% of the tin concentrate, and over 50% of the crude oil. [91] Since these percentages are almost always rising, the Third World is becoming the largest producer of extractive resources. Therefore, the developed capitalist nations, who import most of these resources, are becoming increasingly dependent on the Third World for their industrialization. For example, a U.S. Government commission reported that for 52 of the 62 strategic industrial materials needed by the Department of Defense, at least 40% had to be imported and "three-quarters of the imported materials included in the military stockpile come from the underdeveloped areas." [92] The Third World also supplies 100% of the U.S. consumption of collumbium, chromium, and cobalt, elements required for jet engines. [93] Presidential assistant for international economic affairs, Peter Peterson, reported in his 1971 study, "The United States in The Changing World Economy":

> Developed countries, facing expanding demands for raw materials and limited supplies available domestically, are turning increasingly to less developed countries. Competition for LDC raw materials will intensify . . .
>
> . . .Long-range projections indicate that by the year 2000 we will import 30-50% of our mineral requirements, including a significantly increased share of our oil needs.[94]

Under Secretary of State, John Irwin predicts that by 1980 the U.S. will be importing 50% of the oil it uses, mostly from the Middle East.[95]

What has happened, one might ask, to the panaceas of technology and synthetics which are supposed to be making America self-sufficient? Economists DuBoff and Herman give the following explanation:

> The truth of the matter is that our domestic industrial base and our export sector are becoming *more* reliant on 'high technology products'—chemicals, machinery, aircraft, instruments, office equipment—which themselves require greater proportions of imported raw materials, not less. 'Technological progress,' rather than serving as a bail-out device, appears to be deepening our dependence on foreign sources of metals and oil. This, in fact, is one conclusion of an 18-month study by Commerce Department economist Michael Boretsky, who predicts that in 1980 the United States will be importing 50% of its total raw material consumption compared with 30% at present.[96]

Third World Underdevelopment and Poverty

The happy, "sky's the limit", high-consumption world is a myth. For reasons detailed in the ecology section, everyone in the world cannot become affluent in American terms. Moreover, the world cannot much longer stand even the present levels of production, industrialization and population. On the one hand, not only the United States, but the world is running out of most of the non-renewable mineral resources required for the consumptive life of the now developed nations. On the other hand, the *present* level of western-type industrial production is already so damaging to the environment that the existence of humankind is threatened. The dream of a world without poverty is further restricted by the rapid increases in both world population and the rising consumption of the already-developed nations. Consequently, the per capita levels of consumption which can be attained in the Third World vis-a-vis the developed nations take the form of a zero-sum game. That is, the more one gets, the more the other loses. Preston Cloud, for example, points out that if all the world's poor consumed at the average American per capita level, virtually all the world's non-renewable mineral resources would be depleted within several years.[97] Moreover, both the Club of Rome's MIT study, as well as the "Blueprint for Survival" statement by 33 of Britain's most distinguished scientists, conclude that "all growth projections end in collapse." Even the present world economic growth trends (in which world poverty is increasing) are seen to be short lived:

> Continued exponential growth of consumption of materials and energy is impossible. Present reserves of all but a few metals will be exhausted within 50 years, if consumption rates continue to grow as they are. Obviously there will be discoveries and advances in mining technology, but these are likely to provide us with only a limited stay of execution.[98]

The collapse of economic growth is seen even if population is soon stabilized, pollution reduced by three-quarters, resource reserves doubled and important technological breakthroughs made, according to the MIT study.[99]

The United States, therefore, has two choices: further growth or de-development. In the "further growth" choice, the United States would continue its present course of expanded per capita production and consumption as measured by galloping GNP growth. However, this choice necessitates that the poor nations, at best, maintain their present per capita production and consumption levels as well as their poverty, or, more probably, experience an increased poverty rate. The second option, "de-development", requires that the United States and other developed nations *reduce* their present levels of production and consumption while allowing the poor nations to "semi-develop", i.e., not develop industrially as the present industrialized nations have, but seek a quality of growth which meets essential needs of all their population while curbing their birth rates. America has chosen the further growth option.

MULTINATIONAL CORPORATIONS: NEW AGENTS FOR WORLD DOMINATION BY CORPORATE ELITES

The power to make political and economic decisions which affect people's lives is rapidly moving from people and governments to private businessmen who manage and control a relatively few giant corporations which have successively outgrown the stages of small enterprise, company and national corporation. Some of these corporations are so big that twelve American corporations now rank among the top 38 non-socialist nations in annual revenue.[100] And only 11 nations had GNP's higher than General Motors' sales-income in 1965.[101] It is these giant corporations which have become multinational, dominating the political economies of many non-socialist nations. The foreign operations of the top 25 American industrial corporations, for example, account for between 25% and 30% of their total sales, assets and earnings.[102] *Newsweek* listed 30 big American corporations whose foreign operations averaged 47.2% of their annual profits, including: IBM (48%), Dow Chemical (44%), Squibb (63%), F.W. Woolworth (61%), Boeing (40%), IT&T (35%), J.J. Heinz (44%) and Uniroyal (75%).[103]

The internationalization of business is both growing in scope and becoming more concentrated among the world's big corporations. It is estimated that 15% of the Gross World Product (GWP) is now accounted for by corporations' foreign operations and this percentage is rapidly rising.[104] Moreover, over half of the world's internationalized business is conducted by American corporations, and 40% of American foreign earnings are made by only 16 firms.[105] Recall that in Brazil, the world's 10th largest non-socialist nation in GNP, 82% of the industry is foreign owned. And Canada, with the world's 8th largest GNP, has over two-thirds of its resource and primary manufacturing industries controlled by foreigners, and over three-fifths of its secondary manufacturing industry. Most of these are owned and controlled by large United States multinationals.[106] Moreover, the multinationals' hold on the non-socialist world's economy is increasing so rapidly that professor Stephen Hymer, of Yale University's Economic Growth Center, predicts: "We will soon have a regime of 300 or 400 multinational corporations controlling 60 or 70% of the world industrial output."[107] Since economic power is political power, the political and economic lives of the "free" world's peoples are increasingly undemocratically controlled by a relatively few private corporate elites.

INDEPENDENCE: A PREREQUISITE FOR THIRD WORLD FULL DEVELOPMENT

To achieve full development of life-sustenance, esteem, and freedom[108] for their poverty-stricken masses, the poor nations must achieve independence from the developed nations.

The Development of Underdevelopment

The Western colonial nations played a crucial role in the historical process which led to the present underdevelopment of the now poor nations. The militarily-achieved colonial relationship (1) destroyed traditional economies and societies, (2) established new economies dominated by colonial interests in their own favor, (3) appropriated economic surpluses, including the plundering of human and material resources, (4) established new social and political institutions favoring colonial exploitation, including despotic military regimes, and (5) was ultimately maintained by military intervention.[109]

Some of the colonialized, now underdeveloped nations, were as economically advanced and as capable of
development as the conquering nations. One such area
was India:

> India in the eighteenth century was a great manufacturing
> as well as a great agricultural country, and the products of the
> Indian loom supplied the markets of Asia and of Europe. It is,
> unfortunately, true that the East Indian Company and the
> British Parliament, following the selfish commercial policy of a
> hundred years ago, discouraged Indian manufacturers in the
> early years of British rule in order to encourage the rising
> manufactures of England. Their fixed policy, pursued during the
> last decades of the eighteenth century and the first decades of
> the nineteenth was to make India subservient to the industries
> of Great Britain, and to make the Indian people grow raw
> produce only, in order to supply material for the looms and
> manufacturers of Great Britain. This policy was pursued with
> unwavering resolution and with fatal success; orders were sent
> out to force Indian artisan to work in the Company's factories;
> commercial residents were legally vested with extensive powers
> over villages and communities of Indian weavers; prohibitive
> tariffs excluded Indian silk, and cotton goods from England;
> English goods were admitted to India free of duty or on
> payment of a nominal duty ... The invention of the power-
> loom in Europe completed the decline of the Indian industries;
> and when in recent years the power-loom was set up in India,
> England once more acted towards India with unfair jealousy. An
> excise duty has been imposed on the production of cotton
> fabrics in India which ... stifles the new steam-mills of India.
> Agriculture is now virtually the only remaining source of
> national wealth of India ... but what the British-Govern-
> ment ... take as Land Tax at the present day sometimes
> approximates to the whole of the economic rent ... This ...
> paralyzes agriculture, prevents saving, and keeps the tiller of the
> soil in a state of poverty and indebtedness ... In India the State
> virtually interferes with the accumulation of wealth from the
> soil, intercepts the incomes and gains of the tillers ... leaving
> the cultivators permanently poor ... In India, the State has
> fostered no new industries and revived no old industries for the
> people ... In one shape or another all that could be raised in
> India by an excessive taxation flowed to Europe, after paying
> for a starved administration ... Verily the moisture of India
> blesses and fertilizes other lands. [110]

... nearly all our major problems today have grown up during British rule and as a direct result of British policy; the princes; the minority problem; various vested interests, foreign and Indian; the lack of industry and the neglect of agriculture; the extreme backwardness in the social services; and above all, the tragic poverty of the people. [111]

The example of Japan proves the "development of underdevelopment" rule; it was never colonized, and yet, is the only Asian country which industrially developed. [112]

Russia, China and Cuba's elimination of their historical hunger and poverty after achieving political-economic independence from the West offer more recent evidence of the development of underdevelopment thesis, especially when they are compared to the continued poverty in the remaining dependent Third World nations.

Permanent Underdevelopment, Poverty and Domination

Since World War II, most of the colonies have achieved official national independence, yet virtually all of the exploitative political and economic relations of colonialism remain; Rapid economic development is still prevented by the excessive outflow of dollars, investments are in economic sectors unproductive to long-run growth; and there is excessive consumption and hoarding by the small upper class, exportation of resources at unfavorable terms, wastage from large military outlays, underutilization of people, etc. Furthermore, some new exploitative forms have begun such as foreign aid, currency exchange rates, and international monetary institutions like the International Monetary Fund, the World Bank and the Inter-American Development Bank. [113]

Within the international corporate-capitalist sphere, economic power accumulates to the strongest competitors while goods and services are distributed through the market according to ability to buy, that is, in proportion to wealth. These two factors feed one another, forming a spiraling cycle in which power accumulates to an increasingly affluent minority, while, conversely, the political power and economic conditions of the poor deteriorate.

The American-led, free world political-economy, therefore, continues to aggravate inequalities (1) between the developed and the now underdeveloped nations, and (2) between the rich and poor within the underdeveloped nations. During the "development" decade of the 1960's the annual average per capita income for the developed nations increased by $650, but only $40 in the poor nations;[114] by 1970, the per capita income of rich nations was $3,000, but only $200 for the poor nations.[115] Second, The *New York Times* "Economic Survey of Asia and the Pacific" describes the unequal distribution of development benefits within the poor nations:

> For rich Asians—and for a small, but growing middle class in a number of countries—this economic growth has provided more goods to buy, more food to eat, more comfort and more luxury.
>
> But probably the majority of Asians still share little of this growth. In fact, not only is the gap between the poor nations of Asia and the rich industrialized nations still widening, but the gap between rich and poor within the poor counties is widening.
>
> The Asian poor do not yet have the cars and television sets produced by industrialized society. But they do have the new problems of an affluent society: air and water pollution, traffic jams, chaotic flows of population from the countryside into the cities, mushrooming slums, technological unemployment and breakdown of government services.
>
> In some places, old family and cultural patterns have been disrupted without being replaced by alternatives such as social security and welfare . . .[116]

In 1972 the *New York Times* reports on Brazil, "the industrial dynamo of South America, if not Latin America":

> . . . the gross national product should exceed 10% in net growth, keeping Brazil among the fastest developing countries in the world. There are other statistics, however, that are less pleasant. Minister of Finance Antonio Delfim Neto noted

recently that only 5% of Brazil's estimated 100 million people benefited from five years of unprecedented economic growth, 45% actually had their standard of living eroded, and the rest live as they did before the boom started.[117]

Supposedly, one of the primary benefits of American business penetration is the creation of jobs for the poor, but many are not brought into the labor force at all,[118] and, as World Bank President McNamara points out, those who are brought into the labor market have a 20% unemployment rate.[119] Despite extensive penetration of the rich nations into the Third World, McNamara laments, "The basic problems affecting the lives of the developing peoples are getting worse, not better, despite a good record of economic growth. These problems . . . include severe malnutrition, rising unemployment and growth in inequality in the distribution of income."[120] In its report, "Trends in the Social Situation", the United Nations despondently concludes:

> It is tragic that at the end of the 1960's there are more sick, more undernourished and more uneducated children in the world than there were ten years ago . . . malnutrition threatens to get worse in the 1970's.[121]

Although individual corporations are not deliberately malicious, the outcome is inherent in the American-led international economy. American investments inevitably decapitalize Third World nations. If American corporations, for example, invested $500 million in Third World nations every year for ten years at 1971's profit return rate of 21%, in the fifth year the corporations would bring home $525 million in profits. This would be $25 million more than new investments that year. By the 10th year they would appropriate $1.05 billion in profits, thereby decapitalizing the Third World by $550 million that year.[122] Because the purpose of private enterprise is to make maximum profits—not to meet social and human needs—production is geared to customers with the most money, who exist first back in the United States and second, among the affluent minority of the Third World.

The corporate imperative for expansion and hegemony undermines *economic* democracy. The people of the Third World cannot control their own economic institutions and resources when they are owned and controlled by foreign corporations. In addition, economic hegemony not only transfers wealth and resources from the poor to the rich countries, but it transfers political influence and control as well: the more U.S. firms invest, the more political control they have. American firms cannot foster *political* democracy when they demand political stability of an unjust status quo which, in turn, is tied to American business success. Moreover, to maintain their privileged position as economic conquistadors, American businesses have had to allign with military dictatorship regimes. In summary, American corporate activities in the Third World inherently conflict with the achievement of democracy, economic development and alleviation of poverty.

Limits of U.S. Economic System and Technology as a Model

Even if it were politically and economically possible, ecological limits would prevent Western-style development from meeting the needs of the world's poor masses. There aren't enough world resources for the poor nations to much follow the path of Western-type development with its super-affluent investment-class, industrial pollution, high consumption of resources, and general waste— including advertising, middlemen, built-in obsolescence and the baubles of the middle class. They have no "Fourth World" of vast human and natural resources to exploit, and the planet's natural reservoirs and life-support eco-systems are already endangered. For them a full-development economic system must: (1) distribute goods to the masses who have no market demand, (2) achieve relative economic equality for all, and (3) provide planning, cooperation, conservation and resource-sharing. These goals are not possible through the invisible hand of the market place which bestows an inordinate share of resources and political power to a minority. The now subdued and often forcibly idle masses must be both permitted and inspired towards political awareness, cooperation, creativity and activity by which they can contribute to the collective social welfare at levels unachievable in the private enterprise, "me first" system.

Full-development of the Third World also requires a decentralized "middle-technology" rather than the technological giantism and industrial centers of the West.[123] Present-day China probably most approximates the requirements for a fully developed Third World nation.[124]

Limits of philanthropic help

Except for emergency crisis situations, private efforts of philanthropic help have been either unsuccessful or hinderences to alleviating world poverty. Private efforts cannot help being paternalistic, enhancing blind faith in the existing exploitative economic institutions by encouraging self-help within them, building a small middle-class as a buffer to basic change, and distracting attention away from necessary changes in the causal political-economic systems which produce more poor each year than can be ministered to. It also inadvertently places blame on the victims by indicating *they* need rehabilitation through education, self-help, birth control, training, attitude change, etc. This approach is also culturalist by trying to fit people into the "modern", white culture and values when history is increasingly showing that we have much to learn from their cultures.

Two Apologies for Underdevelopment: Overpopulation and Insufficient Resources

In a world capable of ending all poverty, the extreme poverty of over a billion people in the midst of affluence requires justification. Apologists for underdevelopment often say that the two chief causes of underdevelopment are the overpopulation and insufficient resources of the poor nations. They presume that the developed nations have much fewer people per square mile as well as more resources than the poor nations. Their remedy is intensive population control programs. There is strong evidence, however, which contradicts this position. Although overpopulation and insufficient resources do hinder development, these have not caused the *difference* between the underdevelopment in the poor nations and the development of the rich nations.

Exponential population growth is indeed one of several key factors contributing to underdevelopment, depletion of world resources, pollution and eco-systems deterioration. India, for example, cannot be expected to provide for the over one billion people it is expected to have within 25 years. However, high population density is not responsible for the polarity of poverty amid affluence in the world. There is no correlation between high population density and low per capita income.[125] In fact, most of the developed nations are overpopulated in that they are among the highest nations in population density. For example, Belgium has 814 people per square mile, West Germany has 606, United Kingdom has 587, and Japan has 708—all are more than India's 415. On the other hand, most of the poor nations have much smaller densities: Mexico has 62, Indonesia has 195, Burma has 101, and Brazil has only 27 people per square mile.[126]

Moreover, the second apology for underdevelopment, lack of natural resources, is also unsubstantiated. Many of the world's most poverty-stricken nations, such as Brazil and Indonesia, are also among the world's richest nations in natural resources, while many of the developed nations are resource-poor, such as Japan, England and other European nations. The industrialization and high-consumption of the developed nations depends on vast amounts of resources imported (exploited) from the lower-density, underdeveloped nations. Even the United States, with its low density of 56 people per square mile, increasingly relies on poor nations' resources.

We conclude, therefore, that (1) differences in population density and resources have not been responsible for the differences in the levels of development between the rich and poor nations, (2) the developed nations must reduce their own population and consumption to provide adequately for their own populations without exploiting the poor nations, (3) the people of all nations need to reduce their populations, (4) the polarity of affluence and poverty, as has been demonstrated throughout this chapter, is primarily caused by the exploitation of the poor nations by the developed nations as well as by the perverted economies of the poor nations.

What is the solution for the poor nations? The apologists for underdevelopment say with Robert McNamara that the problems of the Third World grow worse "despite a good record of economic growth" largely because of their "growth of population."[127] Their remedy is intensive population control efforts. However, this solution contradicts world-wide experience that population growth has declined only when living standards improve, not before.[128] That is, without prior or concurrent economic betterment of the general population, population control programs have failed. China, for example, is now curbing its population since living conditions are improving for its masses.

Although we agree that intensive population control efforts are needed, they do not substitute for the overriding requirement of new economic structures which benefit the whole population and end exploitation by the developed nations.

Conclusion

The problems of Third World nations are integral to their relationships to the United States and other developed nations. Normal American business and government relations exacerbate Third World poverty, political oppression and underdevelopment. The use of military force is the ultimate outcome of the continuation of these existing relationships. For the poor nations, full develop-

ment requires their political, economic and cultural independence. The United States, rather than continuing
programs of "assistance", must end American ownership
of the poor nations' means of production, end its support
of oppressive dictatorships, and stop its armed interventions. Ultimately the United States must also reduce
its superfluous consumption of resources, waste and
ecological deterioration.

---

[1] For material on Eastern European economic advances, see Zbigniew K.
Brezezinski, *The Soviet Bloc* (Cambridge: Harvard U. Press, 1971), p. 101,
287.

[2] From the 17 point Agreement on the Peaceful Liberation of Tibet,
Signed by Chinese & Tibetan leaders, May 23, 1951. For the full text, see H.
E. Richardson, *A Short History of Tibet* (N.Y.: Dutton, 1962), p. 226.

[3] See Edgar Snow, *The Other Side of the River* (N.Y.: Random House,
1962), p. 665 and Brzezinski, *op. cit.,* p. 409

[4] Brzezinski, *Ibid.,* p. 93

[5] *Ibid.,* p. 237, 286.

[6] *Ibid.,* p. 429. The quote is from a February 29, 1964 letter of the
Central Committee of the Chinese Communist Party.

[7] *Ibid.,* p. 421, From a 1964 letter from the Central Committee of the
Chinese Communist Party to the Communist Party of the Soviet Union.

[8] The term "Third World" refers to underdeveloped nations in the
capitalist sphere. It assumes the world is roughly divided into three groups:
(1) Socialist nations, (2) industrially developed capitalist nations and (3)
underdeveloped capitalist nations.

[9] See for example Peter Peterson, Council on International Economic
Policy, *The United States in the Changing World Economy* (GPO, 1971); p.
4; also John Kenneth Galbraith, *Economic Development* (Cambridge:
Houghton Mifflin Company, 1962), p. 46. "Capital" is used here to refer to
money.

[10] For Latin America, U.S. sources of investment funds were only 11%.
North American Congress on Latin America, *Yanqui Dollar,* 1971, p. 17.

[11] *Jeremiad,* No. 32, July 22, 1971, see pages 6 to 8 for calculations from
government sources.

[12] Harry Magdoff, *The Age of Imperialism* (New York: Modern Reader,
1969) p. 198; also see Peterson, *op. cit.,* p. 36 and Chart 46; and *The Review
of Radical Political Economics,* Vol. 4, No. 1, Winter, 1972, p. 17.

[13] See Paul Baran, *The Political Economy of Growth,* (NY: Modern
Reader, 1957) p. 141 ff., p. 179 and 228-9; A. K. *Cairncross, Home and
Foreign Investment 1870-1913* (Cambridge, England, 1953) p. 180 esp.;
Ernest Mandel *Marxist Economic Theory Volume II* (NY: Modern Reader,
1970) p. 442 ff.

[14] See the Chilean Government's ad in *The New York Times,* January 25, 1971; also see North American Congress on Latin America's *New Chile,* 1971, for extensive evidence.

[15] Pierre Jalee, *The Third World in World Economy* (New York: Modern Reader, 1969) p. 115

[16] *Ibid.,* p. 116

[17] *Jeremiad,* No. 32, July 22, 1971.

[18] From The *World-Wide Industrial Enterprise* by Frederick G. Donner. p. 15. (Copyright 1969, McGraw-Hill Book Co. Used with permission of McGraw-Hill Book Co.) And according to Sweezy and Magdoff, Ford-Canada has grown to an enormous size without any cash investment. *The Dynamics of U.S. Capitalism* (NY: Modern Reader, 1972) p. 32.

[19] The per capita GNP of the poor nations averages $200 while that of the developed rich nations is $3,000. See Peterson, *op. cit.,* p. 50.

[20] $20 Billion to $21.6 billion in 1969. *Survey of Current Business,* October, 1971, p. 34.

[21] *Newsweek,* November 2, 1970, p. 58. A Council of the America's report shows American subsidiaries shipped 41.2% of all Latin American exports in 1966; see NACLA Newsletter, October, 1971, p. 13.

[22] *Newsweek, Ibid.*

[23] David Morris and Philip Weaton, "Questions About Latin American Policy" in *Christianity and Crisis,* June 22, 1970.

[24] *New York Times,* January 28, 1972

[25] The *Survey of Current Business* (U.S. Department of Commerce), Oct., 1971, p. 35.

[26] U.S. Department of Commerce, *Survey of Current Business,* June, 1970; and the Statistical Abstract of the U.S., 1969, as reported in *Economic Notes,* November, 1970, p. 7.

[27] Jalee, *op. cit.,* p. 63., About 75% of Third World nations' trade is with the developed capitalist nations; often one or two primary products make up the bulk of their trade; and most of their trade is usually with one developed nation. Also, many of their corporations are subsidiaries or owned by developed nations' corporations—all of which contribute to extreme dependency on the developed nations. Less than 6% of their trade is with Socialist nations.

[28] The *Wall Street Journal,* July 10, 1969.

[29] Jalee, *op. cit.,* p. 72.

[30] Jalee, *op. cit.,* p. 75.

[31] *Ibid.,* p. 62; also see *New York Times,* November 9, 1971, p. 3.

[32] The *New York Times,* October 20, 1970, "Latins Assured by the U.S. on Aid."

[33] Earl M. Smith, "The Latin American Revolution", copyright 1969, Christian Century Foundation. Reprinted by permission from the May 14, 1969 issue of *The Christian Century.*

[34] NACLA Newsletter, May-June, 1971, p. 8.

[35] Frances Moore Lappe, *Diet For a Small Planet* (NY: Ballantine, 1971) p. 17.

[36] *Ibid.,* p. 17.

[37] Jalee, *op. cit.*, see chapter 2, especially p. 18.

[38] Anne and Paul Ehrlich, *Population, Resources, Environment: Issues in Human Ecology* (San Francisco: Freeman, 1970) p. 90; Also see Jalee, *op. cit.*, p. 20-21.

[39] Georg Borgstrom, *Too Many*, p. 237. Copyright 1969, 1971 by Georg Borgstrom. Copyright 1969 by Macmillan Publishing Co. Inc.

[40] *Ibid.*, p. 245-6.

[41] Pierre Jalee, *The Pillage of the Third World* (NY: Modern Reader, 1968) p. 17.

[42] See Harvey O'Connor, "Venezuela: A Study in Imperialism" in Paul Sweezy and Leo Huberman, eds., *Wither Latin America?* (New York: Modern Reader, 1963; and The *New York Times,* November 3, 1970, "Venezuela Planning Tougher Stock Law."

[43] Jalee, *Third World In World Economy, op. cit.*, p. 53.

[44] *Ibid.*, p. 70.

[45] *Ibid.*, p. 111-112.

[46] Lloyd Free and Hadley Cantril, *The Political Beliefs of Americans: A Study of Public Opinion,* (NY: Clarion, 1968) p. 73.

[47] "Technical Assistance." Final report of the Committee on Foreign Relations, March 12, 1957, as reported in Hamza Alavi & Khusro, "Pakistan: The Burden of U.S. aid," *New University Thought,* Autumn, 1962, p. 15.

[48] Gabriel Kolko, *The Roots of American Foreign Policy* (Boston: Beacon Press, 1969) p. 70-73.

[49] *Ibid.* p. 72.

[50] Kolko, *op. cit.,* 72.

[51] The *New York Times,* September 14, 1971, p. 9.

[52] See Teresa Hayter, *Aid As Imperialism* (Baltimore: Penguin, 1971), esp. Ch. 2, for how the rich nations dominate the international lending institutions; The U.S. has 21% and the ten major developed nations over 50% of the vote on the board of the 110-nation-member International Monetary Fund. Similar percentages occur in the World Bank, see *New York Times* September 25, 1971, p. 35.

[53] *Life,* July 18, 1969. *Life* also notes. "Nixon recently cancelled our requirement of 'additionality' which requires a loan recipient to purchase specified U.S. goods we are trying to peddle abroad. But the 'tied' loan, forcing the recipient to buy in the U.S. or ship in U.S. bottoms, remains a far bigger irritant."

[54] Denis Goulet and Michael Hudson, *The Myth Of Aid* (NY: IDOC North America, 1971) p. 74.

[55] For examples, see North American Congress on Latin America *Newsletter,* May-June, 1971, "Food for Profit"; and *Ramparts,* October, 1971, "Guatemala: Food for Profit".

[56] NACLA *Newsletter, Ibid.,* "The Food For Peace Arsenal", p. 5; also see *New York Times,* January 5, 1971, p. 13, "Congressmen told of $700-million Arms Sales Under Food for Peace Program".

[57] E. K. Hunt and Howard Sherman, *Economics: An Introduction to Traditional and Radical Views* (NY: Harper & Row, 1972), p. 554.; Also see Hayter, *op. cit.;* Magdoff *op. cit.,* p. 128; *New Chile, op. cit.,* p. 45 ff.

[58] *Columbia Journal of World Business,* Vol. 1 (Fall, 1965), p. 23, "The

Domestic Dividends of Foreign Aid."

[59] Kolko, *op. cit.,* p. 73

[60] Agency for International Development, "Fact Sheets on Selected Aspects of U.S. Foreign Economic Assistance," 1972.

[61] The *New York Times,* September 17, 1971, p. 27 His Vietnam reference was to those questioning President Thieu's lone candidacy in the presidential elections; Also see Subcommittee on Economy in Government of the Joint Economic Committee, *Economic Issues in Military Assistance,* 1971, esp. p. 314.

[62] U.S. Congress. Subcommittee on Security Agreements and Commitments Abroad, Committee on Foreign Relations of the United States Senate, "Security Agreements and Commitments Abroad", December 21, 1970, p. 23-24.

[63] Magdoff, *op. cit.,* p. 117.

[64] See Senate Committee on Foreign Relations 5-year Report, September 28, 1971, p. 8.

[65] Statement of The Comptroller General of the United States before the Subcommittee on Economy in Government, Joint Economic Committee, January 4, 1971; and The *New York Times,* June 14, 1971 p. 4, "U.S. Plans to Increase Aid to Foreign Police Forces to Help Fight Subversion."

[66] The United States Declaration of Independence, July 4, 1776

[67] *I.F. Stone's Bi-Weekly,* May 4, 1970.

[68] *Newsweek.* May 13, 1971, p. 45.

[69] Senator Frank Church, "A Liberal Takes His Leave", *Congressional Record,* October 29, 1971.

[70] Seymour Melman, The *New York Times* Op Ed, Nov. 3, 1970, "Pax Americana II: Cost of Militarism."

[71] The *Congressional Record,* June 23, 1969.

[72] North American Congress on Latin America, *Newsletter,* Vol 14, No. 6, Oct., 1970.

[73] Records of American support of coups against unfavorable regimes are extensive. See, for example, the "Pentagon Papers"; The *Philadelphia Inquirer* April 6, 1972, p. 48; Tom Christoffel, et al, eds, *Up Against The American Myth* (New York: Prentice Hall, 1972) p. 245-6.

[74] Statement of The Comptroller General of the United States before the sub-committee on Economy in Government, *op. cit.*

[75] Magdoff *op. cit.,* p. 203 ff.

[76] Dwight Eisenhower, *Mandate for Change,* p. 337-338, as quoted in Kolko, *op. cit.,* p. 108.

[77] *Newsweek,* May 3, 1971, p. 44. Also see Sidney Lens, *The Forging of the American Empire* (NY: Crowell, 1972)

[78] The *New York Times,* March 22, 1971, p. 24.

[79] NBC-TV "White Paper" on Vietnam, December 23, 1971. Quoted President Kennedy's cable to Mr. Lodge, "It is in the interest of U.S. that the Coup must succeed."

[80] In 1953 President Eisenhower asked if "we lost" Vietnam and Malaysia, "how would the free world hold the rich empire of Indonesia?"; And in October, 1967, Richard Nixon said, "With its 100 million people and its 3,000 mile arc of islands containing the region's richest hoard of natural

resources, Indonesia constitutes the greatest prize in the Southeast Asian area."; from "Indonesia: The Making of a Neo-Colony" by the Pacific Study Center in *Pacific Research and World Empire Telegram.*

[81] *The Monthly Review,* June, 1961, p. 51.

[82] See S.M. Miller, et al, "Does The U.S. Economy Require Imperialism", *Social Policy,* September-October, 1970.

[83] Richard DuBoff and Edward Herman, "Corporate Dollars and Foreign Policy" in *Commonweal,* XCVI, April 21, 1972; and *Businessweek,* December 19, 1970. For 80 of the top 200 corporations, foreign operations now account for at least one-fourth of sales, earnings, assets, or employees, and for some, it is over 50%.

[84] *Jeremiad,* No. 35, October 25, 1971: " . . . the September 1971 issue of the Department of Commerce *Survey of Current Business* shows that profits and related returns on U.S. direct investment abroad ran at a rate of about $9 billion per year at the last reading. Other types of investment appear headed toward a $3.5 billion return for the year. Add it up and the profit inflow runs about $12.5 billion. Profit repatriated to the U.S., then, is running at a $12.5 billion rate. Compare it to the profit of all corporations, running at $77 billion and we find it to be about a 16% cut. Yet this is not all . . . The Department of Commerce itself estimates . . . unrepatriated profits at $2.5 billion last year . . . (therefore) foreign earnings ran about $15 billion, and the profits of U.S. corporations are up to $79.3 billion—close to 20% of annual profit of U.S. business originates abroad, a far cry from Connally's 4%."; And Hunt and Sherman (*Op. Cit.,* p. 555) point out that if profits from the military production to defend U.S. interest abroad were added, total foreign-related profits would amount to 25 to 30 percent of all profits. That two thirds of U.S. foreign business comes from Third World, see ref. no. 26.

[85] The *Survey of Current Business,* October, 1971, p. 35.

[86] DuBoff and Herman, *Op. Cit.,* report U.S. foreign profits were 7 to 11% of total U.S. profits in the 1950's but 14-18% in the 1960's; *U.S. News and World Reprort,* October 29, 1969, said growth in volume of goods produced by U.S. overseas affiliates was "increasing at an annual rate of 25%."; *Newsweek,* October 20, 1969, p. 98B: "U.S. industry, in its postwar drive for overseas markets has taken control of 61% of all the foreign investments in the world"; NACLA *Newsletter,* October, 1971; American subsidiaries shipped 11.7% of all Latin American exports in 1957, but 41.2% in 1966.

[87] Thomas Weisskopf, "United States Foreign Private Investment: An Empirical Survey" in Richard C. Edwards, Reich, and Weisskopf, eds. *The Capitalist System* (NY: Prentice Hall, 1972).

[88] Quoted from Heather Dean, "Scarce Resources: The Dynamics of American Imperialism", Radical Education Project, 1965.

[89] Magdoff, *op. cit.,* p. 49-50.

[90] Preston Cloud, "Why Will the Economy Collapse?", in *Ti Estin,* special edition, "Ecology, Pollution, Conservation" (Hamilton, Canada: McMaster University, 1970).

[91] Jalee, *The Third World in World Economy, op. cit.,* p. 37-38.; Jalee, *The Pillage of the Third World, op. cit.,* p. 17.

[92] Magdoff, *op. cit.,* p. 50-51.

[93] *Ibid.,* p. 52

[94] Peterson, *op. cit.*, p. 55.

[95] The *New York Times*, April 11, 1972, p. 13.

[96] DuBoff and Herman, *op. cit.*, p. 162.

[97] Cloud, *op. cit.;* Also see Anne and Paul Ehrlich, *Population, Resources, Environment: Issues in Human Ecology.* (San Francisco: Freeman, 1970), p. 58 ff.

[98] "A Blueprint For Survival" as quoted in the *New York Times,* February 5, 1972, Op-Ed.

[99] Donella Meadows, et al, *The Limits to Growth* (NY: Universe Books, 1972) Ch. 4.

[100] Thomas E. Weisskopf, "United States Foreign Private Investment: An Empirical Survey", P. 434 in Edwards, et al., *The Capitalist System.*

[101] Weisskopf, *op. cit.*, p. 432.

[102] Ibid., p. 432

[103] *Newsweek,* Jan. 3, 1972, p. 38. No oil companies were included.

[104] Judd Polk, "Statement of Judd Polk, U.S. Council of the International Chamber of Commerce" in U.S. Congress. Subcommittee on Foreign Economic Policy of the Joint Economic Committee. *A Foreign Economic Policy For The 1970's Part 4—The Multinational Corporation and International Investment,* 91st Cong., 2nd Sess. p. 770. The GWP includes Socialist nations.

[105] Weisskopf, *op. cit.*, p. 432.

[106] Melville Watkins (Head of the Task Force on the Structure of Canadian Industry), in *A Foreign Economic Policy For the 1970's Part 4—The Multinational Corporation and International Investment, op. cit.*, p. 915.

[107] Stephen Hymer in *Ibid.*, p. 905.

[108] See Denis Goulet, "The United States: A Case of Anti-development", *Motive,* January, 1970 for his description of "full" development; Also see Paul Ehrlich and Richard Harriman, *How To Be A Survivor* (NY: Ballantine, 1971) Chapters 4 & 5.

[109] See E. L. Wheelwright, "Colonialism in Asia—Past and Present" (New England Free Press Reprint); Baran, *op. cit.*, p. 141-150, 179, 228-9; Mandel, *op. cit.*, 441 ff.; Andre Gunder Frank, "Rostow's Stages of Economic Growth" in Frank, *Latin America: Underdevelopment or Revolution,* (NY: Modern Reader, 1971); Hunt and Sherman, *Op. Cit.*, p. 120 ff.

[110] Baran, *op. cit.*, quoting from Romesh Dutt, *The Economic History of India,* London, 1901; Also Mandel, *op. cit.*, p. 442-3; Charles Bettleheim, *India Independent* (NY: Modern Reader, 1971).

[111] Jawaharlal Nehru, in his *The Discovery of India*, as reported in Frank, "Rostow's States of Economic Growth", *op. cit.*

[112] Baran, *op. cit.*, p. 151-161.

[113] See Hayter, *op. cit.*, Chapter 2, describing international financial institutions.

[114] The *New York Times,* November 9, 1971, p. 3 from a documented report of a group of 80 poor nations.

[115] Peterson, *op. cit.*, p. 50.

[116] *The New York Times,* January 18, 1971, p. 41; A similar report on effects of Western penetration in Africa appeared in The *New York Times,*

April 30, 1971, p. 14.; regarding Latin America, see Frank, *op. cit.,* and his *Capitalism and Underdevelopment in Latin America;* Also see Gordon K. Lewis, *The Growth of the Modern West Indies* (N.Y.: Modern Reader, 1968).

[117] The *New York Times,* July 10, 1972, p. 45.

[118] See John Weeks, "Employment, Growth, and Foreign Domination in Underdeveloped Countries", *The Review of Radical Political Economics,* Vol. 4, No. 1, Winter, 1972.

[119] The *New York Times,* September 28, 1971, p. 43.

[120] *Ibid.*

[121] The United Nations, "Trends in the Social Situation".

[122] Recall that decapitalization occurs from many other sources also, and 89% of American investments actually come from monies generated in the Third World.

[123] See Goulet, *op. cit.,* Ehrlich and Harriman, *op. cit.,* Ivan Illich, "Outwitting the 'Developed' Nations" in, John Holdren & Paul Ehrlich, eds, *Global Ecology: Readings Toward a Rational Strategy for Man.* (NY: Harcourt, Brace Jovanovick, 1971).

[124] See The Committee of Concerned Asian Scholars, *China! Inside the People's Republic* (NY: Bantam, 1972); E.L. Wheelwright and Bruce McFarlane, *The Chinese Road to Socialism* (NY: Modern Reader, 1970; esp. Chapter 9; Bronson Clark, "If Ever The Twain Shall Meet", *Saturday Review,* December 18, 1971; Tuddril Johnson, "China Today", American Friends Service Committee, 1971; Ruth and Victor Sidel, "The Human Services in China", *Social Policy,* March-April, 1972.

[125] Hunt and Sherman, *op. cit., p. 541;* also see Mandel, *op. cit.,* p. 442.

[126] The *New York Times, Encyclopedic Almanac 1970,* p. 362.

[127] The *New York Times,* September 28, 1971, p. 43.

[128] See Barry Commoner, *The Closing Circle: Nature, Man & Technology* (New York: Knopf, 1971) p. 233 ff.; Also, Baran, *op. cit.,* p. 237-244.

6

Anatomy of
the Political Economy

The implication of the previous two chapters is that the world is approaching the end of a relatively brief era which had unlimited industrial production. The converging of two historical forces—environmental limitations, and the awakening of the rest of the world to the reality that the more America gets, the less they get—is stopping the dream of limitless opulence in its tracks. The big and ever-expanding American pie has been the great healer of what has been wrong in America. Whether it was poverty, hunger, slums, inequality, discrimination or political impotency, the victims and their supporters were lulled into complacency. "Sure there are problems, but aren't we doing twice as well as the next best nations, and isn't it going to be even better for our kids?" A *Newsweek* economist stated, "Growth is a substitute for equality of income."[1] In the past we have been able to give those with less a little more to pacify them so that they didn't see that those with more were increasing their share also. With the dawning of a new era in which the American pie stagnates and shrinks, people will demand action on their problems because the future can only be worse for them and their children.

In this chapter we will focus on some of our domestic problems—Poverty, Economic Inequality, Political Inequality, American Militarism, and Domestic Violence and Alienation.

POVERTY

Poverty is the deprivation of resources. Until Michael Harrington's book *The Other America,* [2] extensive deprivation in the United States was unthinkable. That is, both at home and abroad, America was considered to be the land of affluence. Furthermore, it was thought that those few who did not enjoy the fruits of the bounty were lazy, inept, or generally not worthy. "Pulling yourself up by your own bootstraps" implied that there was ample opportunity for poor to get out of poverty.

Poverty can be defined in both absolute and relative terms. Relative poverty is the lack of resources by some people relative to the resources of others. The American blue collar worker is poor compared to the Rockefellers, but rich compared to a Brazilian peasant. Absolute poverty, on the other hand, is the extent to which people's basic needs for housing, clothing, food and other necessities meet some minimum standard. However, even poverty defined in such absolute terms is also relative and varies according to the nation, culture and point in time. Despite these somewhat academic problems of definition, we think the general ideas are clear enough for the points we wish to make regarding poverty in the United States. In this section we are concerned with absolute poverty in the United States, and in a later section we will focus on relative poverty—economic inequality.

There are four points we will make regarding poverty: (1) There is extensive poverty in the United States, and it is growing. (2) All mainstream efforts to end or alleviate poverty by government and humanitarian programs are doomed to failure because they focus on symptoms rather than the causes. (3) The primary cause of poverty is the political-economic system, not the lack of individual effort. (4) Universal governmental services which are available to meet basic needs on an equal basis are needed in order to end poverty.

(1) There is extensive poverty in the United States. Following the 1950's decade in which it was thought that poverty in America had been stamped out forever, poverty was "rediscovered" by Michael Harrington's *The Other America.* Subsequent books, government studies and special media reports confirmed that large parts of towns and cities were vast rat-infested, crime-ridden, over-crowded slums; millions of children and elderly were hungry, half the children under 15 years of age had no dental care, millions in farmworker families scraped together a living on meager incomes, and many rural and inner city areas were in deep depression. Especially hard pressed were nonwhites, single-parent families, the young and the old. Poverty was rampant. Everyone was aghast. In response, the Democratic party, in control of the White House and Congress, opened with great pomp and circumstance an all-out offensive which it called the War on Poverty.

That was in 1964. In 1971, the National Urban Coalition's report declared that urban life was as bad as or worse than the conditions cited by the Kerner Commission in 1968:

"Housing is still the national scandal it was then. Schools are more tedious and turbulent. The rates of crime and unemployment and disease and heroin addiction are higher. Welfare rolls are larger. And, with few exceptions, the relations between minority communities and the police are just as hostile." [3]

In the years since then, the position of America's poor has deteriorated as unemployment has increased, workers' wages have declined relative to prices, and government programs and services for the poor have been cut drastically. The war on poverty was lost.

(2) All mainstream efforts to end or substantially alleviate poverty both by government and humanitarian programs are doomed to failure because they focus on symptoms rather than the causes which lie in the political-economic system. Billions of dollars are spent by government and private efforts to "help the poor." Most Americans believe that the problem of poverty lies with the poor themselves; our view is quite the contrary—the problem lies with the political-economic system and, consequently, any efforts to end poverty without changing these social structures will fail. Programs to help poor people are set up for failure, as demonstrated by the history of anti-poverty programs. We have salved our consciences with "we've tried and tried, but the poor just won't help themselves" while overlooking those fundamental problems that trap humans in lives of deprivation. To better understand why anti-poverty efforts have failed we will look at four main approaches to ending poverty: employment, education, income maintenance and "trickle down" from a strong, growing economy.

Anti-poverty approach # 1 — Employment

The first admonition to the poor is "Why don't you get a job?" The employment solution to poverty has been the strongest approach used by both government and liberal social work agencies. Why has it failed?

The first reason for the failure of the "employment solution" to poverty is that its major method, manpower training, has never gotten one additional poor person a job because it doesn't create any new jobs for poor people, it just determines which of the poor people get the limited jobs available. Social work agencies working with "hard-core" unemployed give annual statistics of how many people they placed in jobs, thereby implying that they are reducing those unemployed by that number. They do no such thing. For every poor person that gets a job, there is another that becomes unemployed. For example, if there is a local gas attendant job available, the agency may train Jimmy how to wear his cap, wipe the windshield, and be pleasant with customers; they go with Jimmy for a successful employment interview with the owner; and Jimmy is added to the agency's success statistics. What the annual report fails to mention is that if the agency did not exist someone would still have gotten the job—Billy in the next block who is also a hard-core unemployable. The real beneficiary was the owner who got a trained job applicant who was more likely to hold the low-paying job for a longer time than off-the-street applicants.

Even those unemployed poor who enter and graduate from official government training programs and usually get jobs are not raised out of official poverty as concluded by the government's Joint Economic Committee study "The Effectiveness of Manpower Training Programs: A Review of Research on the Impact on the Poor":

> Manpower programs are not a substitute for income supplement programs. Training does increase the earnings of the poor and reduce the poverty gap, but continued income supplementation is likely to be necessary for the average trainee. Even those studies with the most optimistic results estimate average post-training annual earnings levels well below the poverty line. For example, in a recent sample MDTA trainees averaged $3,200 in post-training annual earnings, over $800 below their poverty line.[4]

A second limit to the employment approach to ending poverty is that the *American economy requires a minimum of 4% unemployment*—and is usually well over that figure. When the unemployment rate drops toward 5 or 4% of the labor force, the economy becomes intolerably inflationary and government efforts are taken to increase unemployment. Consequently, the government and economists have called "full employment" the point of 4% official unemployment and established it as the ultimate employment goal for the economy. In recent years, however, hopes of reaching this low level of unemployment have virtually disappeared. Not only has this rate not been reached in 25 years except at the height of war-time expenditures, but in recent years intolerable inflation occurs with ever higher unemployment rates.

Employment programs are not very effective for those millions at the bottom when the economy requires a minimum of 5 million or so unemployed even in its best years. The unemployed are predominantly the nation's poor and they are also mostly nonwhite, young, elderly, women, less educated, and underskilled. They are the last hired as the economy grows and the first fired when it falters.

Women in particular are at the mercy of the whim of business and industry "cut-backs." Operating on the myth that all women are being supported by some man, employers find ways to give job preference to males.

The percentage of women who work outside the home has risen steadily from 31% in 1950 to 35% in 1960 to 42% in 1970 to 44% in 1973. A large part of the American work force, women are a cheap constant source of labor. The 56% of women who are not "officially" employed are the free labor of the home, providing services and skills without remuneration.[5]

Women's wages are limited by the design of those jobs open to them. Often women can acquire jobs but find that those jobs for which they have skills, or those positions open to them, are at the bottom end of the wage scale. Women predominate in the clerical, service, sales, and domestic jobs (more than 64% of women wage-earners were in these fields in 1968), and men predominate in the professional, technical, managerial, supervisory, craft, or skilled labor jobs (more than 70% of men wage-earners were in these fields in 1968).[6]

Low unemployment is a much higher priority for the governments of many other nations. Sweden, for example, has a target unemployment rate of less than 1% (compared to the U.S.'s 4%), and has traditionally been below that figure. That nation has established a special organization, The National Labor Market Board, with the goal of making sure the unemployment rate is below 1% and has given it a virtually unlimited budget.

Compare this to the fact that in our best year of low unemployment (3.5% in 1969) the official unemployment rate for black teenagers was at the depression level of 19.9%. As the governmental efforts to fight inflation took hold in 1970, the black teenage unemployment rate increased to 24%, and to 33.5% by the summer of 1974, at which time public officials were calling inflation public enemy number one and saying the fight against it would cause still more unemployment.

A third reason why the "get a job" approach to ending poverty is ineffective is that *most of the employ-*

able poor are already employed. Millions of full-time employed people earn poverty wages. According to government statistics, about 42% of the non-aged heads of poor families already worked full-time, and another 31% worked part-time. Most who did not work were unemployable either because they were women with responsibilities for young children or had medical disabilities.

and find themselves in poverty are unable to receive the necessary education and job training to qualify them for anything more than the most meager-paying employment. Stringent welfare laws provide money to exist on for a single mother and her children, but will not allow her to use any part of her income for preparation to climb out of the poverty cycle. The choice is then to remain "on welfare" or become employed at the very bottom of the wage scale, still below the official standard of income.

The seemingly obvious answer to the problem of low wages is to raise the Federal minimum wage. It is argued, though, by both business and government economists that if low wages were significantly raised, corporations would make less profits which, in turn, would cause an economic slowdown and more unemployment. Also, many small businesses would fire many employees because they couldn't afford to pay them. They argue, additionally, that higher wages would cause higher prices, thus setting off inflation which would make many needed products less available to the poor. Another concern is that higher wages would make U.S. products less competitive abroad, causing an economic cutback here with increased unemployment.

Anti-poverty approach # 2 – Education

There is a correlation between education and income. However, more education is not a way open for most poor to get out of poverty—the United States has the best-educated poor people in the world.

Many poor families cannot afford to have their children stay in school because they need the added income. Meeting the cost of college tuition and expenses is unthinkable. Moreover, schools in low-income and minority-group areas usually do not prepare students for college or to take entrance examinations, while schools in the more affluent areas mainly shunt poor and nonwhites into noncollege tracks.

Education to end unemployment has the same limitations as job training—it only determines who gets the jobs; it does not create new employment opportunities.

More education is not particularly helpful for increasing income because as a JEC study found, "There are millions of blacks, Spanish-speaking Americans, other minorities, and women who have all the necessary qualifications to be promoted into better jobs than those they now hold." Full-time employed women with four years college education earned about the same median income as full-time employed males with only eight years of schooling. [7]

Anti-poverty approach # 3 — Income Maintenance

A third major solution to poverty which has been proposed is the assurance of a guaranteed annual income. The argument goes as follows: "Poverty is a lack of money so it can be ended by giving cash to the poor. As the richest nation in the world we can afford it; moreover, it will spur the economy and everyone will benefit. The cash grants will be spent immediately, thereby giving a big boost to the economy, which in turn will provide more jobs and income for everybody. In other words, it will pay for itself."

We believe that any effort for a reasonable guaranteed annual income program, within the political-economic framework of the United States is not only destined to fail, but would impair a successful movement to alleviate poverty.

First, it is inconceivable that Congress would pass a law guaranteeing America's poor a reasonable income within the present political-economic system. Such high level grants would require a redistribution of money from the affluent (obviously including Congresspeople and their financial backers). Although the economic system does permit government cash benefits to the poor, the amount of money given must be limited to punitively low levels such that no unemployed poor person can receive more welfare income than that earned by the lowest-paid worker. It is obvious that high cash payments would undermine and probably collapse the labor market. If the Federal government gave sizeable direct cash benefits to the poor, who would do the dirty work? Who would pick the lettuce, join the Army, type the letters, or run errands for the executives? Clearly, neither Congress nor the President would ever support legislation which would so undermine the foundations of the political economy.

Second, if the pursuit of a GAI is successful in getting legislation passed, such legislation, on balance, will be harmful to the nation's poor. Not only will the guaranteed base income be punitively low, but recipients will have to work, if at all possible, at whatever job is available for whatever wages are available. Since, as we have pointed out, many jobs would go lacking for someone to fill them if high cash grants were guaranteed to everyone, the government would have to attach the "workfare" ethic to any such program. Richard Nixon made it clear: "We are a nation that pays tribute to the working man and rightly scorns the free-loader who voluntarily opts to be a ward of the state."[8] All the GAI plans seriously considered by Congress, such as the Nixon Family Assistance Plan for a $2,400 minimum income, required that the poor accept whatever jobs were offered them. These jobs, which offer insubstantial pay and few benefits, therefore would be sure to be filled so that the economy could continue to benefit those on the upper rungs of the political-economic ladder.

Third, even if achieved, a $6,500 GAI would not provide a decent life or meet many basic human needs of poor people. Many families which already have wage incomes of $6,500 a year cannot purchase decent housing, cannot afford adequate health care, and live in crowded, demoralizing and unsafe slum conditions.

Even more important is that the lives of the nation's poor would probably not be much improved because their increased income would be virtually wiped out by the resulting inflation. If the GAI legislation did not have a forced-work clause, prices would further skyrocket from the higher wages caused by the labor shortage.

Fourth, even if the GAI approach were totally successful in its goals, it would be disastrous for humanity. That is to say, if all the U.S. poor increased their consumption to average middle-class levels everyone would suffer. The great increase in America's national consumption would require increased repression, exploitation and poverty in the Third World from the increased American need for dwindling material resources at cheap prices. There would be a tremendous deterioration of the environment and its life support system with future generations inheriting a drastic lack of basic resources and an even more polluted environment.

Anti-poverty approach # 4 — Economic Growth

Political leaders, economists and businesspeople call for an economically strong America in order to solve poverty and other social ills. However, it is not true that economic growth is a solution to poverty in America. The United States has had the highest levels of production and consumption the world has ever seen (and probably ever will see) during the 1960's, yet it failed to diminish poverty much in the U.S.

The problem is not a lack of government spending. Successive Federal Administrations have called for a strong economy to enable government to spend money on social problems. But the *New York Times* gave the following account of a 1972 Brookings Institute book-length study on national priorities:

> ... they concluded that the multiplication of dollars and programs brought not solutions for such problems as welfare reform, day care and city finance but a multiplication of dilemmas ...
>
> In the end, they argue, the critical lack has not been

money. How could it be when the Federal social spending has soared from $30-billion to $110 billion in 10 years, and when spending for Great Society programs alone has jumped from $1.7 billion to $35.7 billion?[9]

It is clear that economic growth has not alleviated poverty and that if continued, it will diminish resources and jeopardize decent living, if not survival. What is needed to end poverty is not economic growth, but *massive redistribution of resources from the affluent to the poor.*

(3) **The primary cause of poverty is the political-economic system, not the lack of individual effort of the poor.** This conclusion, obvious from the preceding discussion, is mentioned separately here because of its importance. We have shown that the structure of the American economy requires high unemployment and under-employment of the poor (there are 50 million Americans living in families or alone who have income levels designated as poor or near-poor, and another 50 million are not much better off) and provides millions of jobs which pay poverty wages. As Barry Bluestone points out, traditional economic theory is wrong in assuming that the basic structure of the economy provides an equal opportunity for those willing to compete for well-paying jobs.[10]

It is a popular belief that many of the poor are lazy and don't want to work, but the studies by government and university researchers show that poor Americans, including those on welfare, adhere strongly to the American work ethic. The U.S. Department of Health, Education and Welfare estimates that less than 1 % of the poor people on welfare are able-bodied adults and available for work. It has been found that "poor people—males and females, blacks and whites, youth and adults—identify their self-esteem with work as strongly as the non-poor."[11]

The importance of changing institutions and social systems rather than people can be seen by comparing the United States to other nations' battles against poverty.

Virtually all of the other western industrialized nations, with less than half the per capita income of the U.S., have made enormous strides toward the elimination of slums, hunger, high unemployment, beggars, poor health care, and high crime rates.[12] And these conditions are no longer found in socialist nations such as Russia and Yugoslavia or even in the extremely poor socialist nations of China and Cuba.

(4) **The solution to poverty requires governmental services which help meet everyone's basic material needs on an equal basis.** In our view, each of the anti-poverty "solutions" is faulty and unworkable on a long-term basis, and furthermore, added together, they would only serve to multiply our problems. We need an entirely different approach to ending poverty. Richard Titmuss has studied the various approaches and called the one used in the United States "Selective Programs" and the other, used in other Western industrialized nations, particularly the Scandinavian nations, "Universal Services."

The Selective Programs approach selects various population groups in need (black teenagers, elderly widows, handicapped, unemployed youth, welfare mothers, etc.) and develops specific social programs to help them. In contrast, the Universal Services approach creates free or low-fee social services which are available to everyone on an equal basis. Americans already have the Universal Services of free education up to college level, and police and fire department services, but Europeans and socialist nations extend this into many other areas. Sweden, for example, has complete free hospital care for every citizen as a right; free dental care for all children up to the age of 15; job training with pay and placement for everyone regardless of employment and educational background; the same children's allowance for all children regardless of family income; subsidized, low-fee doctors' services and prescription costs. Mass transit is highly subsidized and low cost. There is extensive public housing and rents are controlled. There exists a national program of low-fee daycare centers especially geared to working mothers.

There are some very practical and human reasons why the Universal Services approach has succeeded while the Selective Programs approach to meeting needs has failed. The *Selective Programs* approach, directed solely at poor people, has the following limitations: (1) Benefits must be kept punitively low in order to maintain recipients' incentive to earn their way like the other citizens. (2) They have little political support. The non-poor majority oppose them because they ask why should the poor be given what they have to work for. (3) As a consequence of the first two limitations, a social stigma is placed on the welfare role such that many poor are ashamed to accept what benefits are available, and when they do, they often lose their self-respect. To qualify for benefits, people have to "prove" they are needy by passing means tests, a process which usually evokes strong feelings of failure. (4) Selective programs to help the needy usually have the effect of blaming the victim, the poor, for their condition rather than blaming the social causes of poverty such as the political-economic structures. [13]

The *Universal Services* approach avoids many of the limitations inherent in the Selective Programs approach. Because its programs benefit a broad spectrum of the population they have strong public support. The benefits do not have to be punitive since everyone is given the service. The stigma of being a recipient is greatly reduced because every citizen is a recipient of at least some of the various universal services. From a social change strategic viewpoint, the Universal Services approach is much more effective because it unites the various segments of the non-rich population rather than setting them against each other as do Selective Programs. Moreover, it looks more at the economic structure as a major cause of poverty and assumes that the social order ought to be organized to maximize the meeting of human need.

The diagnosis of poverty and our visions of what we expect our society should be like determine the remedies we use and their chances of success. As long as we diagnose the problems as functions of individuals rather than of the political-economic structure, and as long as we do not expect our social order to maximize the meeting of human needs, then we will always have a major problem of unmet human needs. For this reason we suggest that those groups and individuals focused on ending poverty in America adopt the Universal Services approach. Moreover, a strategy to end poverty must also be seen in the larger context of ecology and relations with the world's poor nations. To end poverty calls for major reductions of American production and consumption of material resources as well as massive redistribution from rich to poor.

The myth of the American middle class. The image of average Americans is that they are college graduates, car owners, hold white collar jobs and earn over $10,000 a year. While not prosperous, they at least are affluent, comfortable, and secure. Only a small minority are seen to be not part of this great middle class, but with some hard work, even their lot is imagined improvable. Upward mobility is believed available for all who wish to engage in hard work, to study and to postpone immediate gratifications by saving.

The average American family is far from the two-car garage suburban house with the picket fence. The average factory production worker brings home in his/her pay envelope less than the lowest of three family budgets worked out by the Federal Government. The U.S. Department of Labor publishes each year descriptions of budgets for American families at three levels of income. In 1973, the middle or moderate budget for a city family of four was $12,000, but the average factory worker made only about $8,000.[14] Morever, the average factory worker, fully employed, brings home a paycheck that is less than the lowest frugal budget worked out each year by the government.[15]

Richard Parker, in his well-documented book *The Myth of the Middle Class,*[16] shows that affluence is limited to the rich and upper middle class and not enjoyed by the vast majority of Americans. In fact, less than 10% of American families earn over $13,000 after taxes—only a little more than the Labor Department's modest budget.[17] Parker points out, for example, that while a college degree is one basic aspect of the middle class American, it is estimated that even by 1985 less than 10% of Americans will be college graduates.

The current state of national and world affairs is further eroding both the reality and the dream of affluence for all Americans. The curbing of growing affluence is seen by the stagnation of the real spendable income of American workers since 1965, and a 10% reduction between 1967 and 1974.[18]

ECONOMIC INEQUALITY

In affluent industrial societies new wants are continually being created and higher goals of individual consumption established. For most people, economic poverty is a question of inequality rather than a lack of getting basic material needs met. A family is considered poor if it can't afford a car, television, central heating, automatic clothes washer and dryer, inside plumbing and toilet, electric toaster, etc. because these are what most other people have. As S.M. Miller points out, "Poverty in America is more than mere substance, it's psychological and social distance between people—relative position rather than absolute level."[19] The economic question in the United States, therefore, is not only whether basic needs are being met, but what is a just distribution of wealth and income?

Economic distribution is a political and moral question. It is a *political* question because the distribution of income and wealth is caused by the roles of government, the political and economic system, and social institutions—all of which are human-made. The ways in which these roles were created were political—i.e., by the power of certain people to influence these decisions in what they thought to be their own favor. Economic power is political power and vice versa. The distribution of income and wealth is also a *moral* question because of the totality of its effect on individuals, society, and the whole world and ultimately the future. Economic distribution plays a great part in determining society's values, ideology, goals, institutions, and other social arrangements. It determines in large part who we are as individuals [20] and how we affect the rest of the world, the environment, hunger, war, and future generations.

Consequently, political democracy and ethical decisions (such as those which are based on the maximizing everyone's well-being rather than looking after the narrow interests of a few) require a fairly egalitarian distribution of economic wealth and income.

Income Distribution. In the United States, the economic distance among people is great. The *income* of the top 10 percent of Americans is equal to that of the bottom 50 percent and this percentage distribution has not changed much in this century. [21] The following chart shows the vast inequality of income distribution in the United States, which has changed little in the last three and a half decades.

Percentage Share of Aggregate Before— Tax Income Going to Families

	(In percent)	1947	1969
Highest 5th		43.0	41.0
4th 5th		23.1	23.4
Middle 5th		17.0	17.6
2nd 5th		11.8	12.3
Poorest 5th		5.0	5.6

Percentage of Population

	1947	1969
top 5%	17.2	14.7
Bottom 5%	0.47	0.68

(U.S. Bureau of the Census, "Current Population Reports, Consumer Income, 1969" Washington, D.C. 1970, page 56).

Kolko shows how even this great income inequality is drastically understated because of expense accounts and other income-in-kind for corporate executives and by under-reporting and non-reporting of income by upper-income groups. [22]

It is not apparent in these gross average-income statistics that there is an affluent mass population. A Joint Economic Committee study, for example, shows that nonwhites, youth, elderly, and women have much lower incomes than their peers. In 1969, for example, the incomes of nonwhite families were only 63 percent that of white families and full-time female workers earned only 59% that of male workers. [23]

While the image of American families and individuals is one of middle class, many cannot meet the minimum standards set up by the Bureau of Labor Statistics. Moreover, there is little economic mobility among the poverty population. [24] The Congressional study concludes that in the future the distribution of family income will probably remain reasonably constant when measured in relative terms, but the gap will continue to widen when measured in absolute dollars. That is, even though the percentage of income acquired by the various groupings of population might remain constant, the rising total national income creates a broadening discrepancy in the amount of income actually available for families.

Wealth Distribution. The inequality of *wealth* in the United States is even greater than income inequality. The top two percent of wealth holders have the same amount of wealth as the bottom 94 percent of the population. [25] Wealth here is being defined as equity in a home or business, liquid assets, investments, value of auto, etc.

Wealth statistics are hard to come by. Even the Joint Economic Committee 1972 study used scanty 1962 figures. One of the most recognized and sophisticated studies was the Lampman study published by Princeton University Press in 1962. Its findings, summarized by

Lundberg, show that less than two percent of the adult population:

> ... owned 32 percent of the privately owned wealth, consisting of 82.2 percent of stock, 100 percent of state and local (tax-exempt) bonds, 38.2 percent of federal bonds, 88.5 percent of other bonds, 29.1 percent of the cash, 36.2 percent of mortgages and notes ...[26]

At the bottom end, Lampman found that 50 percent of the American people owned very little, having only 8.3 percent of the wealth.[27] Not only is the economic distribution of income and wealth in the U.S. an inequitable pyramid of super rich, but historical trends give no hope for improvement in the future. Moreover, as shown in the two previous chapters, the pyramid of economic inequality of the American system does not stop at the borders of the United States, but continues throughout its world-wide sphere of influence.

Economic Ownership and Control. Another important measure of economic inequality is the concentration of ownership and control of the economic system and its institutions. This measure shows even more inequality than the distribution of income or wealth, and the trend is toward increasing disparity. Citing a United States Internal Revenue study, Hunt and Sherman report that a relatively few giant corporations (958, or just 0.06 percent) held a majority of all the assets ($1,070 billion, or 53.2 percent) of the million-plus United States corporations in 1967. At the bottom, a large number of small corporations (906,458 or 59 percent of the total) held a miniscule portion of corporate assets ($31 billion, or 1.5 percent).[28] The top 0.06 percent held more assets than all the other corporations put together!

Senator Gaylord Nelson, as chairperson of the Hearings on The Role of Giant Corporations reports:

"The 200 largest American corporations in the last 20 years have increased their share of all manufacturing-company assets from under 50 percent to over 60 percent. This means that the share remaining for everyone else in the manufacturing sector has gone down from over 50 percent to something under 40 percent." [29]

That comes out to .0001 of the manufacturing corporations owning 60 percent of the nation's assets.

The Question of Power. The "power elite", those who occupy the commanding heights of the most powerful institutions in America, are responsible for much of the trend of contemporary history. [30]

The immediate significance of the concentration of economic power in the hands of these few is that they use their wealth to gain more wealth and control for their corporations and themselves, thus perpetuating the system. *The key economic decisions in our society are made not on the basis of human needs, but rather on the basis of profits.*

If the power is wielded by the "power elite" then those masses of workers and consumers—virtually the entire population of the United States—are not only exploited by the large corporations but are in essence disenfranchised by them. The people have lost their right to decide how economic power is to be used in our society.

This loss of decision-making power is most graphically seen in the use of advertising and a conscious program of planned obsolescence on the part of industry. The consumer is made to believe there is a wide choice of goods, that those goods will make one happy, socially acceptable, and fulfilled, that the goods are worth the price being charged, and that the consumer is the one benefiting from the transaction. The facts are that the corporation does not respond to the felt needs of the consumer; rather, it creates the felt needs. Advertising diverts the consumer's attention from real needs and the individual is caught in the syndrome of consuming more products to achieve status, all for the profit of the corporations.

The Failure of Mainstream Solutions to Reduce Economic Inequality. Because wealth and income are believed to be a result of people's individual efforts, economic inequality is assumed by most citizens to be legitimate and is generally accepted. Attempts to call public attention to inequality have been de-legitimitized and ignored. Perhaps the failure of these attempts is also due to the common belief that the American pie is big and growing ever larger, such that a piece of it is available for everyone who works for it. As a result, economic equality is not considered a national goal, and there are no government or private programs specifically designed to reduce economic inequality. Nevertheless, supporters of the status quo often claim that the pattern of economic distribution is becoming more equal through such means as economic growth, taxation, anti-poverty programs, and education.

Economic growth is probably believed to be the biggest equalizer. However, as pointed out by the report of the Joint Economic Committee (JEC), growth of the American pie is increasing the gap between the rich and the poor rather than decreasing it because most of the increase is going to the most affluent citizens.[31]

Anti-poverty programs have not been an equalizer either. The poor have received very little money from such programs. But even if anti-poverty schemes were entirely successful in raising the poor above the poverty line, the incomes of those poor would still be insignificant compared to the incomes of the most well-to-do Americans, whose incomes would still be 10 to 100 times higher.

Taxation fails as an equalizer because, as pointed out by the JEC,

" . . . taxes reduce everyone's income by the same percentage and leave relative incomes unchanged."[32]

Additionally, it is the super rich who benefit from tax loopholes, not the poor.

Education clearly fails to serve as an equalizer. It does not create jobs, and does not determine which of those persons properly educated receives those jobs. A woman well qualified and educated is still met with the same invidious discrimination against her holding those positions now allocated to males.

Federal regulatory agencies have also failed to stem the tide toward increased economic concentration and monopoly. Most studies conclude that governmental regulatory agencies invariably are controlled by the very corporations they are supposed to regulate. This is not so surprising to readers of Kolko's book *The Triumph of Conservatism* [33] which describes how the idea of governmental regulatory agencies over business was conceived and implemented by the corporations themselves, ironically for the purpose of preventing excessive competition and to maintain high profits.

Three Chief Causes of Unjust Economic Inequality: wages, capital and government.

Wages. Most efforts to correct injustices of wages have been to increase the wages of the poor by raising the minimum wage, bringing more workers under Federal work laws, organizing unions, and providing training. These efforts are important and need to be continued, but they cannot redress the *inequality* of the wage structure in the economy. That can only be done by drastically reducing outrageously high salaries. While millions of full-time workers, such as farm workers and domestics, earn less than $2,000 per year, many business executives get over one-hundred thousand dollars. GM Chairman Richard Gerstenberg has a salary of $923,000 a year. Henry Ford and Lee Iacocca of Ford each receive $865,000.

This wage gap is immoral and unjust. No social order should permit it. A reasonable distribution of wage income requires the establishment of either a maximum ratio allowed between the highest and lowest wages (perhaps 2 to 1) or a low maximum allowable wage income, set at perhaps $10,000 to begin with and lowered at some future time.

Capital. *Business Week* points out the obvious: "Money really does make money . . . the gap between the poorest and the richest Americans continues to widen" because "the rich get rich faster since they start from a higher base. Moreover, most of the capital base of today's rich is inherited." [34]

Capital investment is the main source of income for the rich. A Department of Internal Revenue study found that the top 2% had 90% of their income from investments and only 10% from their work. [35] This super wealth and income is justified on the grounds that it is the very foundation of our economic and social system. The private enterprise system with its freedom for individuals to own and invest and become rich is defended as the heart of our capitalist system. The problem, however, is that this ordering of economic life is unjust in the extreme. If we define capitalists as those individuals who receive at least half of their income from capital ownership, less than 5% of Americans are capitalists. Moreover, 83 out of every 100 Americans own no capital at all.

The American economic system in which the rich few get most of their wealth and income from capital ownership (which is now predominantly inherited) is not unlike the feudal societies where the peasants did the work for the prosperous propertied aristocracy.

Government. The Federal government is a major distributor of wealth and income. Although the Federal government in a democracy would be expected to serve all people equally, the government of the United States distributes economic benefits in proportion to one's wealth, and economic disbenefits in proportion to one's poverty, thereby increasing the economic disparities among the population. There is a rationalization for this economic policy. The Employment Act of 1946 gave the government the responsibility of maintaining a strong economy so that it provides maximum production and employment *through the private enterprise system.* It is assumed that if business is kept strong, depressions like that of the 1930's can be avoided and people will be provided with economic well-being. Through monetary and fiscal policies, the Federal government, so the rationalization goes, must give all the assistance to private enterprise that it needs and this is expected to "trickle down" to the general public. Through a vast system of "welfare to the rich," the government has become a senior partner in the economic system. The following is merely a sampling of the government's unjust role as economic distributor:

(1) Agriculture. The Federal government gave farmers about $5 billion in direct subsidies each year between 1968 and 1970 plus an additional $4.5 billion in higher prices. The wealthiest 7% of the farms received almost 63% of the total subsidies, while the poorer half got only 9.1%. Senator James Eastland, staunch opponent of welfare to the poor, received $159,000 a year for not working on part of his 5,200 acres. The Russian wheat deal in 1973 involving the U.S. Department of Agriculture, was exploitation of the American consumer, taxpayer and farmer. While five exporting firms reaped excess profits, the resulting wheat shortage in the U.S. sent many food prices skyrocketing. A Joint Economic Committee study said that the Russian wheat deal cost the Department of Agriculture about $150 million in subsidies to American agribusiness and caused an inflationary spiral in food costs. [36]

(2) Banks. A report of the House Committee on Banking and Currency concludes that the Federal Reserve "has given away billions to the private banks" in recent years through various policies including free services from the Federal Reserve, governmental protection from competition and the hazards of failure, and the ways government creates new money. In addition, Senator Proxmire estimated that in 1970 the U.S. government had $1,084 million in interest-free deposits of government money in banks. These deposits were mostly in 10 giant banks which did not serve urban and rural poverty areas.[37] Since banks would normally pay a minimum of 5%

interest on deposits, this money amounted to a government subsidy of $50 million per year—$5 million per bank.

(3) The fight against inflation and recession. According to Leon Keyserling, the first chairman of the Council of Economic Advisors, the government's monetary policy

> . . . of tight money and rising interest rates, undertaken in the name of combating inflation, has served only to inflate the fat and starve the lean. I estimate that, during 1953-66, the rising interest rates in themselves transferred close to $100 billion of national income away from those who borrow and toward those who lend, which means in the main away from those who need income supplementation most and toward those who need it least. [38]

A Joint Economic Committee of Congress report states that:

> Most of the current government instruments for reducing inflation, such as creating recessions, limiting interest rates for small savers, and resisting cost of living escalators only serve to make the poor worse off. At the moment, the poor are asked to pay the price necessary to stop inflation for the rest of society. [39]

(4) Prisons and Courts. It is estimated that half the people in U.S. prisons are untried and are there simply because they are poor and can't afford bail, not because of a crime they have committed or because they are especially dangerous to society. Many illegal activities, however, on the part of businesses and affluent individuals are ignored by law enforcement and regulatory agencies. Our court and prison system is bulky, inefficient, and costly. Furthermore, prisoners not only earn little income while in prison, but because of their prison records, are often unable to attain satisfactory income for the rest of their lives.

(5) Housing. "Housing Subsidies," a Joint Economic Committee report, concludes that the overwhelming governmental financial assistance for housing goes to

affluent families. Most of the housing subsidies go to homeowners through tax deductions. Tax savings which go to the upper incomes rather than to the poor serve only to encourage the relatively well-to-do to buy even better housing than before.[40]

(6) Tax Revenue Sharing. President Nixon introduced the Tax Revenue Sharing program in October 1972 at Independence Hall, calling it the New American Revolution. It was to distribute $30 billion up through 1976. The *Philadelphia Inquirer,* in July of 1974, however, reported that a nation-wide survey shows that the revenue money "is going to rich, not poor."[41]

(7) Monopolies. In most major industries four giant corporations control over half the national market and do not engage in price competition. Although this is in violation of the Federal anti-monopoly laws, regulatory agencies do little to make corporations abide by the laws. Moreover, the function of many Federal regulatory agencies is specifically such as to prevent price competition since those agencies regulate the industry by setting prices as, for example, in utilities, airlines, milk, cabs, railways, oil, etc. Every basic economics textbook states that prices (and profits) in noncompetitive industries are much higher than if they were competitive. This causes a major shift in economic resources. Ralph Nader estimates that consumers pay about $23-billion a year in overcharges due to monopoly.[42]

(8) Income tax laws. Many giant corporations pay little if any federal taxes. Corporations with familiar names paid no taxes in at least one year since 1970. Although giants such as Alcoa, Continental Oil, McDonnell-Douglas, U.S. Steel, and Consolidated Edison were paying little or no taxes, all were paying sizable dividends to stockholders. These stockholders, mostly wealthy, were able to take advantage of tax law loopholes and pay a smaller percentage of taxes than persons with less income.

The 16th amendment to the Constitution authorized Congress to levy taxes on "incomes, from whatever source derived." But over the years Congress has passed "tax reform" laws exempting rich citizens from tax payments using all kinds of excuses. Philip Stern has calculated the benefits of these laws, which he calls "tax welfare programs," and who gets them:

Chart I
1972 Tax "Welfare" Program

If You Make	Your yearly Tax "Welfare" will be	You'll get added Weekly "Take-home" of
Over $1 Million	$720,000	$14,000
$500,000 to $1 Million	$202,000	$ 3,900
$25-50,000	$ 4,000	$ 75
$15-20,000	$ 1,200	$ 21
$ 5-10,000	$ 340	$ 7
Under $3,000	$ 16	30 cents

Chart II
Who Gets Tax "Welfare"?

Income Group	Number of Families	Total Yearly Tax "Welfare"
Over $1 Million	3,000	$2.2 Billion
Under $3,000	6,000,000	$92 Million

Chart III
Income From Tax-free Bonds

If You Make:	Your Yearly Tax "Welfare" From Tax-Free Bonds Will be:
Over $1 Million	$36,000
$500,000 to $1 Million	$19,000
$25-50,000	$ 24
$10-15,000	80 cents
$ 5-10,000	10 cents

Chart IV
Favorable Taxing of "Capital Gains"

If You Make:	Your Yearly Tax "Welfare" From "Capital Gains" Will be:
Over $1 Million	$ 641,000
$500,000 to $1 Million	$ 164,000
$20–25,000	$ 120
$5–10,000	$ 8
$3–5,000	$ 1

(All charts from Philip Stern's testimony at hearings on *The Economics of Federal Subsidy Programs*) [43]

The Federal government's dual welfare system, which gives lavish outlays of money to the rich in the name of helping the economy but gives punitively small amounts to the poor while calling them "drains on the economy", has established a unique situation in which the poor people are fighting to get off welfare while the rich hire expensive lawyers to get them on welfare.

(9) Public Squalor. The poor and nonwhites suffer the penalties of public squalor resulting from our industrial growth and political-economic system. They experience, more than anyone else, unemployment, slums, pollution, violent crimes, over-crowding, dirty and monotonous jobs, and a loss of a sense of freedom and self-actualization.

Our economic system's structure of *wages* and *capital ownership,* along with *actions of the Federal government,* are major causes of the immoral and unjust economic inequality that exists in the United States. These are human-made, not God-given, aspects of our social order. Any effort to achieve a just society must directly attack these three primary sources of economic inequality.

POLITICAL INEQUALITY

Americans sing "America the land of the free" and believe it. We believe that we have political freedom and democracy; at least as much or more freedom than anyone else. We point to the freedoms individuals have here: freedom of speech, assembly, and protest. We can actively support the party and candidate of our own choice, even run for office. The slogan "anyone can be president," with images of Abe Lincoln, lurks in our unconscious. The supposed ultimate and primary weapon of citizens is the vote. The mainstream political scientists ("pluralists") claim that the vote is the great equalizer for the mass of citizens.[44] The foundation of the power of the vote is the two-party system. For almost all of the 210 million Americans, democracy is the right to vote for people of their choice in the Democratic and Republican parties.

The reality of the voter's power is quite different from the mythology. On the major issues that affect people's lives, the vote is ineffective. First, there is little difference, if any, between the two parties. It has been said that there is one party, the Property Party, with two wings—Democratic and Republican. While they may differ in methods or tactics, the parties do not disagree on basic issues and goals. Both support the private enterprise system, economic growth, "trickle-down" economic policy, support of dictatorships to protect U.S. foreign interests, and both maintain at least 4% official unemployment rate. Neither questions economic structures that cause inequality. Both parties are financially underwritten by the super rich. The difference is not between Democrats and Republicans, but between the "ins" and "outs".

A second limit of the vote is that many of the important issues are not debated or voted on in election campaigns which are run on personality, grandiose promises, unclear ideology, public relations and dirt. Voters have a choice between candidates, not issues. If citizens disagree with any of the positions of each candidate, they cannot convey which issues they agree and disagree with. The successful candidate doesn't know why people voted for him/her. Consequently, successful candidates interpret the vote any way they want. Richard Nixon claimed that people voting for him were voting for every issue position that he took. He said that he had the backing of the silent majority for pursuing the Vietnam war even though polls showed 73% of the citizenry opposed the war.

Another limit to the power of the ballot is that there is not much choice in candidates for the masses. Virtually all candidates are upper-income people who have the mind and views of the top of the social strata. Additionally, all successful candidates require extensive funding which ties them in to industries and individuals of power. In 1972, for example, the *New York Times* wrote:

> "The most detailed study ever made of campaign contributions to political candidates has confirmed a cynical notion about American elections—that one formidable asset for public office is great personal wealth."[45]

Finally, even when opposing candidates do take opposite positions on important issues they often fail to carry out those promises when elected. In fact, they often carry out the policy position of the defeated candidate. For example, one of the biggest landslides in Presidential voting history occurred when the American people voted in President Johnson ("American boys are not going to fight battles for Asian boys") over Goldwater's position to escalate the war, bomb North Vietnam and mine Haiphong Harbor. After the clear mandate of the American people for Johnson and against the war, Lyndon Johnson carried out Goldwater's program. Johnson not only extended the war, but as the Pentagon Papers show, even *before* the election he had plans to do so. Again, in 1968, candidate Nixon's "secret plan" to end the Vietnam war won him just enough votes to barely defeat Humphrey. Once in office, he continued the war policy.

The base of decision-making in Western parliamentary theory is usually related to the size of the issue involved. If it is a substantial issue, it is considered by Cabinet-level persons, perhaps in consultation with the chief executive. Still larger issues receive parliamentary debate or Congressional review and decision, while the largest questions of all go to the people for decision, because, in a democracy, the sovereignty lies in the people.

Unfortunately, the American political system is approximately the reverse of this model. Instead of increasing the number of people who make a decision according to its importance, we decrease the number. For example, did the people at large have the opportunity to decide on the development of the hydrogen bomb? the re-armament of Germany? the Korean War? the support of the French in Indo-China? taking over the French role in Vietnam in 1954? the bombing of North Vietnam and the involvement of American ground troops? the invasions of Cambodia and Laos? governmental response to the 1973-74 energy crisis? the Russian wheat deal? In most of these decisions, the American people were not involved; relatively few people decided and the rest of us paid the consequences.

In a key confrontation in the 1960's, the Cuban missile "crisis", while the lives of hundreds of millions of people were at stake, the very few of the power elite played "chicken" with the Soviet Union. We are told that there is "no time" for informing the masses of the realities of what is happening and "no time" for public debate. There is no time because political and diplomatic brinkmanship pushes the issues to critical before the public can be informed and make a rational decision. The question is not *time*. The question is *secrecy* and *power* in the hands of a few.

Since Cuba, democracy has, if anything, eroded still further. The invasion of Cambodia was done over the objection of the Senate Foreign Relations Committee. The president did not even tell the friendly head of the invaded nation what was happening. While this tendency for the most important decisions to be made by a small number of people is most dramatically illustrated by foreign policy decisions, it is also a trend in domestic decisions. Health care is a high priority for nearly every individual, yet even by 1975, decades after most European countries have made decisive advances in delivery of free or low fee health care, the American political system is still unable to provide the electorate with an opportunity to decide in favor of universal health care. If the people at large were given the opportunity to decide between spending $50 billion for space races and spending the same amount for making our cities liveable, it would be fascinating. The people are not given such a decision to make, however; perhaps because there is a fear that they might make the "wrong" decision. The powerful few, not the people, decide.

Economic Elite Control of the Political System

Earlier we showed that the economy is dominated by a small number of giant corporations. Now we will discuss some of the *mechanisms* by which they exert control or influence over important governmental decisions.

Perhaps one of the most important ways the economic elite dominate government is through *campaign funding*. Campaigns are expensive. The committee to re-elect president Nixon in 1972 collected over $60 million alone. Campaigns are so expensive that only the rich can really afford it: 90% of the funding comes from the super-rich 1%, while only 10% comes from the great majority of citizens. Large donations by a few undermine democracy because a return is expected on the investment and elected officials are aware of what they need to do in office to assure more donations to cover future campaign expenses. The giant oil companies, for example, gave over five million dollars to the 1972 Nixon presidential campaign and his administration responded in puppet-like fashion during the "energy crisis".[46] ITT pledged $200,000 to the Republican party just before the

Department of Justice settled three anti-trust suits in its favor. Bebe Rebozo's wealth increased seven-fold during the first five years of Nixon's Presidency.[47] Nixon granted a large rise in milk price supports requested by the dairy industries shortly after they pledged two million dollars in campaign donations. Nixon said he knew about the pledge at the time and took "traditional political considerations" into account in raising milk price supports.[48]

The government also reflects a strong bias towards the super-rich because *so many of the highest elected officials and their appointees are themselves rich.* Most of the Democratic presidential candidates such as Roosevelt, Stevenson, Kennedy, and Johnson were wealthy. Richard Nixon, after serving as Vice President, and before running for the presidency, in private law practice became a millionaire in the course of a year. Almost half of the U.S. Senators are millionaires. Ex-president Nixon and eight of his former cabinet members are millionaires. The interests of the rich in government are self-evident.

Another means of corporate control over government is their power over regulatory agencies. Judge Lee Loevinger stated that " . . . the history of every *regulatory agency* in the government is that it comes to represent the industry or groups which it's supposed to control".[49] The fantastic concentration and monopoly in American business is obviously in violation of anti-trust laws, but most cases are settled out of court and rarely is there a penalty. When there are penalties imposed they are usually insignificant. Both Democrats and Republicans are soft on monopoly.

Closely associated with regulatory agencies are *governmental advisory councils* which make policy recommendations to government; these also are usually dominated by the businesses most closely related. Often they hold meetings which are secret and closed to the public despite laws to the contrary.

One of the ways citizens are supposed to participate in the democratic process is through *lobbying.* But lobbying is overwhelmingly the method of the rich and big business. It is estimated that most Congressional bills originate or are written by lobbyists. Only rarely does there exist lobbying on behalf of those people who pay the enormous social costs for the political-corporate decision making.

Although there are many mechanisms and methods by which the government is controlled by and acts for the big corporations and the super-rich, the ultimate proof is in governmental actions, the *actual behavior of government* in maintaining the tremendous economic, political and social inequalities of the status quo. The attainment and maintenance of such an unjust status quo is a political act, or the result of political actions and deliberate inactions. It is obvious that in countries such as China, Cuba, and Sweden where major changes in various sectors have taken place, the changes were made by political decision and power. It is a political act of inequality for the government not to have a law limiting wealth. It is a political act of inequality to decide not to give every person free or low-fee health care as is done in almost every other industrialized nation. It is a political act of inequality to maintain the status quo.

There has almost never been a secret or deception by the government in which the government was serving the masses or the poor. Always they are serving business, supporting dictators, infringing on rights of citizens, or undermining popular governments which oppose U.S. businesses and industry. Never have governmental secrets or deceptions been exposed to find the government hurting Rockefeller, General Motors, or ITT. Never has the government been found to be secretly giving billions of dollars to the poor or more power to the people. The relationship between the super-rich and government is most obvious from the fact that the same top 1% who receive most of the government welfare benefits from tax loopholes and subsidy programs are the same 1% who pay 90% of campaign funds.

A case of General Motors. Economic power is political and social power. A recent study by Bradford Snell, *American Ground Transport,* [50] showed in detail how economic power of one corporation has drastically affected our lives and how the handful of decision makers of General Motors brought the demise of mass transit in America. He shows that since 1925 General Motors bought out electric mass transit systems in over 100 cities and converted them to motorized bus systems. GM accounts for 75% of the American bus production. Moreover, the demise of efficient and updated electrical mass transit systems has also spurred automobile sales. GM is the world's largest auto-maker. GM makes more money on automobiles per passenger; therefore once converting transit systems to buses, GM's best interest was served by converting the bus systems to automobiles as much as possible. Because of bus inconvenience, foul smoke and noise, and inadequate service to suburbs, ridership has declined by three billion passengers and bus sales have fallen by about 60% since 1952. This was the year that General Motors achieved monopoly control of bus production.

The conversion of the nation's transit system from electrical mass modes to an individualized motorized system has sweepingly affected the lives of all Americans. The issue has never come to a vote and has never been allowed to become a substantial public issue. Few people outside the industry knew what was happening. Yet most Americans now require an automobile to go to work, visit friends, or go on a vacation. Automobiles kill thousands on the highways each year and are one of our most dangerous sources of pollution. Hundreds of hours are spent annually by each worker in undesirable workplaces to pay for automobiles and their upkeep. The nation has become addicted to oil such that it creates questionable foreign policies. The resulting high use of automobiles, tires, and oil has led to powerful monopoly corporations and industries and rich individuals which exert considerable control over our local and national governments. Highways and roads take up a considerable part of our land and are a blight. Automobiles are a constant noise pollutant and nuisance in the cities. The situation will become even worse as numbers of cars increase and regulatory agencies drop or fail to enforce pollution restrictions.

The power of GM, the other auto manufacturers and oil companies has been and remains pervasive. Our lives have been drastically altered for the sake of these corporations, against our best interests. This giving of power to so few never came to a vote. Both parties supported it.

Some Consequences of Political Inequality in Economic Life.

Economic life is a crucial aspect of living. Almost everyone depends on work to provide them with income for their necessities and lifestyle. Many spend half their awake hours either in transit or at work. However, neither as citizens nor as workers do most Americans have much to say about their economic life. As citizens they have no control over businesses (and jobs) moving in or out of the community. Those decisions are made by managers and directors. As workers, these local citizens have little influence on what is produced (bombs, bread, cars or clothes), quality, where the company is located, daily production decisions, planning, what percentage of profits go to workers, prices, pollution and pollution control, working environment, hours or benefits. These are all political decisions in the economic sector of society. In the United States there is virtually no participation by the masses of citizen-workers in these decisions. Moreover, the decisions are usually not made on the basis of the best interests of the community or the workers, but of the corporation which is often national or international.

Not only do people not have the right to participate in the decisions in their workplace but the productive institutions, as we have pointed out in this chapter, have grown to such size and strength that they constitute political and economic entities comparable to nations. Most Americans (4 out of 5) do not own any stock in these corporations and 2% of those that do, own over half the stock. Democracy in corporate decision-making is supposed to rest ultimately in the hands of the owners (the stockholders) through the power of their vote—just as the vote is supposed to be the ultimate democratic weapon of the general citizenry. But recent governmental studies debunk this process. Senator Metcalf presented these findings to Congress:

> The corporate election process in America today is as rigged as elections are in the Soviet Union. The outcome is as predictable. The accompanying propaganda is as self-serving.
>
> Consider the procedures for an annual stockholders' meeting. The agenda and the candidates are determined well in advance by the corporate management. It polices the election. It chooses the auditors. Great effort and considerable expense, months prior to the meeting, are required to obtain consideration of the most modest proposals . . . If the attempt to get a candidate or an issue on the ballot is successful, identification of the voting stockholders and timely communication with them is difficult or impossible. The proxies of a few key institutional investors decide the election, which is then publicly construed by the corporation publicists as a ringing endorsement of its past activities and a mandate to continue doing whatever it decides to do. [51]

Control of People's Minds. Almost any story sounds believable if only one side is presented. Court trials have a lawyer presenting the case for each side because either one can usually convince a jury of the rightness of their argument. This is not unlike the political process of a state or nation. The democratic process requires that all the relevant facts are presented and each segment of the population has an equal chance to make their opinions known to the public. Freedom of speech is useless without equal access to communications.

During the 1960's, television became the single most important medium in the United States, with radio and newspapers still widely used. But the mass media are controlled by corporations and affluent individuals, thereby giving the public a one-sided view of the world, a view from the top. Sociologist Morris Janowitz points out:

Available research knowledge suggests that mass communications can be decisive in moments of crisis and tension, but that, in general, influence is limited and has effect gradually, over a long period of time. The influence of mass media . . . is not in dramatic conversion of public opinion, but rather in setting the limits within which public debate on controversial issues takes place. [52]

The first manner in which the media are controlled is through *advertisements*. All the media require income from advertisements; the bigger the media, the more income is necessary from big corporations. National TV news and programs are sponsored by corporations in *Fortune's* top 500 corporations. Second, many of the mass media are *owned* by large corporations or rich individuals, and often are part of a "chain" of media with the same owner. *Time* is the nation's 180th largest industrial corporation and is controlled by upper-class members. The *New York Times* is number 381 and owned by a single affluent family. Lord Thomson of England owns the *London Times* and 150 other newspapers including some in the United States. In 1967 chains owned half of the nation's 1,767 daily newspapers. [53]

While we may stand on a soapbox and tell several hundred people that the United States is secretly bombing Cambodia, flying U-2's over Russia, planning an invasion of Cuba, overthrowing the government of Brazil, Chile, or Iran—the President, Congress, the Pentagon, and corporation public relations departments are able to reach most Americans via media to deny the facts and influence public thought. Edward W. Scripps, founder of one of the nation's top media chains, summarized the role of mass communications as follows:

The press of this country is now, and always has been, so thoroughly dominated by the wealthy few of the country that it cannot be depended upon to give the great mass of the people that correct information concerning political, economic and social subjects which it is necessary that they shall have in order that they shall vote and in all ways act in the best way to protect themselves from the brutal force and chicanery of the ruling and employing class. [54]

Watergate. Over two years ago an office break-in grew from a political blunder to a national crisis. By the summer of 1974 it ended with the resignation of President Nixon in disgrace, and a broad sweep of scores of public officials who, like the President, were guilty of misconduct and illegal acts. Watergate has become the catch-all phrase for illegal infringements on citizens' rights, excessive power in the Presidency, and dishonest, secretive, illegal, and unethical acts of public officials.

Although President Ford had no new approaches to the problems of the economy or the American people, he somehow, in the minds of many Americans, symbolized the downfall of evil and corruption. The battle of Watergate was over—won by the good guys. Faith in America was restored. The growing power of the presidency had been halted, and the proper checks and balances among the three government sectors were on the way to restoration. "The system works" was the phrase that cheered people on after the dark days of Watergate.

Watergate was an important event. But it was not a real radicalizing experience for Americans. It was important that the "excessive abuse" of Presidential powers was checked and we hope that the American public has learned to be more critical and skeptical of political leaders.

Watergate gave us a glimpse of what is wrong with America—power of the rich and big corporations and the lack of a voice by the people. But the Watergate affair could neither cure the illness nor bring about the ongoing consciousness necessary for the real changes that must happen. The power of the rich and the corporations over the economic and political system was neither challenged nor questioned by Watergate. The system of control by the rich was left intact, with only the most flagrant abuses being sternly reprimanded. Democracy by the people was not restored. The loud and extensive proclamations that our democracy is working are merely part of a broader coverup.

Limits to Mainstream Solutions to Political Inequality.

The mainstream solutions to political inequality (the popular vote, good politicians, and "checks and balances") seem hopelessly inadequate. The social order of private enterprise and economic inequality seems to have led to a centralism of power covering economic, social and government sectors acting in unison for the benefit of a minority of economic, corporate and political (including military) elites. The adage of Benjamin Watkins Leigh, 19th century Virginia statesperson, seems to prevail:

> Power and property may be separated for a time by force or fraud—but divorced never. For so soon as the pang of separation is felt ... property will purchase power, or power will take over property.

Social change to a democratic society requires a fundamental change in the fabric of society—its values, social systems and institutions.

AMERICAN MILITARISM

The question of war or peace is a crucial one in evaluating any nation. This is particularly true of the United States because of its position as chief world power. Although the ravages of war have plagued humankind throughout history, peace is even more important today because wars are becoming more devastating—civilian victims outnumber soldiers, more nations and populations become involved in wars, the possibility of escalation of local wars to involve major powers has increased, and "improved" weaponry is now capable of destroying all human life.

In this section we focus on the question, "Does the United States contribute more to world war or peace?" We find that the United States not only is a major force for world wars and militarism, but that it cannot become a force for peace without revolutionary changes.

The United States is a nation of war. Sixty percent

of the annual Federal Budget is devoted to past, present and future wars. We spend twice as much money on war as human welfare, and each year military expenditures increase more than all other uses of tax dollars. Although according to Missouri Senator Stuart Symington the United States already possesses 2,500 times the tonnage of all the bombs dropped by us in World War II,[55] over half of all American research and development scientists and engineers in industry are connected to even more war production.

The U.S. is the world's warlord and policeman. The United States spends about 40% of the world's $200 billion plus annual war expenditures. The U.S. is the world's biggest arms peddler, selling arms regularly to 51 countries. Moreover, American arms sales are increasing exponentially. Most of the world's dictators not only receive their military arms and training from the U.S. but also are protected by mutual defense alliances. An added note of horror is that many of the belligerent nations in high tension areas fight or threaten each other with American weapons, such as India and Pakistan, Turkey and Greece, the Arab states and Israel.

Justifications for American Militarism and the Fallacy of Those Justifications.

Since the end of World War II, American militarism has grown in the name of protecting peace, freedom, and democracy throughout the world. The arch-enemy of freedom and democracy has been singly defined as Communism. Consequently, America's militarism has been justified in the name of the crusade against Communism. This has proven to be more of an ideological rationalization than a reasonable explanation.

Presidential visits, cultural exchanges, and a joint space venture might cause us to question the scare tactics of a few years ago. Our fears about the Communist threat fade in light of the fact that none of the wide-spread poverty and hunger in the world today is found in the 40% of the world which is Communist. Those maladies were extensive in many of these nations in their pre-

Communist periods. For example, about one-third of the world's poor lived in mainland China before their revolution, and now, while no hunger is there, it still runs rampant in the other poor nations.

Also, rather than maintaining peace and stability, the anti-Communist arms race and American military build-up are helping to cause conventional wars and instability while helping lay the conditions for nuclear holocaust. The arms race detente strategy calls for ever-increasing military build-ups and newer and deadlier weapons systems because each side believes it needs more chips at the bargaining table.

The possibility of accidental, all-out warfare is increasing over time. The amount of deadly weaponry available to those humans controlling the buttons makes accidental holocaust more and more likely.

Even without the holocaust-war occurring, humanity might be entirely destroyed or seriously harmed by the arms race itself. As we pointed out in the Environmental Crisis chapter, the atmospheric testing of atomic weapons in the 1950's and early 1960's was threatening human existence by the proliferation of radioactivity throughout the world. Even after the July 1963 conference which agreed to end atmospheric atomic testing, President Kennedy made it clear to the U.S. military and to the Senate that he reserved the right to resume testing in the atmosphere even if the Soviets were abiding by the treaty, should the tests "be deemed essential to our national security .. . "[56]

Nuclear testing increased after the signing of the treaty—by going underground. The A.E.C.'s report in April 1970 was that there had been 90 tests from 1945 until the effective date of the treaty, August 5, 1963. From then until 1970 there were 210 tests—more than twice as many in the seven years after the treaty as in the eighteen years before it.[57] Underground atomic tests (which are not adequately monitored or researched by the A.E.C.) have extreme potential hazard to human life.

Instead of decreasing militarism, the detente with

the Soviet Union has continued the *arms race* which maintains the likelihood of localized limited wars like Korea, Vietnam, and the Middle East; these could at some point cause a confrontation between the two super-atomic powers.

Finally, the arms race perpetuates a social climate and acceptance of violence in American society: it intensifies the culture of death. Just 40 years ago the United States spent little money on militarism; today, it is accepted as our way of life. There is a generally permissive attitude in the culture toward violence. It is not only the followers of John Wayne and Clint Eastwood who celebrate violence; even the churches and universities are committed to it on a deep, non-rational level.

Most clergy defend deterrence and other violent doctrines on the grounds that "there is no alternative," yet they have spent virtually no energy on exploring alternatives. The Swedish Defense Ministry, by contrast, has become sufficiently interested in the potential of civilian resistance as a means of national defense that they have put research and development money into exploring it. Swedish generals are more interested in non-military means of struggle than any major American religious denomination that we know of!

The universities and schools also reflect the cultural addiction to violence. R.O.T.C. units have routinely been part of the campus scene for decades while peace studies courses have only recently appeared, and on only a small minority of campuses. Scholars, including historians, study violence with much more interest than nonviolent struggle. High school students are rarely given information about the significant nonviolent movements in American history.

Another chief justification for American militarism is to help the hundred or so poor nations within the American sphere of dominance maintain their freedom and democratic way of life. Indeed, a big portion of our military expenditures is spent in support of the governments of such nations. It is estimated that in 1971 the U.S. spent $30 billion on defense of the continental U.S.

and $44 billion "to foster our interests abroad" by giving "military assistance (broadly defined)" to other nations.[58] A large part of U.S. militarism is geared to maintaining the status quo regarding the poor nations in the U.S. sphere of dominance.

However, the American people are becoming increasingly aware that almost all of the poor countries whose "freedom and democratic institutions" we are protecting are dictatorships. There is virtually no freedom or democracy available to the citizenry. Those few elections that are held have predetermined outcomes. Only governments supported by the United States have opportunities to win. News is severely censored as are fundamental opponents of oppression and exploitation by the national power elites in collusion with American business, military, and government.

The "freedom" that the U.S. imposes in those nations is not the political freedom to choose the government or political system of their own choice, or the freedom to use their resources to meet the needs of their own people. Rather, it means the freedom of American business to extract resources at cheap prices and freedom for American foreign policy to make sure the peoples in the Third World do not leave the sphere of American dominance and exploitation.

Consequently, the major violence inflicted on the majority of world citizens, who are the masses living in the poor nations under the American sphere of influence, is not the hot war of Vietnam and Korea, but the constant everyday violence of poverty, starvation, disease and hopelessness which continues to grow. The real violence is the quiet, "invisible war" of our normal business and governmental relations of economic exploitation and political oppression. These "normal" relations are ultimately maintained by our militarism.

Limits of Mainstream Solutions to American Militarism.

Proposals for the de-militarization of the United States divide into two fundamental approaches: (1) guns-to-butter and (2) world law. Both of these approaches seem unrealistic and doomed to failure unless some fundamental changes occur within the fabric and culture of the United States. Both require American de-development.

(1) *Limits of guns-to-butter.* The guns-to-butter idea seems rather easy and reasonable at first reading. The U.S. is the richest and strongest nation in the world and our military has a tremendous overkill capacity. Why not merely take half or three-quarters, or all, of our military money and spend it on meeting peace-time domestic needs such as health care, mass transit, guaranteed jobs in social services, housing for low and middle income people, and slum clean-up? Such a proposal is made in the Urban Coalition's popular book, *Counterbudget.* It suggests that rather than stagnate during the transition to a peacetime budget, the economy could boom from a deliberate supplying of jobs, money and services such as low-income housing to America's poor and near-poor.

Unfortunately proposals like that of the Urban Coalition overlook *the enormous power of the military-industrial complex*—those governmental, military, and business groups whose vested interests lie in huge military spending. Military spending has played a key part in bolstering the American economy and staving off depression, while social programs have been ineffective at it. Since the depression, the economy has risen and fallen in concert with fluctuations in military spending. Today, the fastest growing industries are the most techno-logical—aerospace, communications, and electronics—and these are the most underwritten by the Pentagon. "75% of all research and development activity in the country is paid for by the government, and of this, 50% is disbursed directly by the Defense Department and another 38% by the defense-related NASA and AEC." [59] The Military-Industrial Complex has grown to encompass 10 percent of our work force, 22,000 prime contractors and some 100,000 subcontractors. [60]

As one might suspect, giant corporations dominate the Military-Industrial Complex, the same ones which dominate the rest of the economy. The Pentagon's list of its top war contractor corporations reads like a corporation Who's Who: Lockheed Aircraft, AT&T, Grumman, GE, Tenneco, McDonnell-Douglas, United Aircraft, Boeing, Ling-Temco-Vought. These top 10 in 1971 received 35% of the $29.8 billion in contract money that year. General Motors, Sperry Rand, ITT, RCA, American Motors, IBM, Westinghouse, Litton Industries, Ford, Standard Oil, Bendix, General Tire & Rubber, Chrysler, Reynolds, Texaco, and Mobil are among the powerful corporations that made up the top 100 contractors who received 72%, or $21.5 billion, of the contracts that year. The big industries make up the list: aircraft, oil, electronics, automobile and chemical. [61]

These same corporations and industries which are at the top of the economic and political power hierarchy of the country are also the main benefactors of the military boondoggle. Along with the Pentagon, they comprise the Military-Industrial Complex that President Eisenhower warned the nation about.

While the main financial costs of the Indochina War were borne by the American public at large and the troops who fought, large profits went to a small, powerful group of corporations and the Pentagon. The international corporations also benefited by the demonstration effect; that is, the Indochina war served as a warning to other small nations that the U.S. is prepared to sacrifice whole peoples and governments to maintain them within its sphere of dominance. The American corporations and the American economy need the world's resources and markets to maintain their growth rate. Vietnam-type wars are part of the price that must be paid to retain those resources and markets.

The MIC corporations also have tremendous influence over the Pentagon, Congress and the Federal Administration through interchangeable personnel, campaign contributions, and lobbies. A Pentagon study found that in a 3-year period, 993 high-ranking officers (above rank of major) and 108 high-level Pentagon civilian employees moved into industry and 232 former industry executives accepted Defense Department jobs. Senator Proxmire's one-time check in 1969 revealed that 2,122 former top military officers were employed in the defense industry. Retired officers in some corpoiations were: Lockheed 210, Boeing 169, and McDonnell-Douglas 141. [62]

Campaign contributions are considered to be an important means of political influence, and the bigger the contribution the bigger the influence. If this is true, MIC contractor corporations have considerable political clout. Although there exist laws forbidding any corporation to give money to candidates for Federal offices, there also unfortunately exist loopholes to those laws. One loophole is gifts by corporate executives as individuals. In 1968, executives of Department of Defense contractors donated over $1.2 million to political campaigns. This included Litton Industries ($151,000), Ford ($140,000), IBM ($136,250), and General Motors ($115,675). [63] Representative Les Aspin has written that the oil industry gave President Nixon's re-election committee more than $5 million or 9% of Nixon's total.

The MIC corporations not only benefit from the stability of an industry provided by the government (which also concentrates its prime contracts to a relatively small handful of corporations), but they also have unusually high profits. The high take from DOD contracts is shown by the $23-million in profits and dividends made by David Packard during the three years he was Deputy Defense Secretary. This profit (which he donated to charity) was from the Hewlett-Packard Company which he founded thirty years earlier. [64] Almost all of Hewlett-Packard's business is with the Pentagon.

One reason for high profits is that, of prime contracts, 90% are given out by the Pentagon without real competition. [65] Another source is the almost unbridled cost overruns on contracts. A General Accounting Office study in 1973 totaled $31 billion in cost overruns above the original pricetags ($81.2 billion) for the major weapons systems being developed at the time—and their costs were still spiraling. A navy submarine supposed to cost $1.7 billion was then listed at $8.1 billion. The Minuteman ICBM supposed to cost $2.6 billion was up to $6.1 billion. And a torpedo originally priced at $720 million was up to $1.9 billion.[66] In three months of 1974 the cost of the developing B-1 bomber went from $61.5 million to $76 million each.[67]

Beyond the imperatives of the economic system and the power of the Military-Industrial Complex, however, there is a more compelling reason why the United States cannot end its militarism—*the American way of life requires it.* Six percent of the world's population cannot consume 35 to 40% of the annually consumed resources without being the world's number one warlord. In Chapter Five, we saw how the American military keeps in power those governments which allow us to exploit the resources of Third World countries so that we can continue our gluttonous growth.

It is not possible to switch from guns to butter. That is, the United States can't convert from its present high production of military weapons and troops to a high level of domestic peacetime products. As we lower our military capacity, our ability to exploit is lowered, and consequently, our level of consumption will be lowered. Any decreases in American militarism, therefore, require a vast de-development of the United States. Our present high-consumption way of life requires a warfare state.

(2) Limits of World Law. World peace requires a world-wide solution. Betty Reardon and Saul H. Mendlovitz [68] show the limitations of the present approaches to world peace which they call (1) the United Nations model of balance of power between the big nations, (2) protracted conflict model—cold wars, (3) regionalism, (4) rampant nationalism, and (5) the joining together of the United States and Russia. None of these models satisfactorily addresses itself to most of the key issues "beyond the minimal one of human survival." They don't deal adequately with economic development or social justice, or "the most serious shortcoming of all . . . the possibility of further proliferation of nuclear weapons, break-

throughs in military technology, or additional deterioration of world political stability." [69]

Reardon and Mendlovitz say that the solution through world law must include two important notions in order to succeed: disarmament and a collective security system which includes a forum where parties can bring their grievances.

We agree with the key points made by Reardon and Mendlovitz; however, we believe their solution has the same limitations as the guns-to-butter solution proposed for U.S. militarism. A prerequisite for world law is massive de-development of the present over-developed industrialized nations, particularly the United States and Europe. As long as they are fat and gulp the world's resources in a poor and hungry world, there can be no peace with justice, the world must remain a military camp, and people's revolutions must be suppressed everywhere. This point can be seen more clearly when we realize that if there were today, by a wave of a magic wand, a just, world-wide government with enforcement powers, representing all the peoples of the world and future generations equally, one of its first acts would be to reduce the consumption of the United States by about 80 percent. This point is either glossed over or ignored by most world law proposals which still cling to the myths of world-wide western economic growth and development for all.

Conclusions. The goals of disarmament and an end to wars and militarism cannot be achieved simply by organizing a strong World Government or by conversion from guns to butter. The general phenomenon of militarism has, of course, many causes. But the U.S. seems specifically hooked on militarism because of (1) our high consumption levels, (2) our private enterprise system and the power it gives the economic elites which it creates, and (3) the political-economic power of the Military-Industrial Complex. Efforts to change American militarism must focus on massive de-development of the United States, ending the private enterprise system, and ending our assistance to military dictatorships. Such de-development of the United States must be accompanied by massive efforts at redistribution of resources, wealth, and income as well as changing the emphasis of happiness from materialism to "people-ism."

DOMESTIC VIOLENCE

The United States leads the industrialized world in domestic acts of violence. Assault, armed robberies, rape and homicides abound. The streets of American cities are dangerous.

High crime rates are caused, to a great extent, by poverty and inequality. Most of the population cannot legally achieve the upper-middle-class levels of consumption and lifestyle that are flaunted before us as standards of acceptability. Even more importantly, many Americans cannot legally acquire even the basic material necessities or minimum standard of living defined by the government. Tens of millions are doomed to poverty in urban slums or rural backwaters. Consequently, the American jails and prisons are filled with poor people, especially nonwhites.

Most criminal activity and resultant imprisonment are a function of poverty status; and poverty status is a political decision. Governments *can* decide to end poverty and reduce economic inequality. This has been a large cause for the low rate of violence in other industrialized nations. The United States, for example, has a homicide rate 25 times higher than Sweden. Swedish authorities say their low crime rate was achieved only after they virtually eliminated poverty by providing universal social services and guaranteed jobs with reasonable pay scales, and eliminated slums.

Most inmates in American prisons are political prisoners in the sense that arrest and conviction rates for poor people are much higher than for nonpoor who commit crimes. When convicted, poor and nonwhite receive longer sentences for similar crimes than do affluent whites. The "crime" of many persons in

American prisons is that they are both poor and non-white.

The solution to direct crimes of violence within the United States, therefore, is political, not individual. Mainstream efforts, however, emphasize law and order, and police and court enforcement. Humanitarians often emphasize court and prison reforms. But the problem of violence in the streets, by police, in the courts and in prisons, must be approached at its source—by elimination of poverty through governmental action and the end of police and court biases against poor and nonwhite people.

Alienation in the United States

Americans are estranged from themselves, others, and the world around them. The dominant features of the American way of life—materialism, competition, utilitarianism, private enterprise—ignore and suppress human values.

Most Americans are alienated in their *work*. For Americans, work is neither thought of as a means of self-expression nor as a way to contribute towards the meeting of social needs. Rather, it is a means for earning money. Although most adults spend half their waking hours relating to work, it is a disagreeable task for them. The emphasis of work has been on the product and efficient production to increase profits of the owners rather than on the good of the worker. Another dehumanizing aspect of work has been that rather than working for social benefit, much of the production of goods contributes heavily to social problems such as warfare, environmental destruction, excessive baubles and gadgetry. Many of the products are substitutes for human involvement. People need work which is personally and socially useful. Such work is virtually impossible in our economic system because it is less profitable.

The web of *consumerism* has created immeasurable alienation in Americans. Self-identity, success, self-acceptance, enjoyment, sexuality, and social status are to a great extent tied to ownership and consumption of material products. Human needs have been converted to the desire for products. In reality, however, the ultimate purpose of the consumption of products is corporate profits. We suggest that those who haven't, read Vance Packard's *The Hidden Persuaders,* or, especially, *The Waste Makers,* which "exposes the systematic attempt of business to make us wasteful, debt-ridden, permanently discontented individuals. And all under the pretense of 'keeping America strong'." (back cover of *The Waste Makers).*

The foundation of American culture based on economic acquisition and economic growth has a one-dimensional view of human beings as materialistic. Once basic survival needs are met, humans are social beings rather than material beings. Happiness can only be found in knowing oneself and in meaningful social relationships, not in acquisition of material goods.

Women have been one of the least recognized among alienated groups until recently. Our economic system and its needs for aggregate growth feed heavily into the pervasiveness of sexism in the American Way. False images of women have been used to encourage consumerism by men who are attracted to products by the advertising image of women, and by women who want to be that "ideal woman." Women have also provided the cheap labor to keep the industries running. Undesirable and low-pay work has gone to women. Women workers comprise a reserve workforce which also helps keep men's salaries low. And what is perhaps the biggest and hardest required work in the society, housework and child-rearing, has been relegated to women without pay.

Nonwhites are also still alienated from American society. The majority of blacks still hold low-income, low-status, and undesirable work or are unemployed. Stereotypical images and fear keep racial lines drawn and communication difficult.

Both *old* and *young* people are also alienated from the American way of life. Much again can be tied to the stress on economics—the ability to produce and consume as a basis of well-being and status. The old are seen as dispensable in terms of our economic well-being; the young, as future producers and consumers to be molded and shaped to properly fit into the "American way."

Most Americans, as we pointed out earlier, are also alienated from *political life*. Alienation from power, though, cannot be corrected until the sources by which most political power goes to a few people are corrected. This can be traced back primarily to a maldistribution of wealth and income, and to control by these few over the means of production.

In our high-speed, technological, and rapidly growing environment, individuals suffer deeply from *alienation from self*. Fragmentation, loss of meaning, and a sense of futility are the repeated cries for help heard increasingly in our society. People deserve a sense of wholeness, meaning in life, inner peace, and the ability to change what is wrong in a sick society.

A New Economic Order

While the United States is the top producer, consumer and polluter in the world, at the same time many people's needs are not being met. Slums increase, housing is pitiful for many, crime stalks the streets, and even such basic needs as health care are not met.

The main way of solving these problems, according to the U.S. ideology and economic system, is through more development. Economic growth, rather than being able to solve the problems, though, is the major cause of the problems. More economic growth within the private enterprise system (controlled by big corporations and big government) will fail to solve our problems in the future just as it has failed in the past. Moreover, in our view, the solutions to these crucial problems require less production and consumption, less use of the market system, and less private profit as a motive for economic production and distribution. These big problems cannot be reformed away, because they need a new social structure and new ideology: de-development and re-development. That is, reduced production and consumption accompanied by massive redistribution and a new economic order in which the purpose of production is to meet the basic human needs of all rather than the private profits of a few. This new economic order would consider as a major factor the lives of persons in other nations and the lives of citizens of future generations.

---

[1] *Newsweek,* January 24, 1972, p. 62.

[2] Michael Harrington, *The Other America: Poverty in the United States* (Baltimore, Md.: Penguin Books, 1963).

[3] *Economic Notes,* Dec. 1971, p. 7.

[4] U.S. Congress, Joint Economic Committee, *Studies in Public Welfare. Paper No. 3. The Effectiveness of Manpower Training Programs: A Review of Research on the Impact on the Poor,* 92nd Congress, 2nd Session, November 20, 1972, Stock Number 5270-01638. U.S. Govt. Printing Office, p. iv.

[5] Jackie Greenleaf, "Socialist Feminism" (Mimeo, Fall 1974. Available from the author at 4719 Cedar Ave., Philadelphia, PA 19143).

[6] Lucy Komisar, *The New Feminism* (N.Y.: Warner Paperback Library, 1972), p. 49.

[7] Frank Ackerman et al., "The Extent of Income Inequality in the United States," in Richard Edwards, Michael Reich and Thomas Weisskopf (eds.), *The Capitalist System* (Englewood Cliffs, N.J.: Prentice-Hall, 1972), p. 216.

[8] *The New York Times,* December 29, 1971.

[9] *The New York Times,* May 25, 1972, p. 32.

[10] Barry Bluestone, "Economic Theory and the Fate of the Poor," *Social Policy,* Jan.-Feb. 1972.

[11] *Do the Poor Want to Work?: A Social-Psychological Study of Work Orientations* (Washington, D.C.: The Brookings Institute, 1972).

[12] Robert Heilbroner, "Benign Neglect in the U.S.," *Trans-action,* October 1970.

[13] See William Ryan, *Blaming the Victim* (N.Y.: Vintage, 1971).

[14] *Economic Notes,* July/August 1973.

[15] *Economic Notes,* June 1972.

[16] Richard Parker, *The Myth of the Middle Class: Notes on Affluence and Equality* (N.Y.: Harper and Row, 1972).

[17] Peter Passell and Leonard Ross, *The Retreat from Riches: Affluence and Its Enemies* (N.Y.: The Viking Press, 1973), p. 7.

[18] *Jeremiad,* May 27, 1974 and February 1972.

[19] *Social Policy,* Sept./Oct. 1971, p. 36.

[20] See Peter L. Berger and Thomas Luckmann, *The Social Construction of Reality* (Garden City, N.Y.: Doubleday Anchor, 1966), p. 173.

[21] For a discussion of the widening of the gap in *absolute* income, see U.S. Congress, Joint Economic Committee, *The American Distribution of Income: A Structural Problem,* 92nd Congress, 2nd Session, March 17, 1972.

[22] Gabriel Kolko, *Wealth and Power in America* (N.Y.: Praeger, 1962), chapter one.

[23] Joint Economic Committee, *op. cit.,* Table 3, p. 9; *ibid.,* p. 11; and see also Greenleaf, *op. cit.,* for information on the gap between male and female earning power.

[24] Joint Economic Committee, *op. cit.,* p. 13.

[25] Herman P. Miller, *Rich Man, Poor Man* (N.Y.: Thomas Y. Crowell, 1971), p. 156.

[26] Ferdinand Lundberg, *The Rich and the Super-rich* (N.Y.: Bantam, 1968), p. 8, summarizing Robert Lampman, *The Share of Top Wealth-Holders in National Wealth, 1922-1956* (Princeton, N.J.: Princeton University Press, 1962).

[27] *Ibid.,* p. 9.

[28] E.K. Hunt and Howard J. Sherman, *Economics: An Introduction to Traditional and Radical Views* (N.Y.: Harper & Row, 1972), p. 268-9.

[29] U.S. Senate Select Committee on Small Business, *Role of Giant Corporations: Hearings before the Subcommittee on Monopoly, Part 2— Corporate Secrecy: Overviews,* November 9 and 12, 1971.

[30] In an earlier version of this book we followed C. Wright Mills in identifying these "most powerful institutions" as "the corporations, the military, and the executive branch of government." We expressed the belief that "major control is in the hands of the corporations," but felt "space is too limited to fully document our case." Since then the research of Gabriel Kolko in *The Roots of American Foreign Policy: An Analysis of Power and Purpose* (Boston: Beacon Press, 1969) and G. William Domhoff in *The Higher Circles: The Governing Class in America* (N.Y.: Random House, 1970) has confirmed our belief and made possible advances in our understanding. Their well-documented studies reach similar conclusions on the following major points. First, in the making of foreign and military policy, the military is clearly subservient to civilian leadership, showing little or no independent initiative. (Kolko, introduction, chapters 1 & 2; Domhoff, chapter 5). Second, the executive branch policy-makers are substantially the same people as corporation owners and executives (Kolko, ch. 1; Domhoff, ch. 5 & 6). Therefore, third, the power elite may be defined as the politically active members and high-level employees of a sociologically definable and self-conscious upper class comprising no more than .5% of the population, a group who own a disproportionate share of the nation's wealth—who are, in short, the corporate rich. (Domhoff, Intro. to Part Two & chapters 1 & 4). Fourth, and finally, although disagreements on some points occur (as in the 30's, over whether to accept unions—see Domhoff, ch. 6), they are united in their commitment to the system; and while the ultra-right view of them as an omnipotent conspiracy is overdrawn, they are more than just one of several interest groups in society—the liberal/pluralist position is untenable (Domhoff, ch. 8 & 9). It is important however for strategy to see and point out contradictions within the power elite so that we never begin to view it as an impenetrable block.

[31] U.S. Congress, Joint Economic Committee, *op. cit.,* pp. 13-14.

[32] *Ibid.,* p. 5; see also Miller, *op. cit.,* and Kolko, *Wealth and Power in America* (N.Y.: Praeger, 1962).

[33] Gabriel Kolko, *The Triumph of Conservatism* (N.Y.: Quadrangle Books, 1963).

[34] *Business Week,* August 5, 1972.

[35] Hunt and Sherman, *op. cit.*, p. 219.

[36] U.S. Congress, Joint Economic Committee, *The Economics of Federal Subsidy Programs, Part 7 – Agricultural Subsidies,* April 30, 1973.

[37] *The New York Times,* January 12, 1972, p. 55.

[38] Leon Keyserling, "The Problem of Problems: Economic Growth," in Robert Theobald (ed.), *Social Policies for America in the Seventies* (Garden City, N.Y.: Doubleday Anchor, 1968), p. 17.

[39] U.S. Congress, Joint Economic Committee, *The American Distribution of Income, op. cit.,* p. 45.

[40] U.S. Congress, Joint Economic Committee, *The Economics of Federal Subsidy Programs, Part 5 – Housing Subsidies,* October 9, 1972, p. 585.

[41] *The Philadelphia Inquirer*, July 7, 1974, p. 1-A.

[42] *The New York Times,* January 25, 1972.

[43] U.S. Congress, Joint Economic Committee, *The Economics of Federal Subsidy Programs,* January 13, 14, and 17, 1972, pp. 82ff.

[44] See, for example, Robert Dahl, *Who Governs?* (New Haven: Yale Press, 1961), p. 243.

[45] *The New York Times*, April 19, 1972, p. 28.

[46] See Rep. Les Aspin, "Big Oil and the Nixon Campaign," *The Nation,* Feb. 17, 1974.

[47] *The Philadelphia Inquirer,* August 25, 1972, p. 6-A.

[48] *The New York Times,* January 9, 1974, p. 1.

[49] Cited in G. William Domhoff, *Who Rules America?* (Englewood Cliffs, N.J.: Prentice-Hall, 1967), p. 108.

[50] A study submitted to the U.S. Senate Subcommittee on Antitrust and Monopoly; summarized in *Just Economics,* May 1974, available from Movement for Economic Justice, 1609 Conn. Ave. NW, Wash., D.C. 20009.

[51] *Congressional Record,* June 28, 1972.

[52] Morris Janowitz, *The Professional Soldier* (N.Y.: The Free Press, 1960), pp. 401-2, cited in Domhoff, *op. cit.,* p. 80.

[53] Robert Cirino, *Don't Blame the People* (N.Y.: Vintage, 1971), p. 64.

[54] *Ibid.,* p. 63.

[55] Friends Committee on National Legislation, *FCNL Newsletter*, March 1974.

[56] I.F. Stone, "The Test Ban Comedy," *New York Review of Books*, May 7, 1970.

[57] Stone *(ibid.)* also reports that the Stockholm International Peace Research Institute's Yearbook on World Armaments for 1968-69 believes that U.S. nuclear testing has been understated by the Atomic Energy Commission. Judging from seismic recordings, the true figure on the number of tests could be up to twice as many as announced.

[58] The National Urban Coalition (Robert S. Benson and Harold Wolman, eds.), *Counterbudget* (N.Y.: Praeger, 1971), p. 269.

[59] Michael Reich and David Finkelhor, "Capitalism and the 'Military-Industrial Complex' : the Obstacles to 'Conversion,' " in David Mermelstein (ed.), *Economics: Mainstream Readings and Radical Critiques,* 2nd ed. (N.Y.: Random House, 1973), p. 187.

[60] Sidney Lens, *The Military-Industrial Complex* (Philadelphia: Pilgrim Press, 1970), p. 45.

[61] Department of Defense, Directorate for Information Operations, *100 Largest Defense Contractors and Their Subsidiary Corporations : Fiscal Year 1971* , October 29, 1971.

[62] *The New York Times,* January 8, 1972, p. 13.

[63] *The Philadelphia Bulletin,* September 20, 1970, p. 1.

[64] *The New York Times*, December 21, 1971, p. 1.

[65] *The New York Times*, April 19, 1972, p. 61.

[66] *The Philadelphia Inquirer,* March 27, 1973, p. 1.

[67] *The Philadelphia Inquirer,* October 2, 1974, p. 3-A.

[68] Betty Reardon and Saul H. Mendlovitz, "World Law and Models of World Order," in Charles R. Beitz and Theodore Herman (eds.), *Peace and War* (San Francisco: W.H. Freeman, 1973).

[69] *Ibid.,* p. 157.

Part III: Prescription

7

A Sound
Economic System

Our economic system is not the only source of
sickness in America nor the sole barrier to the creation of
a more just society. However, as we have noted many
times in this book, its pathology is a major force for
injustice here and around the world. Therefore, we begin
this section on "Prescription" with thoughts on what a
healthy economic system might look like.

What kind of economic system will give the greatest
encouragement to people to become full, loving persons?
What kind of system will help to develop persons who
care deeply about the sanctity of human life everywhere
on earth? What economic framework will do the most to
promote the criteria of a healthy society we listed in
Chapter 2, e.g., ecological harmony, democracy, physical
security, equality, non-exploitation, freedom, and world
community?

Limits and Potential of Systemic Change

It should be obvious that no economic system, in
and of itself, can guarantee that the persons participating
in it will act in terms of the above values. Human
power-seeking, pride, greed, apathy, and self-interest can
distort and undercut the most visionary systems. If
people do not change inwardly and adopt a healthy set of
values, then a new economic system will only tend to give

163

continuation to oppression in new guises. Mahatma Gandhi said that we have to beware of dreaming of systems so perfect that no one will need to be good.

It should be just as clear, however, that an economic system can do a great deal to help or to hinder the development of full, loving human beings. Anthropological studies (e.g., of the gentle and cooperative Arapesh of New Guinea [1]) show that there is an altruistic, cooperative side to human nature which can be encouraged by a non-competitive, other-regarding, mutual aid-oriented social and economic structure. Visitors to modern China have been impressed with the mutual reinforcement of egalitarian economic institutions and a "serve the people" spirit which dampens competitive individualism and encourages the search for mutual well-being. The British socialist, Victor Gollancz, once wrote:

> If a society is characterized by a well-established system of cooperative production and distribution, then the members of that society are likely on the whole, and positively by reason of the system being there as well as negatively by reason of its alternative, the competitive one, being absent—they are likely to be gentler, more tolerant, less envious and so on, than they would have been if the atmosphere had been different.
>
> People's characters are powerfully affected by the pattern of culture characteristic of their society, and no element in the life of a society can do more to fix the pattern of its culture than its economic system—save only its religion; which in turn, if it is real religion, will involve an economic system compatible with it. [2]

The present United States economic system runs counter to the values we have identified with "good health." It demands that people who participate in it take a "me-first" attitude, competing individualistically to achieve their own security, even at the expense of others. It is also structured to promote inequality between super-rich and super-poor, to create insecurity for most people, to exploit other nations, and to destroy the environment at an ever-increasing pace.

Given this fundamental contradiction, we believe that the nonviolent movement should dedicate itself to the creation of a new kind of economic system in America, which will be more supportive of social justice and which will encourage the cooperative side of human nature.

We do not believe that such a system can be described in "blueprint" form. No one can foresee at this point the future events which may require economic institutions quite different from those that would seem desirable today. Much of the development of better, more human institutions should most properly lie in the hands of those millions of persons who will become involved in the movement for fundamental change. As William Domhoff has written:

> You need men and women with years of experience—in farming, small business, teaching, city planning, recreation, medicine, and on and on—to start discussing and writing about ways to organize that part of society they know best . . . . You need to provide outlets via forums, discussions, papers and magazines for the pent-up plans and ideals of literally millions of well-trained, experienced, frustrated Americans who see stupidity and greed all around them, but can't do a thing about it.
>
> You need to say, for example, "Look, Mr. and Mrs. City Planning Expert, trapped in this deadly bureaucracy controlled by big businessmen, draw up a sensible plan for street development, or park development, in your town of 30,000 people." "Look, Mr. Blue Collar Worker, working for this big corporation, how should this particular plant be run in a sensible society?" [3]

What we are setting forth here, therefore, is a very general picture of what seems to us to be a more desirable economic system, based on our present limited knowledge and experience. We are sure that there are both general features and important specifics that we have ignored, and we look to the growing social change movement and to the further development of our own thought for a fuller rounding out of the picture.

An Ecologically Sound Economy

Limits to world resources and to the pollution-absorption capacity of nature put severe limits on the material abundance which can be created by an economic system. As we have argued in Chapter 4, "Environmental Crisis," there is no way that poor nations can "come up" to the average U.S. standard of living; nor can the present U.S. economic growth rate be sustained for long without ecological disaster. To achieve a just distribution of the world's resources and a balance between economic activity and the ecosystem, super-rich nations like the U.S. must "de-develop" their economies, then re-develop them along ecologically harmonious lines. We must "take from the rich and give to the poor." Wealth must be redistributed on a world scale.

From the perspective of ecology, the basic purpose of a healthy economic system should not be the pursuit of affluence or ever-higher growth of the GNP. Rather, its purpose should be to provide a simple, adequate, economically secure way of life for everyone in the society, in which there are neither rich nor poor, exploiter nor exploited, where attitudes of cooperation and mutual aid are fostered to the utmost, where everyone has a voice in the decisions affecting them, and in which economic activity is carried on in harmony with environmental requirements.

At first blush, the de-development of the American trillion-dollar economy may seem an impossible dream. Given the fact that we now have tens of millions of Americans living in poverty, how could everyone have an "economically secure way of life" if our GNP were cut by one-half or more? Wouldn't things be just that much worse off?

It is instructive in this regard to look at modern China. John Roderick, writing in the *New York Times* about his return to Shanghai after twenty-five years, is one of the many Western visitors who have commented on the truly amazing physical and social accomplishments of the Chinese:

It was a city of underfed rickshaw boys, filthy slums, and dying poor. Outside the Broadway mansions, where I lived for a year, the teeming sampans, crowded with the starving, made many well-fed Americans avert their faces. The extremes of wealth and poverty were appalling.

Today there are no beggars, no rickshaws, no poor dying in the streets . . . . The rich and the poor are no more . . . . Where once millions died of famine, everyone—at least in the areas visited—seemed to have enough to eat. The ordinary people appeared sturdy, healthy, and content. [4]

The astonishing thing about the Chinese leap from extreme poverty to material adequacy is that it was done with a population about four times as large as ours and with a GNP of about $100 billion, approximately one-tenth the size of ours.

We have deep disagreements with some aspects of the Chinese political economy and are not suggesting that the U.S. should adopt the Chinese system. What the Chinese experience *does* strongly suggest is that the U.S. *should be able to get along with a much smaller GNP while meeting the basic needs of its people.* Our own belief is that the U.S. GNP should be cut drastically, perhaps by as much as nine-tenths, and then that the economy should be held in a "no-growth" state, with the focus on ecological harmony and just redistribution of wealth, income and services.

Many studies are now coming out[5] showing how a de-developed, no-growth economic system could be structured, and we will not attempt to go into all the details here. The features of an ecologically harmonious society listed below, however, indicate the direction in which we believe our economy should move.

What we now have: Our Ecologically Faulty System	What we'll need for an Ecologically-orientated Economic System

Values

Growth, "big-is-good", complex technology, maximum production and consumption, planned obsolescence.

Steady state, "small is beautiful," intermediate technology, adequate production and minimized consumption, equilibrium, conservation, frugality, durability.

Lifestyles

"Keep up with the Joneses", conspicuous consumption, nuclear family, desire for highest possible income, eating meat and living off the top of the food chain.

Simplicity, communal living (with sharing of housing, furniture, appliances), greatly reduced consumption, delight in living with minimal income and possessions, vegetarianism.

Planning

Mostly by business firms to maximize their profit and economic growth.

Developed through democratically-controlled bodies and aimed at governing production by social and ecological criteria.

Capital

Maximum accumulation of capital through search for maximum profit. Maximize GNP and *quantity* of capital stock.

Capital investment rate set equal to depreciation rate. Production for social use rather than private profit. Minimize GNP and maximize *quality* of capital stock.

Resources

Used in wasteful way – use rate increasing exponentially. Planned obsolescence leads to very high resource consumption. Unnecessary duplication leads to wasted material, time and energy resources, e.g., having many private insurance

Drastic reduction in resource use per unit of industrial production. Products built for durability, repairability, recycling. Minimal "throughput." Goal of waste elimination, e.g., instead of several competing private drug companies making almost companies with enormous sales staff, rather than handling insurance through Social Security.

identical products with enormous advertising outlay, have a few regional drug companies making standardized drugs.

Pollution

Ecologically faulty technology (about ½ of post-World War II productive enterprise) pollutes air, water, soil. Introduces synthetics (chemical pesticides and fertilizers, synthetic fibers, plastics, detergents, etc.) which require high inputs of energy in their manufacture and which cannot be recycled by the earth's natural mechanisms.

Replace ecologically faulty technology with ecologically harmonious one. Essentially complete recycling of all reusable metal, glass and paper products. Synthetic products replaced by natural ones, wherever possible (e.g., using biological pest control). Essentially complete containment and reclamation of wastes from combustion, smelting and chemical operations. Make smokestacks rare.

Technology

Wastes resources, creates high pollution products & non-biodegradable synthetics. Geared to maximizing business profits. Focus on quantity.

Seeks processes that conserve materials and energy, are non-polluting, durable, labor-intensive, intermediate. Geared to social needs and ecological efficiency. Focus on quality.

Services

So minimal and haphazard that people feel no real security from them. People feel they must struggle to achieve their own economic security by accumulating possessions and money.

Provide floor of guaranteed minimum universal services (free health care, job re-training, etc.) to entire population. Give people assurance that de-development will not mean loss of economic security.

Advertising

Accounts for about $18 billion of GNP. Aimed at getting people to purchase more and more, be dissatisfied with what they now have.

Eliminate private advertising industry. Public research agencies test and rate products, distribute consumer information to the public.

Autos

Account for $80-90 billion of GNP, highways for $15 billion. One-fourth of economy now dependent on them and their infrastructure. One-fourth to one-third of city land area devoted to streets and parking lots. Very high resource users and pollution creators. (Energy outlay for cement and steel in roadways estimated at 3 to 4 times greater than that required for building a railway, and uses 4 times more land.)

Largely replaced by widespread mass transit system, bicycles, walking. Build no more roads. Any remaining autos powered by steam, wankel, or other non-polluting, low resource-using engine. Cars available through public car-rental facilities. City streets and parking lots torn up and planted with gardens, grass, trees, bike paths, walkways.

Military

Approaching $100 billion of GNP.

Replace with nonviolent civilian defense force.

Consumers

"Consumer goods and services" accounts for about $400 billion of GNP — much is baubles and luxuries like electric carving knives and hair spray.

Elimination of luxuries and non-essentials. Focus on provision of essentials of food, clothing, housing (in simple but adequate way) to whole population. Recycling clothing and furniture through large increase in second-hand shops.

Food and Agriculture

Agribusiness moving heavily into farming — family farms disappearing. Developers and speculators using farm land for industry, housing, commerce. Inorganic fertilizer and chemical pesticides polluting soil and water. 78% of grain harvest fed to livestock, wasting about 18 million tons of protein per year (which approaches the world's protein deficit). Government programs to reduce agricultural surpluses, even though half-billion of the world's people are chronically hungry.

End agribusiness and re-establish family farm. Rural new towns and other services (e.g., training programs in ecology, botany, entomology) to encourage "back to the farm" movement. Strict land use planning to prevent speculation; encourage farming, green belts, wilderness area preservation, protection of wetlands and estuaries. Greatly reduced use of inorganic fertilizers and chemical pesticides. Treated sewage and garbage transported to farms and used for fertilizer.

Grain harvest used to provide vegetarian diet. (Feed raised on 1 acre of land and converted into beef will meet 1 person's protein needs for 77 days; soy beans on same acre can meet one person's needs for 6.1 years.) Diversion of capital into food production to assure sufficient food for the world.

Energy

Exponential increase in use, reliance on uses which pollute. Turning to nuclear power plants, with their lethal radioactive wastes.

Great reduction in use. Reliance on energy sources which cause minimal or no pollution, e.g., solar power, wind power, etc.

Population

U.S. population growing slowly, but high per capita use of resources and pollution impact means that each additional American has a much more damaging effect on the ecosystem than each person born in poorer countries.

Reduce U.S. population by setting birth rate lower than death rate until optimum size (measured by ecological impact) is reached. Then stabilize at "no-growth" level. Encourage adoption. Free contraception, mass education on population issues.

Physical security: Meeting Basic Needs

The prospect of "de-development" heightens the insecurity that many Americans already feel. It seems to imply that everyone will have to cut back, and doesn't that mean becoming even more insecure, dropping back into the poverty out of which so many have struggled to rise? David Rockefeller may be able to cut his $200,000 salary and his $600,000 stock dividend income, but if I am a blue collar worker, struggling to pay off a mortgage, wondering where I will get the money to pay a big medical bill, and worried about layoffs at the plant, the words "de-development" and "simplification" may seem a real threat. If I am an auto worker, the need to replace cars with mass transit can only bring the fear of long-term unemployment.

Unlike many other countries, the United States has not provided its citizens with a publicly guaranteed floor of income and services below which no one can fall into destitution. There are Americans who are not even covered by programs and guarantees such as minimum wage legislation, pensions, and medical insurance. There is a pervasive fear of unemployment, due to the minimal provisions of workmen's compensation, the fact that 15% of the labor force is not even covered by it, and the spottiness and inadequacy of personpower re-training programs. Welfare and Social Security payments often fall below the poverty line. Health care is based on ability to pay and high medical bills can wipe out a family's savings in an instant. Millions of Americans have no health insurance, and those who do find that it does not cover many needed services. Costs of college education are skyrocketing. Almost no housing is being built for people of low or modest income.

Because of the paltriness of public income support and services, Americans know that they must strive to achieve their own economic security through accumulating possessions, money in the bank, insurance policies, etc. If they do not, the abyss of poverty yawns at their feet. There is no incentive to live simply, since moves in the direction of simplification seem to greatly increase the risk of falling into impoverishment.

Basic to our idea of a healthy economic system is that there must be communal or governmental programs which undergird every member of society. There must be a floor of income and services which are universally available to the whole population and which remove the fear of poverty. They must be provided either free or at a cost so low that everyone can afford them. They must be equally available to men and women and must be provided without any racial, religious, or ethnic discrimination.

A healthy society must be one in which children can grow up without fear of hunger, where women and men can live in dignity, and where the elderly can live out their final years without fear of destitution. Everyone should be assured of at least a minimum standard of living for their entire life. All should be protected against misfortunes so that they need not fall into economic misery through no fault of their own. There should be an "Economic Bill of Rights" legally guaranteeing to every citizen the basic needs of nutritious food, meaningful work, a decent minimum income, adequate housing, needed education, good quality health care, sufficient leisure, and a secure old age.

These assurances are vital in a healthy economic system, because such a system is one in which risks are shared, people in need are cared for, and poverty is eliminated. They are also crucial because they can help provide the base of economic security which will enable people to simplify their lifestyle without having to worry about impoverishment as a result. Meeting basic needs and de-development thus go hand in hand.

Entire books have been written on each of these needed services. Suffice it here to simply list a few of the crucial ones which must be provided to meet people's basic needs.

1. Guaranteed *work* for everyone who is able to work. (Much can be learned from other countries, e.g., the experience of the Swedish Royal Labor Market Board. This government agency's policy is to assure to any unemployed worker either local work, mobility to a new place of work, or re-training for a different type of work. The Board has broad powers to create public service jobs if none are available in the private sector. Workers who cannot find local work are paid to enable them to move to another part of the country where work is available. If a worker needs re-training, the Board offers a wide variety of opportunities, which includes free instruction, free teaching materials, free travel to the place where training is given, and tax-free funds to help support workers and their families while they are undergoing training. The knowledge that jobs or re-training for a new job are always available undergirds the worker's dignity and economic security.)

2.   A guaranteed basic minimum *income* for everyone who is unable to work. (This will probably best be provided through some form of negative income tax, under which people with an income below a certain minimum automatically receive payments back from the government to bring their income up to a decent standard of living.)

3.   Guaranteed *health care* based on medical need, regarded as a basic right and provided without regard to ability to pay. (Many countries already have such a program. The basic choice is between a full-coverage, government-operated medical insurance system, such as that of Canada or the Scandinavian countries, or a more completely socialized system, such as England, the USSR, Cuba and China.)

4.   Adequate *leisure* and the guarantee of at least a month's paid vacation for every working man and woman. (Sweden already has such legislation.)

5.   Freedom from the fear of old age through the guarantee of universal and adequate *social security,* with payments high enough so that the elderly can look forward to old age as a time of fulfillment and enjoyment. (In the Norwegian system, persons who have earned a low income during their lifetimes actually receive a higher social security benefit than they received in wages or salaries before retirement.)

6.   The guarantee of decent *housing* for every citizen and the opportunity to participate in decision-making through cooperative management.

7.   The guarantee of a good *education*, as far as individuals' abilities carry them.

8.   As soon as it is economically feasible, the institution of *free goods and services,* e.g., free public transportation, utilities, a healthy diet, prescription drugs. (Cuba is already experimenting with free milk, China with free work clothes, theater tickets, haircuts, medical services, etc.)

Social Ownership of Productive Capital

In our society, a relatively small number of private individuals own and control the nation's productive capital (e.g., factories, mines, income-producing land, etc.) and use this capital to produce goods which are sold for the profit of the owners. In earlier chapters, we have described the extremely harmful impact of this profit-motivated, privately owned system.

Our picture of a better economic system is one which no longer relies upon the private ownership of productive capital and its use for private enrichment. It is one in which all economic enterprises are coordinated by democratically-controlled planning, which relates production and distribution to human needs and which coordinates the de-development and simplification of the American economy.

Public Ownership and Democratic Control: This will require a large extension of public ownership into fields now dominated by private corporations. Such ownership need not take the form of bureaucratic administration from Washington, a la the former U.S. Post Office. Government corporations, such as the original TVA, can be set up under strict legislative control, yet with enough autonomy to be able to make decisions without undue red tape and to avoid the temptations of patronage.

All public utilities can be owned by municipalities, rather than by larger government units, and can be administered by boards made up of workers, consumers and local government appointees. Other enterprises can be owned and run by local communities in much the same way businesses are operated in the Israeli kibbutz. The present giant corporations should be broken up and geographically decentralized so that they will no longer function like autonomous nation-states, but will be brought under the control of workers and community people. Instead of a few people running a few giant enterprises, we see a great many people running a great many small enterprises. Large economic units will be needed only for very large tasks, such as national mass transit and heavy industry.

In a healthy society, neighborhood and community government will be revived and as much resources and power will be transferred to the local level as possible. This will provide the basis for local community ownership and control of many productive resources, and people will be engaged much more in face-to-face decision-making, rather than dealing with anonymous bureaucracies. Basic self-governing units will be community councils in neighborhoods and workers' councils in economic enterprises. Every institution can be self-managed by those who participate in it, e.g., a theatre might be managed by a council made up of representatives of actors, directors, writers, stage hands, etc.; a social agency by a council made up of social workers, administrators, and social welfare recipients. Every decision should be made by the smallest unit that can deal with it adequately. Decisions should be made at a higher level only if they can't be handled at the lower level. Neighborhoods would be federated into communities, communities into regions, regions into a cooperative commonwealth. Representative government would link each level together.

We have criticized our present economic system for making the worker powerless. How can economic democracy be made real in a system in which public ownership has been greatly extended?

One thing that jumps to people's minds when public ownership is mentioned is the economic system known as "state socialism," such as is found in the Soviet Union. This is *not* what we have in mind. Under state socialism, factories are viewed as owned, not by private individuals, but by the whole people collectively through the state. Enterprises are controlled closely by the centralized state economic plan and by state appointment of managers. All, or nearly all, of their earnings are paid directly into the state budget.

We understand the reasons for the development of this system in many parts of the world as a reaction against the built-in injustices of economies organized around private ownership and private profit. Public ownership can be an important step in the direction of economic democracy, but just as important is the workers' participation in day-to-day democracy through direct involvement in immediate work-place decisions. Soviet-type state socialism has sometimes meant that workers find themselves laboring under state-appointed managers who act in just as arbitrary a fashion as the old capitalist boss. "A change in the formal ownership of industry," wrote Seymour M. Lipset after his study of Western Canadian socialism, "does not end the basic social frustration of the industrial worker if he feels he is merely a puppet in a dictatorially controlled industry."[6]

The Yugoslav experience with "workers' councils" suggests to us that a system can be devised in which the basic ownership of industry resides in the people as a whole, but in which particular enterprises are managed by the workers who are involved in them on a day-to-day basis.[7] In Yugoslavian "self-management," all the workers of a particular enterprise vote directly by secret ballot to elect worker candidates to a two-year term on a Workers' Council, which is the supreme management body of the enterprise. This body in turn elects a Management Board, which, within the framework of Workers' Council policy and legislative enactments, determines all issues of policy. It hires and fires a managing director for the firm, decides what to produce and how, what wage levels to set, where to purchase raw materials and equipment, when and how to borrow money, how to reinvest earnings, etc. The Workers' Council also holds meetings of all the workers and organizes worker referenda on important matters, so that the entire work-force can make continual input on policy. Workers rotate on and off the Council so that, over a period of time, a large percentage of the employees of a firm have the experience of direct policy setting. Unions retain the right to organize and strike.[8]

Workers' self-management thus provides the *internal* controls of the enterprise; the lowest worker has a direct say about conditions of work and methods of production. *External* controls—to assure that the enterprise acts in the public as well as in the worker's interest—are also provided. Local government, for example, participates in the choice of the firm's manager and has a great deal to say about financing (e.g., through approval or disapproval of loans from the local bank). Prices cannot be raised without the approval of the local assembly, and the latter body can make recommendations to firms in its area and even dissolve ones that it feels are not meeting their business or social responsibilities. Other external controls are federal and regional laws, national and regional planning decisions, and such market mechanisms as the influence of customers, suppliers and competitors on costs and prices.

We do not suggest that the Yugoslav system is without problems or that it necessarily provides the perfect model of industrial democracy. However, it does suggest how workers themselves can manage their own enterprises and participate in vital economic decisions. Instead of being subordinate to absentee private owners or an inaccessible state, workers elect and control those at the top of their own firm, set their own policy to a large degree, and exercise control over decisions which immediately affect them. The Yugoslavs have created a system in which worker self-management is joined with community self-government to create a high degree of industrial democracy.

As the American people build a new economic system, we will want to draw on experience like that of Yugoslavia, and also look at worker participation schemes being developed in Europe, at the highly democratic self-management of industry in the Israeli kibbutz, at the participatory management of the Chinese revolutionary committees, and at the worker owned and controlled factories already existing in the U.S.A. (Olympia Veneer Company, in Olympia, Washington, for example, is one of 23 worker-owned plywood manufacturers in the Pacific Northwest.)

One other area which we believe would benefit from public ownership is land, where the speculative market is one of the most potent sources of injustice in the present economic system. All of the nation's natural resources and corporate and absentee-owned land should be brought under social ownership, with regional planning agencies giving general guidelines as to how land is to be developed, and local planning agencies having specific control over how local land is to be used. The millions of acres now held by big corporations should be redistributed in a new Homestead Act to individual farmers, farm coops, and land trusts. As in industry, any agricultural enterprises larger than a family farm should be worker-controlled or run as a cooperative. New rural towns should be developed, rural electrical cooperatives should be greatly extended, and every encouragement should be given to interested people to return to an ecologically sound form of agriculture.

Cooperative Ownership and Control: We are opposed to private ownership which takes the form of the large-scale, private, profit-making corporation, but we see an important role, in a better economic system, for a large sector of non-governmental ownership by cooperatives. Such ownership would not only provide an important counter-balance to the possible misuse of power by the state, but would also inject into economic life the significant humanistic values which cooperatives, at their best, have always sought to embody.

The very term "cooperative" symbolizes the mutual aid principle as it applies to economic life. Rather than being a business which seeks to make a profit for one group of people—from sales to other people—the co-op is owned and controlled by, and exists to serve the needs of, its customers. Co-ops are democratically controlled, one-person, one-vote, rather than through the power of individual aggregates of stock. They are non-profit and are created to serve specific needs of the people who take advantage of their services, returning any excess earnings to the very people whose purchases supplied the funds in the first place. By and large, they have been very consistent in meeting the needs of consumers, producing high quality products and services at a reasonable cost.

In a better economic system, practically all housing

could be constructed by housing co-ops and could be owned cooperatively, thus taking tenants out from under the thumb of the private, profit-motivated landlord. (About 25% of all new housing in Sweden is now produced by cooperatives.) Consumer co-op stores could take care of food retailing, relying on ties to co-op wholesalers and farm co-ops as sources of products. Farmers could extend their own co-ops in farm equipment, feed, seed, fertilizer, electricity, marketing, etc.

The American banking system should belong to the people—the people who save and who need loans—rather than to rich investors who collect high interest and use the people's money to create profit for themselves. All banking should be run on cooperative lines, similar to the 23,000 cooperative credit unions already existing in the U.S. The Federal Farm Credit system and the Canadian co-op banks—called "Caisses Populaires" in Quebec— show the feasibility of running banks along cooperative lines.

These are only some of the examples of the ways in which co-ops could play a vital role in a better economic system.

Individual and Small Group Ownership: Personal property, as distinct from productive capital, should be able to be owned by individuals. We see no harm in individuals, families and communes being able to build and own their own homes. Family farms seem to us to have been a positive influence in the American economic system, and we would hope to see more of them.

There may even be a role for a small private business sector in manufacturing, retailing, and other areas. Such a sector would be another counter-balance to the possible misuse of power by the state and would provide opportunities for innovation and craftship. Even though this sector might be inclined to carry forward the individualistic, competitive orientation of the earlier economic system, its size would be so small that it would have relatively little impact on the system as a whole. Also, since it would exist within a general economy of social and cooperative ownership, it would tend to adopt the more positive values of the larger society.

We see a need for this sector, not only because of the needed diversity and flexibility which its existence would lend to the total system, but also because we see no need to bring under public or cooperative ownership such people as the small farmer, the small book or magazine publisher, the craftsperson, or the small business entrepreneur. Also, we see an important role for private voluntary associations and organizations, which need a separate power base, shielded from the state, from which they can act to protect civil liberties, promote academic freedom, experiment with new lifestyles, engage in muck-raking, social criticism, and nonviolent social change, and provide services to areas where public agencies fear to tread.

In summary, therefore, we see three basic sectors in the better economic system: (1) a large sector of public ownership, but with the emphasis on decentralization, localism, and worker/community control; (2) a large sector of non-governmental, cooperative ownership; and (3) a small "private" sector.

Equity in Economic Life

Since concentrations of wealth lead to inordinate concentrations of power, a healthy economic system will strive for a high degree of equality of people's income and assets. The only differentials in income should be to reward those who engage in particularly boring, danger-ous, or demanding jobs.

A healthy economic system would eliminate in-comes based on exploitation of the labor of others (e.g., income from stocks, bonds, land rent, etc.), leaving only incomes from wages and salaries, rebates from coopera-tives, and social security transfer payments. It would design a system of taxation on income, gifts, assets and inheritance which would prevent wide and unjust dispari-ties between the wealth of various citizens.

Economic Planning

Essential to our idea of a better economic system is that the people as a whole, rather than profit-motivated corporations, should be able to decide how America's natural resources will be used to meet important goals.

In a preceding chapter, we have described how American "planning" today centers around achieving the narrow economic goals of privately-held corporations. Galbraith goes so far as to say that modern firms actually "replace the market with planning."[9] Much of public sector planning, rather than providing for public needs, is aimed at providing a reliable context in which the "mature" corporation can pursue its goals.[10] Economist William Loucks writes:

> Many private interests that are financially strong, astutely policied, skillfully managed, and sometimes in possession of effective kinds of political influence, do their own private economic planning for the achievement of their own private economic goals. Meanwhile, neither government regulation nor any other institutionalized authority or influence can assure that the aggregate of such private economic planning bears a consistent and reasonably close relationship to society's or the nation's economic needs.[11]

We see no magic in "planning" in and of itself. One of the most effective planning instruments in the U.S. is the Program Planning and Budgeting System developed by the Department of Defense. Planning can be a servant of anti-human ends as well as of human well-being.

Yet, if human values and a response to human needs are to characterize our society, there must be planning which guides the total economic system by conscious, intelligent and humane choice—a system which is popularly controlled and which serves human (rather than corporate) needs. Ecological soundness, zero growth, and provision for human needs cannot be achieved by an economy based on twelve million relatively independent business units, each seeking to grow and to maximize profits.

It is impossible to describe at this point the exact planning system which will best fit the needs of the future society. But perhaps the description—for illustration purposes only—of one possible planning system will make clear the kind of general approach to planning which we have in mind. The specifics will have to be filled in by Americans as they reshape American society along more human and ecologically sound lines.

Every human being does planning to one degree or another. We have individual goals that we want to attain and some sense of how we plan to act in order to achieve our goals. In a sound economic system, each work unit, each consumer entity, each neighborhood council will also have its plan, drawn up by its own participants, to achieve agreed-upon goals. Many aspects of these plans can be achieved locally, through the efforts of workers and local citizens and through the expenditure of tax money or earnings from enterprises.

But it is obvious that there is a need for linkages between all these plans so that there can be coordinated action toward the achievement of overall goals desired by all members of society. In order to maximize the fulfillment of human needs, to eliminate waste, and to achieve ecological harmony, an overall planning system is needed. It should be developed from the bottom and approved by the electorate. Each local unit would formulate its own ideas for a broad plan and submit these to the Community Council, which would work out differences and make them into a coherent whole. The Community Plan would then be re-submitted to the local level for approval, and then sent up to the regional level.

At the regional level, the Regional Planning Office would receive the various community plans and would work on a very general, simply-worded planning document for the total region. Two kinds of people would work on this Draft Regional Plan. One is the staff of the Regional Planning Office. These would be people who are trained in the more technical aspects of planning, but who spend part of each year travelling in their region, working in factories, farms, hospitals, neighborhoods, etc.

They would not be planning bureaucrats, isolated from the people, but individuals who are close to the concerns of the people and chosen for their work by workers' councils and community groups. Their personal goal is to understand the needs of their region as deeply as possible and to share any kind of work, no matter how menial, that will enhance their understanding of human and ecological needs.

The other kind of people working on the Regional Plan are workers and citizens who are elected by their co-workers and neighbors to serve on a Regional Planning Council. They are selected to represent the concerns of their work groups and communities, but also to help fit these local needs into the broader regional plan. The R.P.O. staff meets periodically with the R.P.C. and together they hammer out the Draft Regional Plan. The Draft Plan includes such matters as:

1. A statement of *economic and social goals for the region.* Economic goals might include such matters as economic and price stability, a more equal distribution of income among individuals, more rapid elimination of ecologically harmful products or processes, creating better mass transit. Social goals might include matters like improvement in medical care, setting up more day-care centers, etc.

2. A statement of *strategies to achieve regional goals.* This might include setting production goals for agriculture and industry, stipulating the investment level needed to achieve such output, determining how much income government will need to finance its programs and how this income can best be obtained—e.g., through taxes, bond sales, earnings of public enterprises, etc.—and suggesting legislation and a regional budget needed to implement the plan.

The Draft Plan is then sent back to the local level where it is discussed and where further suggestions are drawn up. These are then fed back to the Regional level, where the R.P.O. and R.P.C. work up the final Regional

Plan for presentation to the regional Government.[12] There the people's representatives have a final debate on the plan's provisions, make any final changes, and pass implementing legislation and funding.

We have not taken the planning system beyond the regional level because we believe that the de-development of the U.S. probably requires breaking up this enormous nation-state into several autonomous regions. It is clear, however, that the same planning system can be used for national, as well as regional, planning.

Also, we have not described plan formulation on the neighborhood or community level, but the same kind of back and forth of plan consideration, from local to a broader level, and then back again, applies to neighborhoods and communities also. In fact, the only planning that should be done at the regional level is around broad issues that cannot be handled through local planning.

Certainly more discussion of the specifics of a planning system needs to take place, but we believe that a planning system similar to the one here described—when combined with the other institutions of a sound economic system—could provide for real citizen participation in formulating and carrying out societal goals. Our resources could be mobilized, not to meet the profit-orientated goals of the large corporations and their wealthy owners, but to end hunger and poverty once and for all, to create a balance between the economy and ecological needs, to end exploitation of foreign countries, and to achieve the other goals which are worthy of a person-centered, democratic society.

[1] See Margaret Mead, *Cooperation and Competition Among Primitive Peoples* (N.Y.: McGraw-Hill, 1937).

[2] Victor Gollancz, *My Dear Timothy* (N.Y.: Simon & Shuster, 1953), p. 346-7; (reprinted by permission of Victor Gollancz: London)

[3] G. William Domhoff, "How to Commit Revolution in Corporate America" (speech re-printed in Jeremy Rifkin and John Rossen (eds.), *How to Commit Revolution American Style: Bicentennial Declaration* (N.Y.: Lyle Stuart, 1973)

[4] "China Visit Shows Change of 25 Years," *New York Times,* April 19, 1971, p. 10.

[5] Some of the books on de-development and ecological harmony are:

Dennis Pirages and Paul R. Ehrlich, *Ark II* (San Francisco: W.H. Freeman, 1974)

Ivan Illich, *Energy and Equity* (N.Y.: Harper and Row, 1974)

The Ecologist, *A Blueprint for Survival* (Middlesex: Penguin, 1972)

Herman E. Daly, *Toward a Steady-State Economy* (San Francisco: W.H. Freeman, 1973)

Barbara Ward and Rene Dubos, *Only One Earth: The Care and Maintenance of a Small Planet* (Middlesex: Penguin, 1972)

E.F. Schumacher, *Small is Beautiful: Economics as if People Mattered* (N.Y.: Harper & Row, 1973).

[6] Seymour M. Lipset, *Agrarian Socialism* (N.Y.: Doubleday, 1968), p. 285.

[7] "Yugoslavia is the only country in the world where a serious effort has been made to translate the old dream of industrial democracy into reality," says Robert A. Dahl, moderate political scientist from Yale University. "If Yugoslavia is less democratic than the United States in government of the state, it is more democratic in the government of the enterprise." Dahl, *After the Revolution?* (New Haven: Yale U. Press, 1970), p. 130.

[8] "Yugoslavia has developed an economy which is basically sound and has supplied a steadily rising standard of living for her population, against odds which initially must have appeared insuperable." William N. Loucks and William C. Whitney, *Comparative Economic Systems* (N.Y.: Harper, 1969), p. 312.

For further reading on Yugoslavia and workers' councils, see: Sidney Lens, "Yugoslavia's New Communism," *The Progressive,* (December, 1968); M. George Zaninovich, *The Development of Socialist Yugoslavia* (Baltimore: Johns Hopkins Press, 1968); Jiri Kolaja, *Workers' Councils: The Yugoslav Experience* (N.Y.: Praeger, 1966); Gerry Hunnius, G. David Garson, and John Case (eds.), *Workers' Control: A Reader on Labor and Social Change* (N.Y.: Vintage, 1973).

[9] John Kenneth Galbraith, *The New Industrial State* (N.Y.: Signet, 1968), chapter 3, "The Nature of Industrial Planning."

[10] Ibid., p. 315.

[11] William N. Loucks, *Comparative Economic Systems* (N.Y.: Harper, 1965), p. 723.

[12] It would also be just to consult with Third World nations and with other groups concerned with international economic development, since choices made in the American economy have so much to do with economics elsewhere in the world.

8

Contributing to
Global Health

Since our concern is with human life as such, we must think in terms of the growth and development of the whole human family, and not simply with a more human society in the United States alone. Our eventual goal is a world community in which problems are resolved nonviolently and in which there is an equitable distribution of wealth, power, resources and services. The same guarantees of personal and family security which we have insisted upon for us—such as a nutritional diet, adequate medical care, guaranteed minimum incomes, good education, decent housing—must be made available to every member of the human family. Economic institutions and planning organs which focus on meeting human needs rather than enhancing private profit must be spread world-wide. Political economies throughout the world must enable humans to live harmoniously with the environment. "Spaceship earth" as a whole must become a place where there are no longer tremendous gaps between rich and poor, in which individuals are enabled to participate in the decisions which affect them, and in which they can develop into full and loving persons.

Many thinkers are addressing themselves to the task of describing how a global society of the future might realize these goals. W. Warren Wagar's *Building the City of Man,*[1] for example, outlines a unitary republic of humankind in which the nation-state system is ended and people are joined in a democratic, socialist, liberal world civilization.

Our task at this point, however, is not to say how such a grandiose vision will be brought into actuality, but rather to describe the beneficial impact on world society of a radically changed U.S.A. Our assumption is that one of the major barriers to creating a decent world is the way U.S. society (and especially the U.S. economy) presently operates. (Much of what we say applies with varying force to other "over-developed," industrialized, high consumption countries besides the U.S.)

Let us imagine that the kinds of changes that we have outlined in the foregoing discussion of a sound U.S. economic system actually took place. What would be the impact of such changes on the world scene?

The most positive result would be the termination of the tremendously detrimental impact the present U.S. political economy has on the Third World. It is difficult for most Americans to accept the stark reality that their nation's normal relationships with the world's poor countries are overwhelmingly harmful to the masses of people there, as was shown in Chapter 5, "The Exported Plague." The United States can do nothing more important for these peoples than to stop draining their capital, depleting their natural resources, invading their territories, supporting their military forces, and dominating their governments and economies.

Here are some specific ways in which a socially-owned, democratically-planned U.S. system could reverse our presently harmful relationships with other nations:

1. *New Values:* American people, working through a wide variety of democratically-planned, cooperatively-orientated institutions, will be much more imbued with the values of mutual aid and cooperation. With a cooling of our passion to consume, we will be less likely to see other nations as having the resources we need to fuel an affluent lifestyle. With the lessening of dog-eat-dog, competitive, me-first values (which are a major source of violence and alienation), it will be easier for Americans to view other countries, not as enemies or competitors, but as co-travellers on the "spaceship earth," co-members of the human family. With a heightened ecological con-

sciousness, we will see the need for all people to work together to prevent the destruction of humanity through ecocide.

We recognize that the development of these values, and their application to world conditions, is neither easy nor inevitable. Historically, there has been a tendency for nations which have had their own revolution to go ahead and exploit other nations. Some "socialist-bloc" nations, for example, have engaged in practices similar to capitalist ones, e.g.: (a) importing primary products and raw materials from poorer nations and exporting only finished industrial goods to them; (b) cutting back on imports of products from Third World nations when their prices rise; (c) levying excise taxes on poorer countries' exports; (d) promoting foreign aid in the form of loans rather than grants; (e) putting political "strings" on foreign aid; (f) following practices which increase the indebtedness of poor countries.

Changes in U.S. economic institutions will make it easier to relate creatively to poorer lands, but the American political and educational system will also have to play a strong role, consciously developing in citizens a sense of world citizenship and global responsibility.

2. *De-development, Ecological Harmony and Simplicity:* An economy dominated by large, private, profit-orientated corporations cannot deal with the basic injustice of the U.S. using up such an inordinate portion of the world's annually consumed resources. Such corporations seek to grow and to become still more profitable, and they use mass advertising as a basic method of creating a high level of consumer demand for their ever-larger flow of products. This stance not only heightens the dichotomy between rich lands and poor; it also adds ever-increasing amounts of pollutants to air and water.

In a better economic system, the value stress will be on personal simplicity and on compassion for those who suffer from lack of life's necessities anywhere in the world. The planning system will coordinate the economy in such a way that we can achieve a "stationary state," at a much lower level of G.N.P. Perhaps this will involve a reverse flow of "aid" *from* poorer nations *to* the U.S.— experts in meditation from Buddhist cultures to help us explore "inner space," weavers from Guatemala to restore our weaving craft, Chinese acupuncture and sewage-recycling experts, Yugoslav self-management specialists, Japanese intensive agriculturalists, etc.

Socially-owned enterprises will produce products with maximum durability (rather than with planned obsolescence) so that they do not have to be constantly repaired and replaced. Enterprises will recycle everything recyclable and planning will provide for the replacement of ecologically-harmful technologies. There will be a shift toward vegetarian diets so that land now wastefully used for animal feed and livestock can be planted with grains and legumes that can be consumed directly by humans, giving them many times more protein for the same acreage.

All of this will drastically reduce the demand of the U.S. for world resources and will cut back on the ecologically-harmful effects of pollution. Not needing such an unjust share of world resources as the present economic system demands, these resources will be much more available to the nations where they now exist. We will not make covert or overt war on them to keep control of their wealth.

3. *The Impact of Planning:* The American economy will be a regionalized, planned economy which consciously and democratically chooses its goals. Planning in the U.S. can be tied directly to the development planning of other nations and to worldwide planning systems initiated by the U.N. or other international and transnational organizations. It can participate in the development, for example, of a World Ecological Planning Administration, which will work out a more just and ecologically-sound method of using non-renewable resources and reducing world-wide pollution. It can correlate with a World Security Service, which will assure to everyone adequate health care, basic minimum incomes, nutritious food, and other essentials to meet basic human needs. It can tie in with other global planning agencies in

such fields as population, climate, the oceans, etc. Once planning in the U.S. is lifted out of the context of the private corporation and put at the service of human need, it can not only develop a strategy for eliminating poverty in the U.S., but it can also spell out how the immense resources of U.S. farms and factories can contribute to the elimination of poverty throughout the world.

4. *The Impact of Social Ownership:* The present U.S. economic system hurts other nations through multi-national corporations, the military, and a foreign aid program which serves the needs of the private economy. This inevitably means exploiting world resources to provide a high standard of living for a minority of the world, while holding in check the social aspirations of the poor majority.

An economy owned and controlled by the people, through cooperative and other public enterprises, will have a very different effect on the life of other lands. The private, profit-making corporation will no longer exist, either in its national or multi-national form, and will not be available to penetrate other nations' economies. When the famed American know-how is made available to other lands, it will be to set up healthy enterprises which are owned and controlled by the workers and consumers of those lands, rather than by financiers in New York or Chicago.

5. *Eliminating the Military:* Under a better economy, there will be no need for a gigantic military to protect the interests of the corporations that operate overseas. There will still be difficult problems of international trade and equitable access of each country to world raw material reserves, but the economic motivation for stationing U.S. troops in countries all over the world will be removed. This will mean: (1) fewer resources being burned up in military production (e.g., the immense amounts of steel, aluminum, etc. now used for tanks, aircraft carriers, and planes); (2) cutting back on the pollution associated with big industrial military technology; (3) no U.S. military training programs to support

dictators and their armies and police; (4) no use of the U.S. military to hold back the social change efforts of Third World peoples.

Clearly, the vision of a non-militarized, de-developed, planned U.S.A. does not project a vision of a world in which everyone achieves material luxury or even what we now call affluence. It is a world in which members of the now-poor countries are enabled to meet their basic needs, but members of "over-developed" nations will have to give up the luxuries they have been conditioned into believing are necessary to the good life. The slogan of the latter will have to be Thoreau's: "People are rich in proportion to the number of things they can afford to leave alone."

Life will be simple and frugal, but all people will know a new richness. They will have the security of knowing that their needs will be met. They will live harmoniously with a beautiful environment. They will participate in the decisions which affect them. They will experience a deep sense of community. They can shift their focus to growth, not in material things, but in things like creative work, personal development, meaningful human relationships, deeper understanding of life's meaning, and contemplation of the depth of life from which the impetus for truth, beauty and goodness springs.

---

[1] W. Warren Wagar, *Building the City of Man* (N.Y.: Grossman, 1971)

9

A Sensitive Body Politic

Evolution has often been on the side of the sensitive. The enormous, armor-plated dinosaurs died out along with the saber-toothed tigers; their brute strength was no help to them when they failed to find an ecological niche which would support their life.

A theme of brute strength has run through male-dominated politics for a long time. We agree that politics is about power. But we return to our initial statement of values and ask, power for what? For us, the new society must be on the side of continued growth and development of the human potential. Sensitivity of political institutions will help that.

From mass politics to participation

Politics in America approximates a movie theater, in which many individuals react to the film but little to each other. The political parties seek to engineer support through images and slogans which usually avoid the basic issues. Candidates "sell themselves" to a market of consumers, rather than engage in genuine dialogue with a group of citizens.

It can hardly be anything else in "mass society", a large social order dominated by high mobility, mass communications, centralization, and swollen cities. The essence of participative democracy—discussion among peers of the great issues of the day—is eclipsed by one-way communication via the press and television. Mass society can only result in the politics of manipulation.

Our vision of the new society is, therefore, decentralist. We see major economic institutions, cities, and nations becoming decentralized.

An objection immediately arises: do we not need large aggregations of people to support great achievements in civilization? Would not decentralization simply put the cultural clock back and make us all rude provincials without the riches of modern life?

A glance at Iceland answers the objection. Iceland supports theater, music, opera, art, quality education, excellent health care for all, social security, a government with embassies around the world, and even an airline. Icelands' population? 200,000 people.

By that standard, it is hard to find a good reason for any city to be larger than 200,000. A monstrosity the size of New York City could be avoided through a socialist economy which was intent on decentralization and ecological soundness.

Even small cities can usefully be decentralized for some functions. Neighborhoods might provide the best unit for the operation of schools, welfare, peacekeeping, recycling. Even some economic enterprises could be owned and operated by the neighborhood organization.

This idea is not as far-fetched as it may seem. Senator Mark Hatfield proposed an idea in the direction in 1972:

> It is clear today that the great experiment of our cities is a failure. We must return to a scale of government which is comprehensible to our citizens. By developing neighborhood government—not by fiat but by an organic evolution from community organization—we can develop a sense of community through the state and a sense of individualism and neighborhood through the nation. To date, the centralization of government has destroyed community self-management and citizen participation. We must reverse this trend and develop our cities along the lines of neighborhood government and inter-neighborhood cooperation.

Once the question of scale is set right, other problems become much more soluble. Representative government can get a new lease on life when the representatives are close to the people. A way of ensuring that closeness is to do as in Yugoslavia: at regular intervals representatives must appear before meetings of the electorate. If by 2/3 majority the constituency agree on a piece of legislation they desire, the representative is legally required to introduce the bill in the legislature.

Face-to-face discussions are a strong antidote to massification. When peers together consider the issues, democracy becomes stronger. The Swedes have developed a system which encourages that process and at the same time develops a high degree of consensus on many decisions. In Sweden a new program or policy often starts with a small group of concerned people who gain attention for their idea through public debate and lobbying. When the idea has achieved some credibility a governmental commission is set up to investigate it. The commission holds hearings and stimulates research on the subject. (At any one time there are hundreds of these commissions operating in Sweden.) Out of this investigation comes a report which is circulated to all the individuals and groups in Sweden known to be interested in this subject. They have a period of time to discuss the report and give feedback. Then the commission goes back to work, sifting the feedback, starting new research if necessary, trying to find answers to the unresolved questions. When its next report comes out, another round of discussions and feedback may occur. Finally the piece of legislation is ready for the parliament. Usually there is a very high parliamentary vote for it, because it has already been discussed so widely among Swedes with that concern.

A number of the specific abuses of democracy which we are now used to in the U.S. will be eliminated because of the change in the economic system. Aspirants for public office will not be able to turn to the rich for campaign financing, because there will be no rich people. Today, super-rich create foundations and special organizations (e.g., Council on Foreign Relations, Ford Foundation) which exercise inordinate influence on government policymaking. Equitable distribution of income will also eliminate this practice. High-priced lobbies maintained by the corporations will dissolve along with the corporations.

In short, the Watergate, ITT, and Soviet wheat deal scandals of the Nixon Administration could not happen in the sort of society we envision.

Over time the individualistic, me-first, profit-orientated values of today's business world will lose some of their power. That will in turn help politics develop a service ethic. The social values of cooperation, community well-being, mutual aid, and simplicity will have a chance to dominate political life.

Further checks and balances can be instituted to insure democratic participation. Referenda can be used for really major issues. Compulsory rotation in roles of authority can occur. (The Yugoslav system of rotation under self-management has meant that, over the past 20 years, 75% of the workers have been elected to the workers' councils or other decision-making elective bodies in factories. Why not the same in political life?) Many more posts could be open to public elections rather than subject to appointment. The system could allow for the fall of governments, as in parliamentary democracies, rather than the present near-impossibility of Presidential impeachment.

In this situation the freedom of individuals to participate in the decisions which affect their lives would be enormously greater than today. Of course the guarantees of the Bill of Rights would be there, but the social emphasis would be not so much on freedom from government interference as on freedom for political participation. In this way the body politic will be most sensitive to the new insights of the citizens themselves.

Conflict in the new society

Conflict will be much less rampant in the new

society than in the present one, we believe. Economic change which meets basic needs and promotes equality removes the foundation of class conflict and will at the same time drastically reduce most kinds of crime. (A comparison of crime rates in Sweden and the U.S. is revealing on this score, even though Sweden has not yet reached full equality.) Cultural change for equality reduces the basis for the attacks on individual dignity made by sexism, racism, and other forms of elitism. Political change toward equality and participation means ending the frustration of going unheard.

We disagree, however, with those on the Old Left who have imagined that "come the revolution" conflict will disappear in the harmony of a classless society. We expect that this heterogeneous world will be a seedbed of conflicts forever. We do not envision a static society in which people no longer care enough for their perceptions to struggle for them. As many a commune has discovered, even in a relatively homogeneous group conflict can arise which leads to splits for lack of means of resolving differences.

How, then, shall we wage our conflicts? Clearly there is a contradiction between our values and the use of violence, but is there an alternative means of open struggle?

In the past century or so, workers, students, colonized peoples, and others have increasingly tried a social invention for waging conflict which does not depend for its effect on destruction and death. This invention has overthrown dictators, stopped occupying armies from breaking the popular will, and gained national liberation from empires. In the form of the industrial strike it has changed the condition of millions of people, so that unionized workers today can scarcely imagine the wretchedness of factory labor in the 19th century. Like some other inventions, this one has failed to realize fully the hopes of many of its users; it is still in an early stage of development.

When the automobile was introduced it was called a horseless carriage. An innovation, it was defined by what it was not, as well as by what it was. So, too, with this innovation in social struggle called nonviolent direct action. It is a conveyance but it manages without the horse. It gets people places by another source of power. It is action, but it is not violent (although governments often feel so threatened by it that they respond with violence).

A wide variety of tactics are a part of this invention: boycotts, civil disobedience, strikes, sit-downs, marches, picketing, occupations, counter-institutions, haunting, street-speaking, reverse strikes, and so on. The invention itself has been given many names: civil resistance, positive action, satyagraha, civilian insurrection and pacific militancy, are a few.

The invention is generally used when conventional, institutional means for change fail. People get tired of writing letters or making polite requests, or find that the law courts are not just, or that the election process is unresponsive. *In*direct action having failed, people try direct action.

Violent forms of direct action have been popular, but they, too, frequently fail. In El Salvador in 1944 an unsuccessful violent revolt against dictator Hernandez Martinez preceded a successful nonviolent insurrection. Bernardine Dohrn announced in 1970 the decision of the Weather-people to move into unarmed struggle; after experimentation with terrorism they decided, "the town-house [explosion] forever destroyed our belief that armed struggle is the only real revolutionary struggle."

Sometimes people use nonviolent action because it seems so consistent with the highest insights of religions and moral teachers through the ages. Whatever their reasons—frustration with conventional means, impracticality of violent direct action, ethical or pragmatic preference for nonviolent action—people using this invention put their bodies on the line and create a sometimes dramatic confrontation which forces the real issues into the open.

Conflict in three dimensions

Nonviolent direct action can be viewed in three dimensions: political, economic, and psychological. Political conflict frequently spills over into direct action, ranging from anti-war civil disobedience to parents blocking traffic at street corners where stoplights are needed. Economic direct action is common in the form of strikes and boycotts. But there is also a psychological aspect which develops particularly in protracted struggles. This psychological dimension is extremely important for our vision of the new society, since it encourages the growth of community through conflict.

People using nonviolent direct action are usually vulnerable to retaliation; they underline the humanity of their demands by the live humanity of their own presence, in contrast to the saboteur who wrecks and runs away. By their very vulnerability they put pressure on the opposition to make a decent response, as in the Mississippi civil rights struggle of 1963-64 when black freedom workers found the best defense against white terrorism was to keep no weapons. As Robert Moses, head of the Mississippi Summer Project, put it, "One reason we've survived is that we haven't had guns and everyone knew it."

The strategy worked, and the bombings diminished and the Ku Klux Klan declined.

Another reason for the community-building nature of this invention is that it leaves room for the creative response. During the 1931 national Salt Satyagraha campaign of civil disobedience in India, the police wearied of beatings and arrests of mass marches and decided on one occasion to try a drastically different tack. The police sat across the middle of the street, blocking the way of the marchers. The nationalists also sat down. A stalemate developed, and as the hours wore on supporters went to get blankets and food for the marchers. When the marchers got the food they passed it on to the police. That was too much for the police, who retired from the scene leaving the march to continue to a triumphal midnight rally.

In the face of a nonviolent tactic of opposition, the Indians escalated their nonviolence! It is hard to find a better model than this for a truly human way in which to wage conflict. This incident has hardly become a habit for Indians or any other people, but occuring as it did in the midst of a heated conflict in which Indians had already been killed, it gives us a glimpse of what may one day become a pattern.

Increasing sensitivity

Four factors seem to us to make possible a more sensitive political system: equality, decentralization, participation, and nonviolent conflict. Precisely because it is more sensitive, it will be more demanding of individuals. One of the very few "advantages" of being oppressed, after all, is irresponsibility. One can passively watch the machinations around one knowing that intervention from oneself is not expected (indeed, might be suppressed). Self-management, on the other hand, means taking responsibility, refusing the cop-outs and distractions, becoming an aware and cooperative individual.

Just because that sort of political system expects that sort of citizen, it is a force for human growth.

The new society may develop more sensitivity by going beyond the head-counting approach of one-person/one-vote. Certainly representative democracy based on equal vote is an enormous advance on differing amounts of power depending on differing wealth or ancestry. The new society will, we expect, need to depend on the one-person/one-vote principle for large-scale decision making. But we cannot be satisfied with that process because it gives equal weight to the view of a person who has not thought about the issue and cares little about it and the view of a person who has thought deeply and cares passionately. Reducing persons to numbers is bound to leave us looking for something better.

Consensus decision-making provides a partial answer. In the consensus style, creativity and conviction count for more than numbers, since the goal is not simply a decision, but instead a decision which is accepted by all the group's members. Rather than rush to a vote, a group seeking consensus seeks new, creative ways to move ahead. That may involve a compromise, but it may also be a new solution that no one had considered prior to the encounter.

The consensus style is only partly satisfactory, however, because there are too many conflicts which cannot be fully resolved. They can only be settled. The settlement finally relates to the depth of conviction of those who are struggling. Fortunately nonviolent action provides some possibility here.

Conflict will continue around issues which matter deeply. A revolutionist who works for a new society needs to propose new ways of waging these conflicts. The only means we know which can express full determination and conviction, and still be essentially affirmative of community, is the way of nonviolent action. Education in that set of skills and attitudes will make possible a more sensitive body politic.

Happily, this is an area where we can put into practice right now the patterns of the new society. There is no need to wait until after the revolution to practice decentralization, participation, equality, and nonviolent action. The campaigns we develop now, the organizations we build now, the style we adopt in relating to each other can give a taste of what it would be like to live in a nonviolent social order.

10

Global Conflict
and the New Society

The new world order will not be very orderly. True, many of the present causes of violence will be on their way to resolution: the economies of most societies will be socialist, redistribution of wealth between societies will be occurring because of the elimination of the giant corporations and their profiteering, equality of consumption will be more often the pattern, ecological principles will be pervasive. Before the second American revolution takes place, many of the countries now dominated by capitalist and bureaucratic elites will probably have moved considerably toward liberation.

But even assuming sweeping changes toward equality, we accept the likelihood that major conflicts will continue.

One reason is the immense variety of cultures. Pick any issue—equality of the sexes, use of technology, religious and ideological freedom—and you see differences which will not likely be resolved in the immediate revolutionary struggles ahead.

A second reason is the variety of institutions which will develop in the different new societies. New institutions are powerfully shaped by history, and the histories of different societies are unique. Clashes between these unique societies can be expected.

A third reason is conflicts of interest over the distribution of wealth and over environmental impact of production. How much of the wealth of the industrialized nations which was expropriated from the Third World should be returned? Should an industry producing needed goods in one place be allowed to discharge waste which affects life in another? Should a region lucky to have abundant geothermal energy object to the use of nuclear reactors in another region?

So, even if we assume that capitalism and bureaucratic centralism will have lost most of their power, conflicts will flourish. In one sense, we would not want it otherwise. A world without conflicts, a world of bland homogeneity, would curb the growth of the human potential. Life implies struggle; goodness implies the clashes of individual and group exploration.

However, the use of violence for waging conflicts cannot go on; as we have argued before, ethical values when combined with the enormous ecological and human destructiveness of war rule it out as a means of struggle. How can this dilemma be resolved?

Usual proposals are inadequate

A number of proposals which are commonly made are inadequate in fundamental ways: world-wide socialism, increased understanding, compromise, negotiation and arbitration, world government, and avoidance of provocation.[1]

People used to dream that *world-wide socialism* would provide the solution to the problem of international conflict. Since war sprang from the private ownership of the means of production and distribution, since it was exacerbated by the capitalist armaments manufacturers, since it fed on rivalries between capitalist nations—eliminating capitalism would also eliminate war. And it was no small corroboration that Russia only got out of World War I when the Bolshevik Party took control of the state under the impetus of that great slogan: "Peace, land, bread."

Unfortunately, war seems to have a more basic hold on humankind than that. The armies massed on the Sino-Soviet border are not there because of the lust for profits of Russian or Chinese capitalists. The Soviet Union does not rank second in the world in arms sales (close behind the U.S.) because its weapons industries are privately owned. [2]

People often assume that *increased understanding* brings peace. The cultural integration suggested by Marshall McLuhan's "global village" will, it is believed, make the difference. Exchanges of people, increased travel, increasingly shared life styles brought about by industrialization will bring a warless world.

Ali Mazrui points out the fallacy here. [3] Large-scale violence has frequently occurred among people who are culturally integrated. Just as racial violence tends to happen most often in U.S. cities where races live side by side, so violence on a larger level is likely where ethnic groups, tribes, or races live side by side. Mazrui cites the large-scale violence in Rwanda and Zanzibar as places where increased communication and sharing brought more conflict. The opponents in Rwanda and Zanzibar shared language, sacred objects, and life style—but they failed to agree which group should rank higher than the other. Increasing closeness on other matters made their disagreement on the distribution of status and power appear all the greater.

Here, then, is the enormous weakness of Esperanto (the proposed world language), electronic media, and other tools for cultural integration taken by themselves.

Compromise is a frequent part of social and political life. Clearly, all the goals of everyone cannot be realized, and trade-offs are made which (in theory) balance the conflicting demands and bring a rough kind of harmony to the system.

While compromise should play a role in conflict resolution, it is dangerous when applied to issues across the board. When fundamental issues are at stake, to compromise is to yield integrity (for the group) and hurt the potential for truth (for the system as a whole).

One of the problems for any group struggling for its just claims is to deal with its own heritage of compromise on fundamental questions. A mystique of compromise so permeates liberal democratic societies that "politics" itself becomes synonymous with "sell-out." Parties and pressure groups choose their leaders partly with reference to whether or not they are skilled in compromise. Harold Wilson, Hubert Humphrey, and Richard Nixon are examples of this practice.

The problem is even clearer on a global level, because cultures vary a great deal in their definition of social justice. Some societies accept extreme degradation of women; slavery is still accepted in some places; some societies consider it just to hold people hostage to force certain actions from their governments. (In the U.S., for example, there are professors of ethics who argue that it is quite permissible for large populations to be held with a nuclear gun against their heads in order to ensure desired behavior from their governments. The theory is called deterrence. If the government misbehaves seriously enough, the gun is to go off.) [4]

On fundamental issues like slavery or being held hostage for nuclear power games, compromise is clearly inappropriate. Better ways must be found.

Negotiation, conciliation, and arbitration are common means of conflict resolution. Frequently they are used along with a test of strength of some kind. They usually result in compromise.

These mechanisms are subject to the same limitations as compromise. In addition, their relation to other levels of conflict pose problems. While negotiations are going on, lurking in the background are the sanctions which each party will impose if the negotiations fail; each party's knowledge of the power available to the other is a strong force on the outcome of the negotiations. Conciliation is more likely to work when the opponents are approximately of equal strength or at least are roughly equal in their ability to disrupt the other's plans. If one party is very much dominant, conciliation is not likely to be helpful except as a face-saving way of giving in for the relatively less powerful. The usefulness of arbitration is also dependent on the relative power of the opponents; if the solution of the arbitrator is unacceptable to the strong party, the conflict can be resumed.

The limitations of negotiation, conciliation, and arbitration seem to us all the greater on the global level. Resuming violent conflict on the global level has worse consequences than one can accept. We must look further for a solution to the problem of how to make a world without war.

The advocates of *world government* argue that the alternative of "resuming the conflict" simply cannot be allowed. To prevent that from happening, the solution should be backed up by the force of law. Law, the argument runs, must be executed by an agency which has a monopoly on the legitimate use of violence, i.e., government. Further, many conflicts could never get to the point of large-scale violence if there were an agency which had as its purpose keeping the peace by heading off and arresting those who would disrupt it.

Without doubt government today plays a very strong role in conflict resolution. The ability to settle disputes with courts instead of guns is a major step forward from the viewpoint of the citizen whose primary concern is with the other citizen or business or agency which is giving him or her trouble.

The behavior of liberal democratic states, however, suggests some complications. The conflict resolution machinery hums along with little difficulty as long as the disagreements are within the cultural consensus. But when they are not, repression is the recourse, sometimes with the troops. The state picks sides in the disagreement (usually the side of the rich even when that is not the opinion of the majority) and tries to enforce that side.

It may not succeed in quickly imposing its own view of the matter and the struggle becomes civil war. Far from keeping the peace, then, the government is killing people in the name of its point of view and of its own authority.

These are problems enough on the smaller scale of the present national states. They will be much larger on a global level. One does not get rid of war by putting a legal framework around it and calling it a civil insurrection!

There is the further difficulty of how democratic control can be kept over a government of such enormous size and jurisdiction. The Swedish government is highly democratic, although important problems remain. The large liberal states such as Britain and the U.S. are nowhere near as democratic. How can the people stay in control of a state apparatus so vast, so distant, and so forceful?

Noting that international conflicts often have a cycle of provocation, each side arming itself more greatly with a threatening effect on the other, some people have called for unilateral disarmament as a solution. *Avoidance of provocation* will, they hope, break the dynamic of threat and counter-threat.

Raoul Naroll did a historical study which found "peace-loving nations are no less likely to be involved in war than warlike nations."[5] Certainly the example of Norway is no comfort: it had a minuscule army and every intention of remaining neutral as the signs of European war increased in the 1930's. Norway was invaded by Nazi Germany, for strategic and probably economic reasons having little to do with Norway's own behavior.

Apparently it is not enough to end imperialism and participation in the arms race, to eliminate the military-industrial complex, and to become decent. Violence needs a functional substitute, a means of direct action which can be used when institutional arrangements fail and fundamental issues are at stake.[6] We need a means of open struggle, we need sanctions which are inherently available (and therefore democratic) to people who deeply disagree.

Pacific militancy

The social invention called by many names—pacific militancy, civilian resistance, positive action, satyagraha —provides that nonviolent means of direct action by which a new world order can be made safe for conflict.

In fact, the proposals reviewed earlier have a new and more viable substance when combined with civilian

resistance. World institutions, compromise, the growth of
a common culture, and disarmament (together of course
with humanist socialism) hold the promise of a global
peace system when transmuted with nonviolent action.

Transarming to civilian defense

People can safely give up the arms race by shifting
their reliance for struggle—if it comes to that—to nonviolent action. There are historical cases of rough, primitive attempts to defend society by non-military means
from which we can learn in designing a defense system
for the new society. In 1923, for example, French and
Belgian troops invaded the German Ruhr in order to
hasten reparations and, ultimately, to annex the area to
France. Military resistance by Germany was out of the
question, so the government resorted to noncooperation.

Without planning or preparation millions of Germans
nonviolently resisted the occupation. The French were
left to try to pick coal with their bayonets. The occupiers
arrested widely and brutally, deported 150,000 people,
and shot into demonstrations with fatal results. Nevertheless, the French were unable to achieve either their
political or their economic objectives. They finally ended
the occupation and agreed to a reparations schedule more
favorable to the Germans. [7]

The Germans paid a high price for their resistance
and the campaign was much less effective than it could
have been had there been advance preparation and higher
consciousness about the means of struggle. The leverage
of noncooperation was shown in action, however; military occupation failed to achieve its goals when confronted with stubborn nonviolent resistance.

How could this be? Machiavelli pointed out long ago
that the regime or would-be government simply cannot
rule against the determined refusal of the population to
obey. Terror does not do the work of the society, does
not turn the lathes in the factory. Repression can succeed
only if it persuades the people to resume their cooperation; if they hold out, the rulers cannot rule.

In military defense enormous sums are spent on research and planning. Armies spend more time training than they do fighting. Civilian defense also requires research and training—nonviolent struggle is not so much easier than military struggle that preparation can be disregarded!

One of the most ambitious efforts to build a civilian resistance strategy for American society is in the book *In Place of War*.[8] Despite the fact that the authors assume the continuation of the unit of the American nation as a whole, we feel that the thrust of the book provides a convincing alternative to the institution of war as a means of defending a community of people no matter what its size.

The writers of *In Place of War* argue that the most effective defense would not be territorial, but social. That is, very little attention would be paid to borders; the "sacred soil of the motherland" is considered mere rhetoric. Instead, the people would defend their institutions at the points where exploitation and domination are actually felt. Workers would defend the integrity of their factories and students their universities. Labor which is demanded by the occupying authorities would be withheld; non-cooperation would be the theme of the resistance as a whole.

The non-cooperation would not, however, be all-out. To respond to invasion by total noncooperation would probably hurt the civilians more than it would the invaders. Noncooperation would be selective, might be guerrilla in style: a transport shut-down in New York, then a steel strike in Gary, then mass civil disobedience in San Francisco. The duration of a particular action would be less important than its unpredictability. Only as a final push to force the invaders out might a general strike and all-out nonviolent insurrection be indicated.

A range of tactics provides means of resistance for all kinds of people, regardless of age or position in the economy. Political sociologist Gene Sharp has uncovered 198 methods of nonviolent action which have been used so far in history.[9] More tactics would probably be invented in the heat of struggle. The point is to make the country ungovernable, which a sizable minority of citizens can do given creativity and determination.

Tactical flexibility is important as well. Suppose that the invader (or the would-be dictator who has staged a coup d'etat) imposed a loyalty oath to be taken by the people. The first response would be to refuse to take the oath. But if the pressure mounted to the point where it seemed unwise to continue noncooperation, the people could reverse gears and take the loyalty oath on all possible occasions. People could take the oath while shopping, or while applying for a driver's license; they could flood the administrative machinery of the occupation with letters enclosing signed oaths, grinding the apparatus to a halt and making a mockery of the oath.

Sabotage seems, on balance, to be counterproductive. Where it was used in European World War II resistance movements it often provided the pretext for substantial repression of the nonviolent activity which was going on. It also involves large amounts of secrecy which should be kept at a minimum if the nonviolent style of resistance is to work most effectively.[10]

These are only a few of the strategic issues. A blueprint for civilian defense still lies in the future, but the increasing amount of research devoted to the problem gives us confidence that, before the revolution occurs, the movement will have a credible alternative to the military solutions of the present.

Compromise and conciliation, plus civilian resistance

Conciliation, arbitration, and negotiation will in our view be important mechanisms of conflict resolution in the new global society, but will be more likely to result in justice than now, if used in conjunction with nonviolent action. Why?

The force of numbers and technological superiority count for less when opponents use civilian resistance than when using violence, so the effect is to make them

more equal in their struggle. Minorities as well as majorities can express themselves powerfully through noncooperation and other nonviolent means.

Armed struggle stimulates bitterness, of course. The
heritage of bitterness brings a negative, irrational force to
the conference table, which may make the compromise
solution quite different from one which would be gained
in a more positive atmosphere.

The destructiveness of violent conflict brings its own
limits to the process of seeking social justice. When
negotiations are backed by the implied threat to return to
the battlefield, it seems irresponsible (to society at large)
stubbornly to reject a compromise. With nonviolent
means, we can more safely return to the struggle, pursuing in open conflict the perceptions of truth to which
one is committed. Later negotiation may proceed with
more respect for the truth as each opponent sees it, and
new understandings of alternatives.[11]

Transnational institutions, peacekeeping, and people's enforcement

Despite the strong criticism of world government,
we admit the importance of means by which the growing
community of interest on a global level can express itself.
There are human issues which cannot reduce to the local
or even continental level: pollution, redistribution of
resources, large-scale violence, use of the seabeds, currency, communication, and more. These irreducible
issues, and the conflicts which accompany them, need a
global arena for decision—but without the most negative
aspects of a world government.

The problem of governmental order is so knotty
because of the confusion of functions which government
assumes.[12] Police are expected to take *both* the role of
peacekeeping *and* the role of enforcer of political decisions. These two roles, however, are often contradictory.
When police enforce a new law against the will of a
minority (or even in some places a majority), they
undermine their credibility as impartial maintainers of

the public peace. On the other hand, when they quell a violent campaign in the name of peacekeeping, the result is often the freezing of the status quo. The latter is illustrated on the global level by the UN peacekeeping force on Cyprus prior to 1973.

These two functions—peacekeeping and enforcing— can be separated. In our conception of a new global society, the job of peacekeepers will be simply that: to channel conflict which has become violent back into nonviolent forms. A particular nonviolent conflict will not be discouraged by the peacekeepers (although it may be discouraged by interested fourth parties or by public opinion). Confident that nonviolent conflict is fundamentally different in its consequences from violent conflict, the peacekeepers will rest when violence has been stopped.

The basis of violent power is destruction. The basis of nonviolent power is noncooperation. While other factors also can play a part in nonviolent struggle, especially the attitude of goodwill campaigners can show toward opponents, the refusal to cooperate is a force which can reduce even tyrants to impotence.[13]

The art of global peacekeeping is still in its infancy. Michael Harbottle, who commanded the United Nations peacekeeping force in Cyprus 1966-68, has outlined some of the experience so far in *The Blue Berets*.[14] His conclusions point away from a professional, military conception of containing violence toward a force of volunteers who come from many walks of life and so have common bonds with those of the community they come to serve. He sees those volunteers, trained and then seasoned with experience in occasional peacekeeping service, able to establish credibility in the area of strife and to blend diplomatic and direct action skills with skills of reconstruction.

Harbottle himself, a career military officer, is increasingly questioning whether armed force is needed in global peacekeeping. We believe it is time to do bold experimentation with nonviolent peacekeeping, under the auspices of the United Nations and/or with other sources of legitimacy. Such experimentation would probably lead to successful unarmed peacekeeping in the new global society of the future, in which an armed policeman or policewoman would be as incongruous as it now is in England.

Our emphasis on maximum possible decentralization means that most peacekeeping should happen on the local level, of course. Regional or global peacekeeping should happen only when local people cannot cope.

There still remains the problem of making and enforcing decisions on the world level. Various proposals have been made for transnational agencies of decision. In our view a solid basis for democracy can be built into such proposals by the concept of *people's enforcement*.[15]

After sifting evidence and clarifying alternatives, the world agency tests the options by public opinion. Finally a decision is reached. While the plan is being put into motion, resistance develops. If negotiations fail to resolve the conflict, the agency publicizes the situation and calls on voluntary associations concerned about the issue to act.

For example, suppose a polluting enterprise refuses to shift to another, more expensive production method and, because of its role in the regional economy, has backing in its area. The pollution is affecting health outside the region. The agency which ordered a change-over calls for the people to enforce its order. Conservation groups inside and outside the region respond by a direct action campaign. The conflict mounts, but whenever it spills over into violence, global peacekeepers intervene to channel it back into nonviolent forms. Finally a resolution of some kind is achieved.

In such a global order as this there would be times when a transnational agency would call for action and get no response; it would, in other words, fail to make a convincing case to the people who might enforce it. At other times an agency might prevail only to be proved unwise later; there is no guarantee that the "right" solution will always or even usually be discovered in the short run. What is "right" in a situation of cultural pluralism? Such a system as this, in contrast to systems which are authoritarian, can afford clashes and mistakes and uneasy gropings precisely because it does not put many eggs in one basket. The energy which otherwise would be spent in repressing conflicts can be put into channeling and resolving them. The widespread use of nonviolent techniques, taught as part of basic education, would make people's enforcement feasible.

Culture conflict and growth in the new world

Although we affirm the value (as well as the inevitability) of cultural pluralism, growth of a common culture is also important. General acceptance of the legitimacy of peacekeeping forces, of transnational agencies, and of techniques of pacific militancy is necessary, at a minimum.

On one level, of course, there is already agreement: a number of religions and philosophical systems include the Golden Rule and the desirability of compassion, honesty, fairness, simplicity.[16] Until the values are expressed institutionally, however, they have little effect on the growth of world community.

The availability of nonviolent action as a means of struggle may, paradoxically, work to encourage cultural commonality and diversity at the same time. Because nonviolent action does not rely on destruction for its leverage, people can more safely challenge each others' hoary myths and sacred symbols. No longer fearing religious or ideological wars, people can with less inhibition attack each others' assumptions and idolatries. In such a dynamic situation the new humanist world culture might arise more quickly. (A common circumstance for the rise of powerful new systems of consciousness is the flux and controversy of two cultures meeting.)

Being freed of the fear of bloodshed will, we suspect, do more than encourage the clashes out of which a common core of values may arise. It should also encourage diversity around non-core issues, because diversity will not depend on military strength for its defense. Martin Luther might not have survived without the protection of the weaponry of German princes. In the new society of our vision, the Luthers who revolt against aspects of the prevailing worldview will not need military protection against violent attack.

A dynamic global society

In summary, our vision of a global new society is the opposite of the static blueprints often associated with utopias. While lethal conflict must be minimized, our peace system retains plenty of conflict. In fact, making violence unlikely may make conflict more frequent even than now.

The usual proposals for minimizing violence (world government, increased understanding and the like) are inadequate because they do not provide a substitute for an essential function of violence—a coercive sanction of last resort. There are times when there seems no alternative to direct action. At such times, nonviolent forms of direct action are needed.

When pacific militancy is further developed and accepted as a basic skill for individuals and groups, transnational institutions, disarmament, cultural integration, negotiation, and compromise all become viable instruments of a peaceful world order.

[1] Much of this list is suggested by Gene Sharp in his essay "The Need of a Functional Substitute for War", reprinted from *International Relations,* April, 1967, by the Center for International Affairs at Harvard University, p. 7-10.

[2] Stockholm International Peace Research Institute, *The Arms Trade with the Third World,* 1972, as summarized in *The Futurist,* Vol. VI, No. 2 (April 1972) p. 48.

[3] Ali A. Mazrui, "World Culture and the Problem of Consensus in Human Affairs", unpublished paper, no date. (Makerere University, Kampala, Uganda).

[4] The comparison to guerrilla movements holding civilians hostage was made by Robin Clarke in *The Science of War and Peace* (New York: McGraw-Hill, 1972), p. 260.

[5] The study was summarized in Robin Clarke, *op. cit., p. 278.*

[6] Gene Sharp, in summarizing the weakness of alternatives to violence which do not include means of waging overt conflict, put the matter clearly: "Whereas violent conflict itself has been used as a means of struggle or ultimate sanction for dealing with the violence of other groups whose principles or objectives were unacceptable, none of these 'answers' serves a similar role." *op. cit.,* p. 10.

[7] For a study of the *Ruhrkampf,* see Wolfgang Sternstein's contribution to *Civilian Resistance as a National Defense,* edited by Adam Roberts, (Baltimore, Md.: Penguin Books, 1969).

[8] James Bristol et al, (in a working party, American Friends Service Committee), *In Place of War,* (New York: Grossman, 1967).

[9] Gene Sharp, *The Politics of Nonviolent Action* (Boston: Porter Sargent, 1973), p. 117-434.

[10] See B.H. Liddell-Hart, "Lessons from Resistance Movements—Guerrilla and Nonviolent" in Adam Roberts, (ed.) *Civilian Resistance as a National Defense* (Baltimore, Md.: Penguin Books, 1969): also Sir Stephen King-Hall, *Defense in the Nuclear Age* (London: Gollancz, 1957).

[11] For the theoretical underpinning of this philosophy of nonviolent conflict and its difference from violent conflict, see Joan V. Bondurant, *Conquest of Violence* (Berkeley and Los Angeles: University of California Press, 1965), especially chapter VI, "The Gandhian Dialectic and Political Theory."

[12] Arthur I. Waskow, *Keeping the World Disarmed* (Santa Barbara, Cal: Center for the Study of Democratic Institutions, 1965).

[13] For two case studies of dictators being unseated by mass noncooperation, see George Lakey, *Strategy for a Living Revolution* (New York: Grossman, and San Francisco: W.H. Freeman, 1973), Chapter II.

[14] Michael Harbottle, *The Blue Berets,* (Harrisburg, Pa: Stackpole Books, 1972).

[15] The idea of *commissions,* composed of respected world citizens with accompanying expert staffs, taking up problems along functional lines, is proposed by George Lakey, *op. cit.,* p. 186-194.

[16] See Aldous Huxley, *The Perennial Philosophy* (New York: Harper, 1970) for a description of common themes running through a number of the major world religions.

Part IV: Treatment

11

From Here to There

Let us review for a moment the ground we have covered thus far.

We began with a concept of health, framing this in terms of the *values* which we believe should be supported in any decent society. We then pointed to what we regard as dangerous *symptoms,* social pathologies which indicate that these values are distorted and mutilated by the present U.S. system, particularly the economic system. We then moved to a *diagnosis* of the sickness, finding much of its etiology in an economic system based on private profit-seeking and growthmanship. Having made this diagnosis, we then boldly suggested a *prescription:* a model of a more healthy political-economic system. We stated our belief that the nonviolent movement should dedicate itself to the creation of a new social order which will be supportive of human life and human dignity.

But how can we move from "here" to "there?" If one is sick, one cannot be cured simply by knowing what is wrong and what a more healthy state would be like. One has to follow a treatment procedure to move from sickness toward health. The challenge of this last section is to think through a treatment procedure for American society. We realize, of course, that the transformation of an entire society is an infinitely more complex undertaking than the treatment of an individual, and that the medical analogy itself has severe limitations. But we cannot be satisfied simply to describe our view of the present American scene and our vision for a better political economy, and to let it go at that. We believe that the American system must be radically restructured, so in this section we are outlining our view of a social change strategy to bring about such a transformation.

The remainder of the present chapter consists of a scenario suggesting how the United States could undergo a fundamental transformation. The purpose of a scenario is not to give accurate predictions about the future, but to bring out some of the key elements of social change and to expand our thinking about the possibilities for such change—in effect, to give a "feel" for how important changes could come about.

The scenario begins with what we think will probably happen without an effective social change movement. Once that is stated, we then explore what a successful movement might look like in a steadily worsening situation. The scenario has two alternative conclusions to read and weigh. The alternatives center on a strategic controversy in the movement: the role of an electoral/political party approach to change versus a differently coordinated, non-electoral, movement structure.

A Scenario*

During the next decade, the crises in the non-socialist world will continue to grow to cataclysmic proportions regarding population, resources, energy, hunger, environment, economic failures, inequalities, war, dictatorships, and police oppression. Within the poor nations, the combination of continued population explosions with diminishing available food cause mass hunger to become mass starvation.

Following the precedent of the oil producing nations (OPEC), the poor nations effectively ban together into cartels according to other products they produce.

---

*For good use of scenarios as tools for strategy, see Martin Oppenheimer, *The Urban Guerrilla* (Chicago: Quadrangle Books, 1969).

Production is cut drastically while prices multiply. This drastically affects the rich nations, causing increased inflation, balance of payments deficits, reductions in gross national products and depression-level economies, replete with massive unemployment and social disintegration. The rich nations retaliate not only with strong economic sanctions and diplomatic attacks, but with a variety of political and military interventions. Social anxiety and unrest at home along with the need for massive military operations abroad send the United States more and more into a military-police state. Civil rights and freedoms are slashed away as violence by the radical left and right increase, and the tens of millions of unemployed and hungry sporadically break out into attacks on food warehouses, supermarkets, banks, and political offices.

By the last decade of the century, not only do these problems grow worse, but they are overshadowed by others. Atomic radiation threatens all life. Accidents at atomic energy plants make several large sections of the United States uninhabitable. Thousands of tons of wastes from atomic energy plants are lost in underwater streams and threaten life with cancer. Skin cancer is the most common ailment because of the virtual elimination of the ozone layer in the atmosphere.

Much of modern industrialization is slowed to a deep depression pace because the reserves of world oil have peaked and are on the decrease while prices hold at maximum levels. The same holds true for many key nonrenewable resources required by the industrialized world.

Venezuela becomes the fifth Latin American nation (and the 35th in the world) to have the atomic bomb. Several suitcase atomic bombs have been exploded in wars between smaller nations—both by terrorist groups. The U.S. considers closing all of its atomic energy plants for fear of attack by terrorists from the poor nations or the American far left and right.

An unknown plague attacking the high-yield wheat seeds increases the already serious food shortage to panic levels.

It is our opinion that without a massive, effective people's nonviolent movement, something like this scenario is the most probable kind of future for the world. The chances of preventing this might be less than one per cent; however, we believe that the one per cent is worth working for.

So let's now see what a successful movement might look like:

The withdrawal of U.S. troops from Southeast Asia, even though slow-paced, undercut the ability of the American peace movement to mount large-scale protest demonstrations against the continuing war. However, the decreasing presence of U.S. combat troops in Southeast Asia began to make more clear the large iceberg under the receding tip of troop presence, i.e., the fact of continued massive U.S. involvement in terms of logistical support, weapons, planes, and political backing for pliable dictatorships. The development of Southeast Asian oil deposits by Western petroleum companies raised the question of the political and military links of the international petroleum companies. More and more, Vietnam, Cambodia, and Laos began to look like only the most obvious symbols of U.S. presence throughout the world—a presence supporting right-wing regimes which were willing to hold their nations open to the presence of American corporations searching for local subsidiaries, raw materials, and foreign markets.

Word leaked out that the Pentagon was training expatriates of Venezuela for counter insurgency action and that the nationalization of U.S. interests in that country had sparked a mobilization of these and supporting U.S. troops. The U.S. needed to return the flow of oil from Venezuela at low prices to help stem the high prices and lack of oil which were contributing to inflation and depression. The strategy was that by cutting Venezuela away they might break the back of OPEC, and return the upper hand to the oil consuming nations. The peace movement held its first large protest rally around the issue of U.S. economic domination of the Third World. Speaker after speaker pointed out that the peace movement must focus, not only on getting U.S. soldiers out of combat in various parts of the world, but also on getting at the root causes of a system which continually feels impelled to intervene militarily all over the world.

Partly as a result of this new consciousness, various peace groups came together in a loose coalition called the Alliance for Basic Change (ABC). One of the main activities of ABC was to develop across the country a network of small study and action groups. These were groups of usually fewer than fifteen people who came together to engage in intensive study of the present American political economy, share visions of how a better society might operate, and do research on a revolutionary strategy for nonviolent social change. As they became more proficient, they shared course outlines with high school and college groups. Soon courses on "Alternatives to the American Political Economy," "The Politics of Nonviolent Action," etc. were cropping up all over the country. A few universities established study and action centers where biologists, political scientists, environmental chemists, economists, and movement people came together to share insights on the ecological crisis, the U.S. political-economic system, etc.

Two east coast ABC groups cooperated in setting up a visitation program which took students on study trips to countries with different political and economic systems and which brought to the U.S. experts from other nations such as Sweden, China, Cuba, Yugoslavia, and Tanzania, to speak about their countries' efforts in economic democracy and in setting up humanistic programs in health, housing, employment, and so on.

In their local communities, the members of ABC groups often lived together in communal households or lived near one another. They adopted simple life-styles, and attempted to "live the revolution now" in their interpersonal relationships, their development of cooperative counter-institutions such as child-care centers, free schools, co-op food stores, and their service projects in the neighborhood. They found that this simpler life style was more satisfying and allowed them to live on less income. Many of them began to work part-time and spend more time on community projects and political action. ABC group members taught each other skills of organizing, housework, simple living, home repairs, public speaking, and tried to make sure that all tasks were rotated. Many people, dissatisfied with institutional slowness to respond to new challenges, found participation in ABC groups a particularly liberating and meaningful experience.

The ABC groups published newsletters and, through the coordinating Alliance, a national newspaper. They also honed their interpretation skills through street-speaking, engaged in local direct action projects, and helped to organize a nation-wide system of training centers for nonviolent action.

Trainees from these centers joined in a summer project organized by the New Populist Organizing Committee, a broad coalition of black, chicano, and native American groups and a mounting number of poverty groups, many whose constituency was drawn mostly from the tens of millions of new white poor, unemployed, and hungry. The project began with a highly publicized march through the U.S. southwest. The marchers saw and reported on widespread hunger and destitution on reservations, among migrant laborers, and in black ghettos. They demonstrated at strip mining sites and before the plants of giant utilities which had pushed Indians off their ancestral lands.

Urban allies, working out of nonviolent training centers, moved onto vacant urban renewal land and used it for the planting of vegetables, a new and satisfying skill for many. The effort seemed small in the early part of the summer, but it grew as participants engaged in nonviolent response to harassment and jailing, and as the country once again became aware of the presence of 50 million hungry people in the midst of its affluence. By the end of summer, ABC's along with significant elements of the welfare rights movement, student groups, and the farm labor movement, were full participants in the decision-making of the New Populist Organizing Committee, which was re-named "The New Populist Coalition."

Several hundred people in a Tennessee town died of radiation sickness which was traced to the leakage of wastes from a nuclear power plant. Real estate values plummeted in waste storage areas around the country as outraged citizens staged demonstrations near the sites (which were discovered by the detective work of radical university people).

An air inversion in Los Angeles caused the deaths of an estimated 5,000 people, and California ABC groups organized demonstrations at industries known to be major polluters. They also engaged in traffic-blocking bike-ins along super-highways to increase the pressure for non-polluting mass transit in the area. Southwestern ABC groups were able to show that similar air inversions were imminent in the small New Mexico valley communities affected by the gigantic coal-fired electric plants, which belched hundreds of tons of ash into the air every day.

Demonstrations at the plants, plus pressure on local government, were so effective that two of them had to close down. This raised the broader question of how California could meet its needs for electrical energy, a question an environmental chemist and members of a local ABC group answered at a large citizens' conference in terms of the need radically to re-think the American political economy and to work for the *de*-development of the U.S. economic system.

The basically liberal people who were part of the ecology movement and who were drawn to the direct action were at first unhappy about the ABC groups' linking of pollution to the basic structure and functioning of the corporate economy, but close contact with intransigent, polluting corporations radicalized many. Although most of the ecology movement did not link formally with the Alliance for Basic Change or the New Populist Coalition (which still seemed too radical for comfort), many ecology action participants joined as individuals.

Further pressure against the corporations (and further education as to their real nature) came with the mounting of anti-corporate campaigns which were joined in by liberal and radical religious people concerned about church investments in corporations engaged in pollution, war-production, overseas exploitation, un-fair hiring, planned obsolescence, etc.

Students had been turning more and more to avenues of personal fulfillment, out of the frustration of political action. Now they began to find ways to use the insights they gained in radical courses, such as the study and action seminars, in direct action. Some participated in broader ecology and consumer actions and others formed student organizations.

Radical caucuses grew rapidly among social workers, miners, scientists, teachers, attorneys, health workers, and practically every other profession and employment group, and there was hardly a convention that was not marked by large protests against a status quo approach to social problems. Caucuses also formed in the major denominational religious groups. Radical religious activists began to sit-in and live-in at churches, synagogues, meetinghouses, and church agencies, demanding that religious organizations divest themselves of defense industry stocks, reduce their property holdings, adopt simple lifestyles, engage in demonstrations at stock-holders' meetings, take a lead in organizing nonviolent training centers, and engage in nonviolent struggles for social justice.

Concerned Jews and Christians began to meet and to re-discover Biblical economics—that the call to a simple, non-covetous life is one of the strongest themes of Biblical faith. More and more religiously-committed people moved into communal living situations, simplifying their lives and sharing economically. New kinds of churches came into being, combining deep spiritual fellowship with prophetic critique of the materialism of American society.

In the early stages of the struggle, workers—especially white workers—stayed at arm's length, complaining about the disruption by "long-hairs" and "welfare bums." But this hostility started to break down as workers began to see how the system of corporations, which so largely controlled them, thrived on unemployment and poverty, hunger, racism and sexism. Events helped to wear down the workers' resentment, such as the United Electrical Workers president's speech before the NewPop convention, in which he drew parallels between these modern populists and the early labor movement. Several study groups brought together New-Pop people and workers. Also, the visit of Yugoslav workers (arranged by an East Coast ABC group) who explained to rapt union audiences the Yugoslav system of workers' councils and social management of enterprises. NewPop's continued support for the unionization of hospital and other workers and ABC groups' support for various strikes helped forge lasting ties with workers. In the movement, derogatory comments about workers as hard-hats and pigs disappeared, and there was an increasing effort to understand what valid concerns the white worker may have against a system which oppresses and threatens her/him in many ways.

When unions began a concerted effort to establish a system of national health insurance, which would provide good medical care to everyone as a matter of right, they were surprised and pleased to receive strong support from NewPop and ABC. They were also surprised at the intensity of opposition from the American Medical Association, which threatened to strike if Congress approved the National Medical Security act.

All of these forces brought a varied response from the government. Where it was possible to justify repression, repression was used. But it was found to be much more difficult to use police power on nonviolent demonstrators than on "trashers" or "urban guerrillas." Police who raided the communes which served as bases for several ABC groups, for example, were greeted by offers of coffee and donuts, beer and pretzels, and were invited to bull sessions on what life could be like in a better society with security in jobs, medical care, old age, and with a more democratic command structure in police departments. Police commissioners found that they were receiving regular reports on the activities of ABC groups, not from their own infiltrators, but from the ABC newsletters that movement people ceremoniously delivered to their offices. When a police bus, rushing to a demonstration, blew a tire and overturned, medical personnel from an ABC group hurried to assist the injured. When the weather turned suddenly cold at a demonstration at an atomic plant, movement people shared food and blankets with police and para-troopers. Police found that they were less and less described in leaflets and speeches as "the enemy" and that movement people appeared to be seriously asking them how they felt the criminal justice system should operate in a decent society.

Perhaps the most dramatic change in attitude was reflected in the movement's revival, at many of its demonstrations, of the old Gandhian discipline which read: "If anyone insults an official or commits an assault upon him, a civil resister will protect such official from the insult or attack, even at the risk of her or his own life."

The establishment on occasion attempted reforms to meet the demands of the advocates of social change. Massive draft resistance had led to the reform of ending the draft and establishing a volunteer, professional army, yet it was soon clear that the professionals were still a threat to democracy, as the former civilian army had been. Massive anti-war demonstrations prevented any commitment of U.S. troops to combat, but the government constantly found it necessary to intervene overseas and it continued its support of retrogressive regimes. The passage of national medical insurance was hailed as a major step forward, but as time went by people began to realize that its financing came through a regressive personal income tax which had no impact on corporate profits and that doctors were using insurance funds to increase their already bloated incomes. Reforms in the food stamp program helped to end the most obvious hunger in the country, but the method of allocating the stamps was still obviously demeaning and unsatisfactory. Anti-pollution laws cut back on corporate pollution to some extent, but scandals of law evasion and continuing ecological break-downs showed the inadequacy of reform.

Thus, the interplay of protest, minimal reform, and public education, and still deteriorating conditions for most Americans led to the development of a more mature consciousness on the part of many people. Whereas in the past people had been either apathetic or concerned only with specific evils—consumer fraud, pollution, militarism, etc.—many people now began to see that the basic structure of corporate capitalism was at fault, and that things *could* be better. As the movement developed, ordinary Americans came to see more clearly the ecological and human irrationality of the political economy and also began to see the movement—with its broad-based, nonviolent, celebrative approach—as a place of sanity.

Closing Scenario #1: The Movement-plus-political party route to change

In response to this new consciousness, new political candidates, running on much more radical platforms than in the past, began to enter the scene. Many of these were old-time liberals who had their fingers to the wind and who believed that a mass political voting base was developing and that this would demand candidates with a more radical posture.

At the fourth annual NewPop convention, it was decided to move into the electoral arena by forming a new political party. Only a few conservatives argued that now was the time to try to convert the existing parties, since most people agreed that these parties were captives of the very forces which were causing the problems. At the other end of the spectrum, some delegates argued for a party based on Marxist-Leninist principles. But the vast majority of the convention voted for a party based squarely on the existing—but almost forgotten—American revolutionary tradition. As a major speaker put it: "We want a socialist party, but it has to be a socialism which comes out of our Populist movement and which is unique to American values and traditions, and not a foreign import. And it has to take account of new historical realities—like the ecological crisis and the need to de-develop the industrial nations—about which Marx and Lenin never dreamed. If it were not such a mouthful, I would call ours a movement for egalitarian, nonviolent, nonsexist, humanistic, anti-racist, decentralized, eco-democratic socialism."

In the first phase of its existence, the new Nonviolent Populist Party did not emphasize winning elections, but concentrated instead on building up its membership, establishing a democratic, grass-roots organization, doing public educational work, getting out a national newspaper. Candidates who *did* get elected to Congress earned the wrath of members of the traditional parties by boycotting most sessions, pointing out the relative powerlessness of the legislative branch, and spending most of their time in slums and rural poverty areas, helping local groups to organize demonstrations and counter-institutions, and joining anti-welfare-to-the-rich demonstrations at the Treasury Department, IRS, and the White House. They also lived austerely and donated large parts of their salaries to social change groups.

To the extent the Congresspeople did join the legislative arena they introduced bills embodying revolutionary reforms such as:

House Bill 1199: to establish a fully socialized medical system financed by a progressive tax.

House Bill 34: to nationalize the banking system and have the banks run by depositor-controlled boards modeled on cooperative credit unions.

House Bill 41: to extend cooperative housing so broadly that the role of the landlord would be eliminated over a period of years.

House Bill 75: to require a national referendum for any military involvement, with those voting "yes" being required to provide the personpower.

Senate Bill 63: to set up a publicly-funded system of educational TV and vastly extend the role of non-profit, subscription radio and TV, with both controlled by mass media workers and by listener/viewers.

Senate Bill 123: to provide comprehensive no-fault auto, home, and life insurance for the entire population through a low-premium policy managed through Social Security.

House Bill 1004: to transfer funds from the terminated space program to the development of new towns in which land and industry are owned by a community trust and worker and community boards govern economic enterprises.

Senate Bill 358: to repeal 54 separate acts providing tax relief to people in upper income brackets and to corporations.

House Bill 1005: No government official or immediate family can own any corporation stock or hold any in escrow or receive any income or favors from any business.

Establishment politicians and business leaders resisted these more fundamental reforms since they dealt not so much with the *benefits* of the system as with the distribution of *privilege and power* within it. But this very resistance, combined with the movement's mass education, acted as a powerful force in educating the public at large about the real nature of the political and economic system. Thus it was not surprising to see the growth of a mass people's movement with a more and more anti-establishment viewpoint—a movement which drew heavily on the NewPop Coalition, the local chapters of the Nonviolent Populist Party, the local ABC groups, the consumers' movement, the coopers and other counter-institutions, the ecology movement, the students, the radical caucuses, the liberal and radical workers and the unemployed, hungry and poor. As resistance to change escalated in the establishment, so did the radical protests and non-cooperation of the people's movement. Because of widespread disruptions, many corporate stockholders' meetings were discontinued. Workers refused to load ships taking materials to dictatorial regimes and foreign subsidiaries of international corporations. Tenant unions demanded ownership and control of their housing, went on rent strikes across the country. As establishment institutions became discredited, some of the radical alternative institutions began to occupy and run them. Free universities occupied and ran university administration buildings. Free neighborhood medical centers took over some hospitals. Parents refused school taxes, paying the amounts instead to locally controlled schools and leaving central administrations without a function. One major TV network had its central office occupied by educational TV broadcasters cooperating with the network's own radical caucus. In some factories, workers elected their own management councils and responded only to them.

The government found itself facing an election, but having to escalate its repression and to bring Green Beret units home from Asia to replace military units whose effectiveness had been undercut by movement fraternization and infiltration. The government seemed to be fighting on every front, but found that increasingly unreliable troops were ineffective against jail-ins, general strikes, massive resignations from government agencies, and mass street sit-ins.

Nonviolent Populists, who were at the forefront of the agitation, swept the Congress and the Presidency in the elections, even though the remnants of the Democratic Party and the Republican Party agreed to back joint candidates in swing areas in an effort to defeat NewPop. For a few weeks after election day there was talk of a coup d'etat engineered by major corporate leaders and the Pentagon, but the formation in most neighborhoods of Nonviolent Committees for the Defense of the Revolution made it clear that a coup would inherit a completely ungovernable populace. The counter-revolutionary elements suffered a setback when several Army units agreed to be retrained as a nonviolent Civilian Defense Force; and the Nonviolent Populist government was able to begin to implement its program.

Although the Nonviolent Populist Party thought of itself as the party of the people, it found it difficult not to fall prey to the dangers of central bureaucracies.

NewPop and other elements of the people's movement had to forcefully remind it, on occasion—with demonstrations and non-cooperation—that the power of government was not just to be *taken* by the people's representatives, but to be *redistributed* to the people as a whole.

Closing Scenario #2: The Movement-without-political-party route to change

As a response to this new consciousness, the liberal wing became the dominant force in the Democratic Party, the party Old Guard standing aside at least temporarily in the face of these strong winds of change. To the trumpets of a major advertising campaign financed by the Harrimans and the Kennedys, the Democrats said they would make America the most just country in the world, vastly increasing expenditures for welfare at home and for foreign aid. "We can all unite," an 18-year-old Kennedy announced against a background of rock music, "behind the ideal of making America loved rather than feared, honored rather than spat upon, the most justly powerful nation in the world."

A minority of the New Populist Coalition hailed this development, but most were skeptical. "The greatest America?" "The most powerful nation?" A vigorous internal debate among the ABC groups and radical caucuses showed that most of them agreed with the Third World peoples that the super-states had outlived their usefulness. "World community will never thrive while the super-states throw their weight around," a Holland, Michigan ABC group stated. "The world community must grow from the people's movements rather than from 19th century relics; we should strengthen our solidarity with the oppressed in the Soviet Union and other states in a mutual effort to build new transnational institutions."

Groups from the American Old Left attacked this position as "infantile anarchism" and "bourgeois individualism." A Bay Area ABC group made the shortest answer: "The Old Left groups and the major parties want

to seize the super-state for their purposes. We see no
genuine democracy possible without dismantling the
super-state—without the people on a grass-roots level
taking power and humankind as a whole enabled to make
humankind-sized decisions."

For six months the debate was heavy in radical and
liberal circles, resulting in the exit of some participants
from the NewPop Coalition and a massive influx of youth
and nonwhites. Many new ABC groups formed, making
alliances with liberation movements in other countries.
Exchanges with radicals in other countries increased.
Direct action projects across national lines also increased
with the new clarity of global consciousness among
movement people, notably, for example, a march down
the Pan American Highway toward the Brazilian police
state, picking up marchers from Mexico and Central
America along the way. Some ABC groups began to draft
plans for transnational institutions which could be built
by people-power, for example the World Protein Equality
Authority.

Pressure on the national government for change did
not stop, however. While the NewPop Coalition did not
form a new party to contest for power in Congress, it did
pressure the Congress through direct action campaigns.
Through non-cooperation, the campaigners were able to
dislocate parts of the country to force the passage of
revolutionary reforms in Washington. For example, an
East Coast rent strike with 55 per cent effectiveness
forced Congress to remove hindrances to tenants buying
apartment houses on a cooperative basis, and establishing
low rent ceilings.

War tax resistance continued to grow since the early
1970s, when it was a tactic of Vietnam war protest. The
protest of most tax resisters broadened to include the
military budget and welfare to the rich. Tax refusal
leagues were organizing to refuse highway taxes as long as
public mass transit remained starved for funds. Religious
groups were refusing to withhold income tax from con-
scientious employees, despite punitive action from the
government.

Intellectual work played a significant role. The historical studies of Gene Sharp *(The Politics of Nonviolent Action)* and others confirmed the gut feelings many activists had had that nonviolent organizing was not only morally preferable, but also their most realistically powerful weapon. Unlike in the 1960's when the failure of nonviolent efforts was often thought to dictate an "escalation" of struggle to violence, turning to stealthy violence (bombings and kidnappings) or open street-fighting came to be recognized as a self-isolating retreat from mass struggle. More disciplined evaluation of both victories and defeats made clear the simple truth that there were no substitutes for sound strategy, well-chosen tactics, and solid organizing. Both "nonviolence" and "violence" failed without them.

More helpful than mere exhortation to do better was the development of specific organizing tools and group processes, and the sharing of experience through collectively written and periodically revised manuals on building nonviolent campaigns, choosing strategy and tactics, and working in efficient, non-elitist ways.

As the movement grew in support, the government and corporations tried to repeat their partial success of 1968-72 in using *agents provocateurs* and entrapment to discredit the movement through sabotage and terrorism done in its name. Most elements of the NewPop Coalition increased their commitment to strategic and tactical nonviolence, and also redoubled their efforts to fraternize with those honest revolutionaries who believed in armed struggle. Two of the agents became disillusioned and publicly admitted that they were being paid—one by the government and another by a large auto-maker—to try to push the movement to violence.

The ruling elite was becoming frantic as its weakness was exposed. High school students held "Reading of the Myths" ceremonies, with material from their textbooks on American democracy. The popular magazines found new ways to show the Emperor without clothes. A government social science crash research program on how to create legitimacy lost half its personnel in a feud which became public knowledge.

In Denver an ABC group made the spark which ignited a national non-cooperation campaign. The activists held a public burning of their insurance policies, to dramatize their demand for socialized, no-fault, comprehensive auto, home, and life insurance to the entire population through the Social Security system.

ABC groups across the nation responded, and black groups angry with the insurance slumlords began to occupy insurance company offices. What seemed like half of New England started to march to Hartford, and rumors began to fly that the entire city might be liberated and become a socialist democracy.

The President acted swiftly, and in the opinion of half his cabinet much too harshly. A state of emergency was declared in New England with mobilization of the National Guard units. Round-ups throughout the U.S. began of those the FBI described as "key agitators." University presidents received telephone calls from White House staff warning repetition of the Kent State tragedy if campus dissent were not controlled. Tight surveillance of the poor and non-white communities was established. Police in six cities forcibly cleared the insurance company offices, injuring hundreds. There were several deaths.

Despite heavy government pressure on the TV networks, one of the news shows mentioned the event briefly. The movement network of ham radios, cable TV, and telephone trees stepped up their activity in spreading the word to the NewPop Coalition, and underground newspapers ran special issues on the government's determination to protect private property even at the cost of many lives.

Although the intensity of conflict was greatest in Hartford for the next months, it continued to grow in the rest of the country. Schools and colleges were occupied or struck, mass demonstrations occurred throughout the country with ABC groups conducting training for direct action around the clock. Forty Congresspeople began a fast for reconciliation, while others flew to Hartford to observe the novel situation of citizens, aided by other

New Englanders, liberating their city from corporation control.

When the U.S. Chamber of Congress publicly urged martial law, industrial workers responded with a wave of sit-downs, accompanied by strikes among the white collar workers. While many of the strikers had specific grievances, they also participated in the general feeling that the system was breaking down, and society needed to be reconstituted on a new basis. This feeling was reinforced by the escalating governmental repression. Workers in several factories began to work again with their own elected councils making decisions, ignoring the corporation management.

Committees sprang up in neighborhoods across the country to maintain order and basic services such as sanitation while the government and right wing put their efforts into stemming the rising tide. The neighborhood committees began to form coordinating councils on city, state, and regional levels and movement people began paying their taxes to the new bodies. Many ABC groups already trained in group dynamics participated in the committees and helped them heighten their inherent democratic tendencies. The intensified efforts at fraternization with police and soldiers and the work of police and GI ABC groups began to pay off. When groups of police began reporting to the councils for assignment, and soldiers in large numbers piled their uniforms outside council headquarters, the President knew the struggle was over.

Repression had been counter-productive, and even the agents of repression were going over to the revolution. Further White House and corporate resistance depended on fresh sources of power—and revolutions were occurring at that very moment in seven other countries which had been until then under American hegemony. Some European governments refused to repress the mass occupations of American corporate property in their countries, because of their own decreasing stability. The President resigned and the Congress formed a special committee to negotiate with the revolutionary councils.

In the next several months, workers, radical caucuses, and coordinating councils began to implement the NewPop program. Parts of the program were strengthened in the give-and-take of vigorous debates among the people. Other parts were set aside for possible use in the longer run. There was local and regional variation as innovations drawing on ethnic and local traditions were tried. Local, regional, and transnational bodies took most of the functions away from the federal apparatus, and May 1 was marked by speeches hailing the historic occasion when socialists actually encouraged the withering away of the state.

12

Why Not
Armed Struggle?

It is difficult to imagine a power shift which opens the way to an egalitarian, ecologically sound, democratic order. We believe, however, that persons who are committed to a severely critical view of the American empire (and, indeed, of the present world order) and to a vision of basic change, *must* try to develop strategies. If the strategies are rough in the beginning, so be it. Dialogue within the people's movements will refine those strategies; self-criticism and creativity will discover strategies which make a closer and closer "fit" to our unique historical situation.

Two common assumptions make strategizing difficult. One is that "nonviolence" is the answer. The other is that "armed struggle" is the answer.

Neither "nonviolence" nor "violence" is a strategy, and debates on a general level are often labelling contests rather than helpful dialogue. Those who say that armed struggle will some day be necessary for revolution may simply be speaking out of a John Wayne culture where the easy assumption is that power requires violence, or they may come to that conclusion from a thought-out choice of strategies. One cannot know until one sees the homework. Those who say that "nonviolence" can bring about revolution may simply be speaking out of a bourgeois idealism which denies the entrenchment of the power elite, or they may come to that conclusion from a considered strategy backed with research. One cannot know until one sees the strategy.

Our strategy suggests that a mass people's movement can force American society to change basically with a range of direct action methods excluding killing or personal injury. It is as specific as we can be at this time. Realizing that people sometimes avoid strategic thinking by debates on "violence vs. nonviolence," we will try in this chapter to clarify our position on the controversy in the hope that readers will be free to return to other strategy questions involved in rapid social change.

Pacific militancy and the people

Perhaps the first task in thinking clearly about methods of change is to question the word "nonviolence;" it is probably too misleading and emotional to communicate at all. The Puerto Rican Independence Party, a socialist liberation movement in Puerto Rico, has coined the phrase "militancia pacifica" to mean methods which go beyond the electoral process. These include noncooperation such as the strike and boycott, civil disobedience, demonstrations, occupations, sit-ins, and so on.

Pacific militancy has been used very commonly in American social change movements because it is particularly the weapon of the people. The government makes sure it has a monopoly of legitimate violence and a near-monopoly of actual means of violence. The methods of pacific militancy are much more available to the poor and the workers, and so American history is full of strikes, boycotts, and demonstrations of various kinds. [1] The fact that many historians have been focussed on this or that military battle should not mislead us any more than the fact that most historians have focussed on white people. The "submerged history" of blacks, and of pacific militancy, is coming to the surface and will gradually change Americans' view of our heritage.

Particularly striking is the shift in tactics in the workers' movements in the last hundred years. The most practical way of getting higher wages was once a matter of controversy, with violence or at least sabotage a leading option. Now there is nearly a consensus that strikes, boycotts, and demonstrations are most effective. Elizabeth Gurley Flynn, one of the great Communist organizers of American history, was eloquent in the strikes she led about the importance of ruling out violence.

The blacks' struggle has also shown the importance, for mass mobilization, of pacific militancy. Since the Montgomery bus boycott of 1955-56, all large-scale black campaigns using direct action have been based on pacific militancy. While there have been sporadic, impulsive riots, they could not be sustained, did not have clear goals, and accomplished little change. In most urban areas one experiment with rioting was enough; the black population and its leadership then worked to prevent future recurrences.

The number of Americans who are suspicious of the power elite is growing. The Potomac Associates did a study for the government which showed that Americans are losing their confidence in government and business leaders and their optimism about the American future. [2] Legitimacy is declining—a classic condition for broad-based struggle movements. However, the movement itself is not yet seen widely as legitimate. Some progress is occurring there, but continuing development of trust in the movement depends on our showing a strong contrast to the violence of the status quo. If the government lies and we are truthful, if the corporations pollute and we are respectful of nature and resources, if the power elite resorts to violence and we act to enhance life, we will deepen the contrast and get the hearing we need. If a mass struggle movement in America wants to go beyond electoral and other conventional methods, it must use pacific militancy. We see no evidence that the masses of people can be or will be mobilized to use arms.

In fact, one of the cultural forces which makes it more difficult to organize a broad movement to use violence is the declining legitimacy of violence itself. Decades ago many politicians romanticized and glorified killing; they said it was "manly," noble, in tune with the evolution of humankind through survival of the fittest. The hymns to killing have gone off-key. Now it is very difficult to find eloquent advocates of the positive virtues of violence: the proponents of violent revolution in America looked to Algeria to find a spokesman and even Frantz Fanon brings in a mixed diagnosis.[3]

Decades ago leaders often *preferred* to use violence because of the positive qualities it was believed to have. Now, however, the trend is to consider violence a *last* resort, a means one uses only for lack of a better alternative. Some liberation movement leaders insist that guerrilla struggle is to be limited, assassination selective, a loving motivation stressed even when it is necessary to kill. "Let me say, at the risk of seeming ridiculous, that the true revolutionary is guided by great feelings of love," Che Guevara declared.

This cultural development away from the legitimacy of war puts pressure on revolutionists if they want to retain the support of the people. In Northern Ireland in spring 1972, the dilemma for the Irish Republican Army Provisionals was very great: should they continue the armed struggle which they regarded as the necessary means of achieving a united Ireland, or should they heed the rising clamor of those who *agreed* with them on their goals but were protesting their means? The radical Catholic women of Northern Ireland—sisters, wives, friends of the IRA—were insisting on a stop to the killing, even by using a public petition.[4] The IRA is a people's movement. How can it ignore the people?

This is the kind of pressure which may force revolutionary leaders into developing a strategy of pacific militancy. When the people say yes to the goals but no to the means, other means must be sought, unless the movement is in fact elitist.

One of the problems of armed struggle is, unfortunately, a tendency toward elitism which is fostered by conspiracy and violence. The "outlaw" nature of violent movements requires secrecy. Martin Oppenheimer in his book *The Urban Guerrilla*[5] shows how anti-democratic the rule of secrecy is: when few are allowed to know, the few will rule. Power flows to those with knowledge. Knowledge must be limited to a few because of the agents who infiltrate the organizations. (Not that even the tightest conspiracies can prevent infiltration; even Lenin's central committee had a Czarist spy on it for years.)

There never has been a democratic army, although armies have varied considerably in their relations between the officers and the rank and file. However evenly the privileges might be distributed, orders are orders, conscription is conscription, and there is still one group of men who decide and a much larger group who go out and risk their lives without participating in that decision. In struggles based on pacific militancy there has also been much elitism. Just as guerrilla struggles have sometimes focussed on the charisma of a Mao or a Castro, so nonviolent struggles have sometimes focussed on a King or a Chavez. Gandhi was named commander of the civil resistance campaign in India and had a pyramidal command structure under him.

Nevertheless, there seems to us more room for participation in decisions in pacific militancy. Conscription is virtually impossible, so the voluntary nature of participation is a foundation of struggle. Widespread debate about the nature and timing of a campaign can occur before decision, since the success of noncooperation rarely depends on surprise. The sanctions available to leaders for dissent in the ranks are more limited; a Gandhi or Chavez finds himself fasting, a King personally going from poolhall to poolhall to ask for the destruction of weapons. Unlike generals, they cannot send orders from map-filled rooms to be implemented by a rigid chain of command.

The emphasis *within* the revolutionary movement on persuasion rather than coercion bodes well for the new society after the shift in power, if the movement's vision includes participatory democracy.

Armed struggle is likely to fail

Whatever may be said about revolutions in other countries at other times, armed struggle does not offer hope in the modern context. We suspect this is why there is such a conspicuous absence of strategies which show the role armed struggle is to play here.

In *The Urban Guerrilla*, Oppenheimer outlined two alternative strategies for revolution by means of violence: one was popular insurrection, and the other was inter-urban terrorism. He spelled out the nature of the strategies carefully because this is so rarely done by radicals. The first strategy seemed most likely to lead to a continuation of the status quo except for a more highly militarized social control apparatus in large cities. The second strategy seemed most likely to lead to a fascist state. Oppenheimer concludes that, however little hard thinking may have gone into it so far, democratic radicals are forced to develop a strategy for nonviolent revolution.

Several obstacles seem in combination to be overwhelming. First is the massive military power of the state and the constant refining of technology (electronic sensing devices, for example) which facilitates repression. If the military arena is to be the crucial one, the Establishment has gotten there first.

It is far from clear where the military hardware would come from as the struggle advances from homemade and seized weapons to a higher level. Strategy for protracted guerrilla struggle expects a final state of conventional war, as in China or in Vietnam. At that point a massive arms supply is necessary. From where would the arms come? From outside sympathetic nations? The role of the Soviet Union in power politics is not reassuring, nor the support of China to the bloody dictator Yahya Khan of Pakistan against the people of Bangladesh.

Second is the difficulty of getting massive popular support for armed revolutionary struggle. The revolutionaries should be to the people as the fish are to the sea, says Mao, but that is unlikely for the reasons described earlier.

Third is the lack of a privileged sanctuary. There is no refuge now or in prospect, no contiguous land area where the revolution has already been made and which would be safe from retaliation from the government. This condition could change, but it does not seem likely.

Some difficulties of pacific militancy

Our negative view of the prospects of armed struggle in America does not mean that we are sure that our strategy, or any strategy based on pacific militancy, is bound to succeed. Just as most guerrilla struggles have failed in history, so have most nonviolent struggles failed to achieve their objectives, at least in the short run. There are no historical cases of a successful nonviolent *revolution* (although there are cases of dictators being overthrown by pacific militancy).[6] No one can be sure, embarking on a road, that he or she will reach the destination.

One difficulty is precisely that we cannot point to a historical model and say, "There it is; our revolution will be like that." In this respect we are like Lenin in 1915; he too was proposing to try an approach without past historical success. Although revolutionists should by temperament be open to the new and unprecedented, our experience has been that some are rather conservative and prefer the old ways. The image of barricades and molotov cocktails fits into a well-worn groove in many a radical's mind. We hope, however, that even the old-fashioned revolutionists will be forced to examine new possibilities by the rapid change of post-industrial America and the ferment which that produces.

Pacific militancy is sometimes held to be too slow a technique; violence more nearly matches the sense of urgency which we all feel. There is little evidence, however, that military is speedier than civilian resistance. In addition to all the cases of guerrilla struggles which failed entirely, as in the Philippines, Malaya, Greece, Guatemala, and so on, there are others which took many years. Mao claims that the Chinese revolution took a hundred years. Allowing for exaggeration and dating it from Mao's own period of leadership, we still have twenty-eight years. The Vietnamese are still being pounded after twenty-six years of struggle against the Japanese, French and American empires. For decades there have not been any cases of protracted, popular armed struggle within western industrialized countries, so it is impossible to say how speedy a process that is if it can happen at all. [7]

Comparing cases of struggle in different cultures and different times is of course a terribly complex process, and we know of no one who has done this seriously and arrived at the conclusion that violence is more quickly effective than pacific militancy. It remains one of those untested assumptions which hampers the development of an effective strategy for fundamental change.*

One problem in developing the effectiveness of pacific militancy is too great a stress on its psychological dimension. If the power of civil disobedience lies in "melting the heart of the opponent," as Gandhi used to say, what happens when the opponent takes precautions to avoid seeing the campaigners? Government officials have the means of isolating themselves; even the agents of repression can sometimes work by computer and electronic weapons rather than face-to-face with the demonstrators.

Much of the power of pacific militancy springs, in contrast to the psychological view, from noncooperation. The campaigners create a problem (social dislocation of the industrial city of Birmingham, Alabama, for example) which *forces* the decision-makers to deal with the movement. Decision-makers meet with movement leaders because they must in order to do their job.

---

*Another untested assumption is that property destruction adds power to a nonviolent struggle movement. The question of timing and other variables are discussed by George Lakey in *Strategy for a Living Revolution* (New York: Grossman, 1973), chapter five.

But neither should the psychological side be discarded as meaningless. The psychological basis operates alongside this political/economic basis in many campaigns. The press and television often convey the flavor of a campaign to the officials involved, in whose interest it is to learn more about the nature of their "problem." The interaction of campaigners with other governmental people has had some effect even in these pre-revolutionary days; Daniel Ellsberg credits his decision to publicize the Pentagon Papers to the example of two young pacifist draft resisters, Bob Eaton and Randy Kehler, whom Ellsberg met shortly before they were sentenced to prison terms. A group of sailors who jumped off their ammunition ship into the sea as it was departing for Indochina said they took that risk because of fellowship with demonstrators who sought to block the ship by canoes and by sitting on the railroad tracks on the loading pier. Larry Bearman, one of the sailors, wrote: "We had to show the public how 7 sailors felt about the war . . . There were others who attempted to jump but were repelled. All of us could not sit back watching your non-violent fleet's efforts for peace without the support from us."

Another obstacle in the path of pacific militancy is the feeling of many people in government and other Establishment structures that they have no responsibility to take an active moral stand because they can do little to change the course of these giant institutions. One way the movement can reach these people is through the power of example, as in the case of Daniel Ellsberg already described. Another way is through developing a variety of roles which people on the "inside" can play that help the movement: organizing radical caucuses, giving information, being inefficient, doing quiet support work while off-duty.

Of course individuals cannot by themselves change large institutions. Individuals can amplify their power enormously, however, by working in concert with a revolutionary movement. This is the message we must communicate.

There are many liberals within the institutions of social control, however, who think that in doing their jobs they are making a positive contribution to social change. They argue that "inside" is where the power is, and that if they do not occupy those positions, other, less humane, people will do so.

The movement can ask these people for proof that they do in fact make any difference in their individual capacities, that someone else could have made a difference for the worse. The tragic example of some Jews in Germany during the Hitler period cooperating in their own oppression with such rationales should put the burden of proof on those who assist in the stabilizing of the status quo.

We also challenge the idea that much power lies within the lower and middle levels of bureaucracies of American institutions. The directions are set by the power elite, as we tried to show in chapter VII. The impotence of former UN Ambassador Adlai Stevenson, or of a number of liberal State Department officials, in the direction of American foreign policy is fairly clear. When even as powerful a man as former Defense Secretary Robert McNamara changed his own mind about Indochina policy, someone else replaced him and the policy went on. Further, we ask what kind of power can come from endless compromise; integrity is a superior source of power in the long-run influence of an individual, especially when he or she is linked to a people's movement for change.

Relation to violent liberation movements

However preferable a strategy employing pacific militancy is to the one using armed struggle, there is nevertheless sure to be violence in the American future. Even though there was a strong majority sentiment among Indian independence movement people for *satyagraha,* parallel to the majority movement were terrorist campaigns. There have been some movements where complete unity was reached on pacific militancy, but we do not expect that in the foreseeable future in the U.S.

The problem of relationship between the mass non-violent movement and the adherents of armed struggle is complicated by the existence of *agents provocateurs*.

Again and again in recent U.S. experience the government has hired individuals to infiltrate a non-violent movement and seek to turn it toward violence. Apparently the government considers it easier to repress a violent movement than a nonviolent one, and therefore promotes violence among those it seeks to suppress. The movement must, of course, be vigilant about this danger and expose whenever possible the provocateurs who might lead the unwary into acts of sabotage and violence. [8]

It is wrong to think, however, that every organizer of violence is a paid agent. There are a number, perhaps a growing number, of completely sincere humanist revolutionists who believe that violence is necessary, although regrettable, and that only through armed struggle can the powerful American Empire be toppled.

The precise posture of the mass movement will of course depend on the situation, but we feel it is important that we express our basic solidarity with all those who share our goals, even where we differ on means. We feel that the old pacifist tendency to measure everything in terms of means is mistaken; it led to support for any nonviolent movement no matter how reformist its goals and dissociation from a violent movement no matter how desirable its goals.

Martin Luther King's posture strikes us as sound: he deplored the acts of violence but expressed his sympathy with the activists. King expressed on every occasion his own view that nonviolent action was best for social change, even though that implied criticism of violent means.

Even while refusing to condemn those who are driven to violence, and therefore resisting factionalism, we do seek to dissuade them from their course. Their violence endangers us as well as them; it slows the pace of social change and throws allies of the movement into confusion; it plays into the hands of the power elite.

Life against death: Beyond pragmatism

When a movement decides that open struggle is necessary for change, it usually adopts either pacific militancy or violent tactics for pragmatic reasons. Elizabeth Gurley Flynn was not trained by her Marxism to reject violence; she worked to keep strikes nonviolent because that made sense in the situation.

The ecological crisis heightens the pragmatic case for nonviolent strategy. The margin of life for humankind is steadily shrinking. The old image of clearing room for the new society by widespread destruction, then building the new institutions in the vacant space, is obsolete. Each year makes it less likely that human life can survive the destruction which guerrilla war can trigger. We cannot expect the power elite to be ecologically responsible in its means of struggle—it is irresponsible even when unthreatened—so the revolutionary movement must add this dimension to its calculations.

These various practical reasons for pacific militancy—and more could be added—are not for us the whole picture. Civilian rather than military resistance is also a moral question.

Nonviolent struggle is probably the moral *preference* of all humanist revolutionists. That is, given alternative strategies for liberation, they would prefer the nonviolent one. However, few revolutionists seem to take the trouble to develop a nonviolent strategy so they may actually be in a position to choose between alternatives. In fact, we know of no liberation movement which has actually developed a coherent strategy for radical change based on pacific militancy, and then compared it with armed struggle. When a movement claims "We found no alternative" to armed struggle, one must ask whether it looked.

When armed struggle movements say they tried nonviolence, they usually mean that it was tried in the early, reformist days, or that a few nonviolent tactics were tried without a strategy or without knowledge of the other 190-odd nonviolent tactics which have been used historically, or that they expected that the government would not respond with violence when it was threatened nonviolently and therefore the methods were given up when repression came. [9]

Certainly the advocates of nonviolent action are partly to blame for this situation. There has not been nearly enough research or hard-headed thinking in strategic terms; frequently the effectiveness of nonviolent action has been overstated, leading to disillusionment and abandonment of the technique.

Although we are deeply conscious of the inadequacies of pacific militancy as now practiced—it is in the bow-and-arrow stage of development—we find it an ethical imperative that we continue to experiment with it.

Nonviolent struggle seems the best way to raise the truth in a situation of injustice. One's perception is, of course, only relative truth at best, yet to develop a change movement means continually to expose that truth as one sees it. Violence is like a dust-storm; the flurry of discussion of who did what to whom obscures the real issues at stake.

Pacific militancy puts the people first. A strategy based on it will not require us to shell populated areas and conscript people in the *name* of the people. Even the leaders can identify with "the least of these" Jesus's brothers and sisters, rather than regard them as pawns in a struggle for justice.

Pacific militancy affirms the sacredness of life. Even in the heat of conflict we can try to see the enemy as "thou," a fellow human being and a member of one human family.

Nonviolent struggle provides means consistent with humane ends. The classic credibility gap of revolution—today's killing for tomorrow's life-centered world—is closed when we find means which clearly are ends in the making.

No one is in a position to predict the outcome of this or that strategy. A nonviolent strategy may succeed or fail, as may a violent strategy. One cannot make a clear moral judgement between a violent and a nonviolent strategy in terms of consequences, because these are at best informed guesses. One can, however, make an ethical judgement between means, between the character of the actions taken.

Put it another way: people are most responsible, ethically, for what they have most control over. The *outcome* of revolutionary struggle is beyond the control of participants in the movement; the outcome is intertwined with large historical forces beyond anyone's control. What we do have control over, and therefore are responsible for, is the methods we use.

Even in the toughness of struggle against the Empire, we can find celebration. Even in the sorrow of prison terms and death, we can find life. For us, that celebration connects organically to the ability, in the heat of struggle, to affirm life.

[1] See for example Staughton Lynd, *Nonviolence in America,* (New York: Bobbs-Merrill, 1966).

[2] The study, "Hopes and Fears of the American People," was cited by William Moyers in *Newsweek,* October 4, 1971, p. 46.

[3] In *The Wretched of the Earth* (New York: Grove Press, 1966), Fanon discusses, in the appendix, the case of a guerrilla fighter who was afflicted neurotically with nightmares about his killing, by a bomb, people with whom he later was able to identify.

[4] *New York Times,* 7 June 1972, p. 6.

[5] Martin Oppenheimer, *The Urban Guerrilla* (Chicago: Quadrangle Books, 1969).

[6] Patricia Parkman and George Lakey have done historical case studies of several of these incidents. The overthrow of Carlos Ibanez del Campo in Chile, 1931, is described in *New Christian,* 25 December 1969. The toppling of General Maximiliano Hernandez Martinez in El Salvador in 1944 is described in *Peace News,* 14 November 1965. Both these cases are more briefly described, plus a similar civilian insurrection in Guatemala, in *Resistance in Latin America: The Pentagon, the Oligarchies, and Nonviolent Action* by A Quaker Action Group (Philadelphia: American Friends Service Committee, 1970).

In two of these cases a military revolt was tried first, and when it failed, the people resorted to nonviolent struggle.

[7] Hungary might seem an exception here in the revolt of 1956. The revolt could not, however, be sustained for any length of time. It is interesting to note that the Hungarians' general strike had greater staying power than the armed struggle and persisted for some time after the Soviets were able to crush military resistance. See United Nations, *Report of the Special Committee on the Problem of Hungary,* Supplement No. 18 to the Official Records of the Eleventh Session of the General Assembly (N.Y.: United Nations, 1957).

[8] One of the clearest recent cases occurred in Camden, New Jersey, in which Robert W. Hardy stated that he had worked with the F.B.I. at the same time as he was a leader of an anti-war group who planned to destroy draft files. Hardy said the raid, which took place 22 August 1971, could not have taken place without his leadership. The twenty-eight persons at one point seemed to drop the idea until he rekindled it by instructing them on the tactics of carrying out such a raid. *The New York Times,* 16 March 1972.

[9] For the widest survey of nonviolent methods so far undertaken, see Gene Sharp's book, *The Politics of Nonviolent Action,* (Boston: Porter Sargent, 1973). Dr. Sharp has catalogued about 198 tactics so far.

13

Organizing for Social Transformation

CONSCIOUSNESS-RAISING

The success of the struggle for fundamental change in America depends upon the extent to which a large number of people develop an understanding that their "personal" problems are widely shared public issues and acquire a determination to bring about a radically new society. Assuming that there can be no radical change without radical consciousness, the primary goal of the movement must be to bring about a situation where a majority of the people demand that the present system of corporate capitalism be replaced by an entirely new society which might best be described as nonviolent, nonexploitative, democratic, eco-socialism.

Defining and Choosing Issues

In an ideal body politic, problems experienced by individuals would frequently be translated into public issues. But in America, as C. Wright Mills pointed out, the prevailing ideology insists on the reverse. We are supposed to see crime as a personal aberration—and jail the offender and put extra locks on our doors.

In any struggle for change it is necessary for individuals to come together and realize that many of their private troubles will not respond to personal solutions but are political issues which require basic change. Consciousness-raising groups in the women's movement serve this function: women come to see that "it doesn't have to be that way" and that rather than learning how to play the game better, they must change the rules.

Choosing an issue on which to work is not always a clear-cut matter. It may be obvious what the chief source of oppression is in a person's life, but many of us are affected by far more things than we can work on at once. Rather than working on simply any issue we become aroused about, we must learn to deliberately choose issues through which it is easy to generate awareness of structural problems.

Some issues lend themselves better to this than others. Poverty, for example, can be defined in terms of the poor themselves, treating their characteristics (unemployment, low income, high birth rate, etc.) as the cause of their poverty. The resulting programs are then geared to rehabilitate the poor, as in job training, birth control, family counseling, self-help housing, etc. By contrast, we see poverty as a lack of resources relative to others in the society. We notice the rich as well as the poor, and see that 2 percent of the U.S. population holds 85 percent of all stock, nearly 100 percent of state and local bonds, 32 percent of privately-owned wealth, 29 percent of cash, and 36 percent of the mortgage notes. The problem then becomes the gap between the rich and the poor, and the cause lies in the basic social organization, not in the efforts of individuals. We assume that the social institutions of the political economy are the primary distributers of both social benefits (employment, profits, etc.) and social costs (slums, unemployment, etc.). Defining poverty this way translates private troubles into basic issues which must be faced if social justice is ever to inhabit this country.

Ecological crises are also often defined in such a way that their causes are traced to activities of individuals or groups of "others". Remedial programs are then proposed such as picking up trash along highways, buying unleaded gas, and recycling containers; and the world's poor are urged to reduce their birth rates in order to conserve dwindling world resources and end their poverty. Programs such as these, however, direct attention away from the real structural causes of ecological crises: a political economy of technological and industrial overdevelopment, over-production, and over-consumption. Our skyrocketing GNP and the very burning of fuel, regardless of additives, are *ipso facto* villains of the ecological crisis. And the problem of dwindling world resources is not the result of Third World population growth—200 million U.S. citizens consume the equivalent of what 10.5 billion Indians would consume.[1] We need to choose our issues and define them in such a way that it becomes obvious that individual solutions are no longer sufficient and we need structural change.

Putting Forward Alternatives

In addition to having an analysis of issues as requiring systemic change, however, it is crucial that visions of a fundamentally new society be introduced into the political debate. The vision of what life could be like under the new society must continually be projected so that people will become increasingly aware of the difference between life as it is in America today and life as it can be with a new social organization of the political economy and a new set of social values.

This model for fundamental social change is a drastic departure from most traditional humanitarian efforts in the United States, which have assumed that successive incremental changes within the present social system would eventually bring about the good society. It is a model, however, much more firmly supported by social change theorists. James C. Davies, for example, in his historical study of radical social change, concludes that social change requires new consciousness—that people demand change only if their perceived actual social conditions do not meet their expectations.[2] And Thomas Kuhn, in *The Structure of Scientific Revolutions,* found that people will continue to believe in the old, "accepted" model, even if it no longer makes sense to them, until an entirely new system is clearly presented to them as a viable alternative so they can (1) compare the presently accepted system to reality, (2) compare the new alternative system to reality, and (3) compare the present and alternative systems to each other.[3]

Mass Education Movement

One important method to develop mass consciousness is direct education. What is required is a nation-wide movement consisting of perhaps thousands of educational programs, varied to fit different ages, class backgrounds, cultures, etc. Mass education of this type has played an important part in social revolutions in a number of societies. The learning process might include: (1) sharing oppressions participants feel personally and locating their causes;[4] (2) sharing information and viewpoints on the present United States' and other super-powers' political-economic systems; (3) weighing histories and theories of revolutionary change against the actual situation we are facing; and (4) relating each of the above to immediate possibilities for social change action.

Seminars, games, and audio-visual aids are already being developed which cover these topics.[5] Also, speaking tours could be arranged for persons from nations such as Sweden, China, Chile, Yugoslavia, Cuba, and Tanzania. These would be augmented by "experiential" educational methods such as street-speaking, speakers' bureaus, participation in direct action campaigns, and work-learn visits within and outside the United States.

BUILDING ORGANIZATION

"The revolt [of the American colonists] against the British government was not a vast, spontaneous movement. Instead, it was carefully planned by shrewd men (sic) and laboriously and sagaciously executed by some of the most active spirits on the continent. *It could never have succeeded if it had been left unorganized.* It was in part because the patriots were well organized, and because the Tories or loyalists were not, that the former won the day."

—Allan Nevins and Henry Steele Commager,
A Pocket History of the United States

Power

Power is necessary for change to a new society. Changed attitudes alone will not change institutions: no matter how many individuals "have their consciousness raised", the structures they participate in will remain essentially oppressive and unyielding.

A frequent mistake of idealists is to think that ideas by themselves have power. Even the best ideas require years of advocacy and organizing before they come into popular consciousness. There must be organization of large numbers of people to incarnate an idea and give it a form which can sustain struggle.

A majority of Americans were in favor of strong gun control measures in 1936, according to a Gallup poll, but today we are still endangered by millions of loose guns in the U.S. The gun lobby, with a highly organized constituency, has power, while unorganized public opinion does not.

Sometimes an aroused public taking action in the streets can force change. It seems clear that the widespread protests in May 1970 against the invasion of Cambodia and shooting of students at Kent State and Jackson State Universities forced President Nixon, against his will and military logic, to withdraw U.S. troops from Cambodia. This is probably the first time in recent U.S. history that anti-war sentiment forced a major reversal of wartime strategy in midstream.

Without organization of power, democracy is impossible. A spontaneous rising is liable to manipulation by a vanguard elite or by a charismatic leader. A mass of people who are not organized into small communities of trust and political discussion results in demagoguery, not democracy. Democracy requires consensus, which requires discussion, which requires ground rules, which requires structure. We can structure a movement to be elitist or to be populist, depending on whether or not we stress open communication, rotation in leadership roles, explicit conflict mechanisms, and education. While all organization tends, under "the iron law of oligarchy", toward bureaucratization, checks can be built in and decentralist structures devised. When power is organized, democracy is at least possible; when decision-making is left to impulse and circumstance, democracy is impossible.

Why a Mass Movement

We advocate a mass movement as the agency for fundamental change. Some people argue for a strategy of *permeation*—that individual radicals should join existing structures in order to bore from within. Permeation assumes a more hardy human being than we are familiar with, however. Individuals bombarded each day in their work situation entirely by pressures to conform would have to be moral giants to avoid co-optation; so many sad examples of sold-out left liberals dot our political landscape that we need hardly argue further. The only hope we see for a permeation strategy is when people within existing structures consciously join together in mutual study, support, and action groups—sometimes called "radical caucuses"—to struggle for far-reaching change.

Another alternative is keeping our own base clearly outside the framework and using that point of moral clarity to speak truth to power. Unfortunately, that alternative assumes that ideas have more impact than they actually do in the rough-and-tumble of politics. People practicing this alternative sometimes adopt the establishment's basic framework to communicate with establishment representatives, and over time find themselves accommodated to the status quo as it basically is.

We might hope that the route to fundamental change lies through one of the major political parties, since these are highly legitimate in our society. As we have pointed out previously however, the parties are controlled by the rich who support them, and are therefore unlikely agencies for basic changes such as eliminating wealth as well as concentrated power, socializing the means of production, and de-developing our affluent American life-style. (Later in this chapter we discuss some of the arguments for and against a revolutionary political party.)

Social movements in the United States which have been mass movements have, however, made broad changes: the movements for the abolition of slavery, woman suffrage, industrial trade unions, and civil rights are examples.

Mass movements mean mass struggle as well as organization. While some might argue for many small-scale campaigns rather than large-scale struggles, the latter provide a multiplier effect because of the greater publicity around them. People in other parts of the country (and outside the country) are more likely to be inspired to act by major conflict, as when the 1936 industrial sit-downs in France touched off similar sit-downs in Michigan.

We are urging that power is necessary for fundamental change and that power should be channeled by mass democratic movements. The question remains: in what forms might the revolutionary movement productively be organized?

Organizational Forms

Organizing is already occurring in the consciousness-raising process, in study circles, street-speaking groups, and travel seminars. We suggest four local and immediate organizational forms which serve educational needs as well as being units for struggle: (1) nonviolent revolutionary groups, (2) radical caucuses, (3) counter-institutions, and (4) training centers. These are only four among many other possibilities.

(1) *Nonviolent Revolutionary Groups* (NRG's) arise from already existing friendships, workplace ties, religious affiliations, etc., and range in size from about three

to twelve individuals. They grow as cells grow, by division, and can proliferate rapidly when conditions are ripe. They seek to live the revolution *now,* sharing simple life-styles even while preparing for the emergence of a mass revolutionary movement. The Groups serve the people, teach a revolutionary perspective, and develop their ability to use direct action.

The Nonviolent Revolutionary Groups should have enough analysis and broad strategy in common that they can help each other at critical points. They are not directed by a central committee, however, and they develop their own particular strategies in the light of their varying circumstances. Some will want to work within the coalition of poverty and anti-war groups, helping in that way to build a mass movement with radical goals. Other NRG's may focus on frontier issues such as ending U.S. support of Third World dictatorships or gay libera-tion.

The team as the building block of a mass movement makes sense because it meets the dilemma of collectivism versus individualism. Unlike some of the old communist cells it is not secret or conspiratorial; therefore, it cannot hold individuals to it rigidly with implicit threats. On the other hand there is sufficient community to give the individual support and criticism, to overcome the isola-tion of an individual stand, and to allow for sharing of skills, insights, and analysis as well as common action.

The often criticized tendency in mass movements for a kind of mob hysteria to sweep people away is not likely in a movement made of teams. On the other hand, the positive movement feelings of joy and celebration of community can be captured by teams. The solidarity which enables people to withstand the terror of repres-sion is even more likely in teams than in an unstructured mass facing waterhoses or bullets. Studies of combatants in battlefield conditions have shown that the solidarity of the small unit is crucial in conquering fear and withstand-ing attack. Fear, of course, is the central weapon of repression. In a movement of small groups we may hold hands against repression and continue to resist.

(2) Another form which serves the movement is the *radical caucus*. Many occupational groupings now have radical caucuses within them: social workers, miners, scientists, teachers, auto workers, health workers, lawyers, and so on. The radicals function as what the British call a "ginger group": they combine to press the group to take more advanced stands on political and social issues. The pressure often includes direct action at the national conferences and conventions of these occupational groups.

The importance of the radical caucus is the close linkage to the non-radicals in the occupation; this ensures a dialogue and reduces the chance of isolation. Revolutionary ideas can in this way influence important elements of society, especially if the radical caucuses do not get distracted into mere power games with the leadership of the association or union.

(3) *Counter-institutions* provide another fertile area for organizing. Alternatives such as expanded families (communes), free schools, land trusts, community medical clinics, and producers' and consumers' cooperatives teach people that our goals can be reached through cooperation rather than through me-first competition; discovering that we have untapped power has revolutionary implications. Counter-institutions also make it possible for many people to live more frugally by sharing resources, avoiding middlemen, and spending time rather than money on needed services. Over time, counter-institutions may develop into total counter-communities where not just one but many common resources are developed.

Alternative economic enterprises by themselves are no match for multi-national corporations. They also require capital, skills, and/or time commitments that are more readily available to middle class people than to poor and working class people. But as long as counter-institutions are seen as *part* of a strategy for change rather than as the whole program, and as *means* to fundamental change rather than wholly as ends in themselves, they can provide a source of discipline and solidarity for sustained struggle.

(4) *Training communities* are springing up in the United States, taking the form of schools for social change or nonviolent training and action centers. Like Gandhi's ashrams they can provide "staging areas" for action campaigns, in which the necessary skills, strategies, and solidarity are developed. By developing thousands of "graduates" who are committed to non violence and who are skilled in developing nonviolent strategies and tactics, such centers can reduce the movements' dependence on charismatic individual leaders. Movement for a New Society, with training/action communities springing up in many parts of the country, is combining several of the organizational forms described here.

Unifying the Movement

A scatter of organizations is not enough to contest the entrenchment of the power elite. Since the mid-sixties in the United States there has been a growth in the tendency toward unity, taking the form of coalitions. One major effort was the Poor People's Campaign of 1968, which brought native Americans, blacks, poor whites, Chicanos, and others into alliance for a short period. Another was the anti-war coalition which embraced a variety of issues including poverty, war, and racism.

The growth of coalitions is a welcome development, but it does not yet reflect a very high degree of unity, and therefore cannot communicate a fundamental analysis of our society nor a vision of a better one.

We look forward to the development of a revolutionary movement which can link NRG's, radical caucuses, and other revolutionary groups. A *network* of communication, gatherings, exchanges of people, and sharing of literature can (1) foster the articulation of radical analysis and vision, (2) provide a broader base of support for local autonomous groups through mutual aid, and (3) coordinate the struggle in its mass phase.

Linkage could take place in this way: local groups

could share their views on analysis, vision, and strategy through newsletters and intervisitation. As a local group engaged in a nonviolent action campaign neared a confrontation on a significant issue, resources from the network of groups and communities could be put into the struggle to make it successful. Sometimes the struggle would achieve national or even international proportions. The groups working at the local level would define problems in terms of the way society is organized at the national level. Solutions to local problems would be defined in terms of a new political economy—a new society.

Eventually it might be important for this kind of loose linkage of groups involved in struggle to be regularized into a regional or national council system to interrelate their efforts on the same issues, to lend credibility to small local groups, and to deal with oppression in a concerted way. Of course, even with representatives at every level elected by the people they represent and with discussion of major decisions at every level, problems of bureaucracy are bound to surface in the long run. It would be possible to ensure that constituents' wishes were followed by having representatives bound to vote as their constituencies decided (by referendum or other procedure); but the need for a rapid, responsive process in the councils militates against having bound representatives. Full prior discussion of issues and mandatory regular reporting back to constituencies may be a satisfactory mechanism. In any case, if the movement is not to become deadened with bureaucracy, it must be prepared to lay down its structures every few years and seek out new forms.

A Revolutionary Political Party

One organizational form that has not been discussed here and that is an historically tested route for changing societies is the revolutionary political party. You will recall that in our scenario we were not clear about the role of the political factor in the movement for revolutionary change—political in the sense of an organized movement that works to mobilize a majority behind its program in order to elect candidates for public office.

This issue is put in its sharpest form by the question: Mustn't there be organized, at some point, a mass-based, democratically-controlled new party, a revolutionary party which will advocate an American form of humanistic socialism, run candidates for national office, and try to gain control of the government?

We feel that advocates of radical change should not try to form a political party now or in the immediate future. The task of the years immediately ahead is to do a great deal of organizing and educational work to develop a strong, nonviolent people's movement committed to fundamental change in America's political economy. We also feel that, if a party is ever formed, it should be intimately related to the nonviolent people's movement i.e., a political wing of the people's movement. (This would be in contrast to the times in history when people's movements have been dominated by a revolutionary party.)

Thus, we feel relatively clear about timing and about the form of a party, *if there should be a party at all.* But this latter point is one of the important matters that we have not been able to resolve. Would it be valuable for the people's movement to have a political wing, and should it engage in electoral campaigns?

Arguments FOR a Political-Electoral Approach

1.   We are intrigued by countries such as Chile, Finland, and Sweden, and by Canadian provinces like Saskatchewan and Manitoba, in which socialist-oriented governments have gained power by nonviolent, electoral, and/or parliamentary means and have been able to use the leverage of governmental office to bring about far-reaching changes. Although the economies of these areas are still largely capitalistic, the economic sector has been humanized to a high degree and the governing parties are pressing for full-scale socialism. These historical examples

suggest that the electoral route can be an important lever in working for fundamental change.

2.   An electoral approach is basically democratic. Rather than relying on coups or other elitist forms of change, it requires education of the public and winning a majority to support a revolutionary platform. Also, as Engels pointed out[6], electoral politics makes possible counting supporters, judging the strength of the opposition, getting in touch with the public and doing educational work, and having opportunities for debate with other parties in public view.

3.   It has been observed (by Che Guevara among others) that people won't support revolutionary methods until reforms within the system have been exhausted. Until the electoral route has proven itself of no further value, people will look to it rather than endorsing a mass nonviolent movement.

4.   Once governmental power is achieved, the legal and administrative structure of government can be used to bring about and to sustain fundamental change, e.g., the setting up of the comprehensive system to guarantee income, work, health care, etc., which are part of the new society's vision. While unusual, it is not unknown for a central government (e.g., Yugoslavia) to implement decentralized people's power, which we also see as crucial to the new society. A party could run on a platform calling for both decentralization and transnationalization of many of the functions and powers of the central government.

5.   In one sense, an electoral party approach is inevitable. That is, if a nonviolent people's movement begins really to gain mass adherence, there *will be* a political response in the form of candidates who will run on platforms embodying the people's concerns and in the form of political organizations which seek to represent the people's new consciousness. So, we might argue, there will be a political-electoral response anyway; why not take advantage of it and try to influence it in the right direction?

Arguments AGAINST a Political-Electoral Approach

1.   Almost the entire thrust of liberal and socialist thought during the past century has focused on strengthening the nation-state as a way of moving forward. But we have grave reservations about the nation-state, particularly a state which encompasses 200 million people. Its vast power makes it almost inevitable that it will use up far more than its share of world resources and that it will be tempted to military adventurism. Perhaps the goal of a nonviolent people's movement should be the *dismantling* of the American Goliath, rather than taking it over. Yet the goal of the electoral process is the achievement of control *over* the nation-state. Would such control be an advantage, or an albatross around the movement's neck?
2.   The party-electoral route facilitates control at the center. It tends to validate and sanction central bureaucracies of government and party. Yet the challenge of the kind of social change we have been describing is to build *people's* power, rather than make people subservient to power centers far removed from their daily lives. The issue shouldn't be posed as "taking power", but as "redistributing power". The goal is not to elect a benevolent vanguard who run the central government for the benefit of the people, but to return power to the people.
3.   Leaders of a people's movement should achieve legitimacy, not in partisan debate, but in leadership in the streets; not for their skill in traditional parliamentary games, but for their ability to facilitate a shared group process. People need to learn the skills of mass nonviolent action, and electoral action will divert their energies from this important task.
4.   Politics inevitably involves compromise, or watering down of goals and objectives. This can be true of people's movements as well as parliamentary debates, but the technique of nonviolent direct action gives a people's movement a tool for accomplishing nonviolent change without compromising its principles. Its nature is large-scale open struggle, where the people can see what is going on. Electoral politics, on the other hand, is based

on compromise, often behind closed doors. Revolutions are betrayed, not by the people, but by their leaders.

5.   Even if candidates running on a people's platform were elected to Congress, they would find that they have very little power, since so much real decision-making in the country now emanates from the Pentagon, the White House, and the corporate hierarchy. Yet, in order to get elected, candidates would need to promise that they can deliver meaningful changes—when they fail to do so, demoralization sets in. The choice seems to be between strong radical candidates who don't compromise and don't get elected, or candidates who are elected but find that they don't have any real power.

6.   When radical candidates do achieve political office, they find that the immediate imperatives of staying in power demand policies that prevent the flight of capital, maintain growth, and so on. For this reason, many radical parties are more radical when they're not in office.

The Transition in the Two Routes

Because of our inability to reconcile these two points of view, we wrote our scenario in Chapter 11 with two endings, one brought about by a people's movement with a political wing using electoral methods along with direct action, the other brought about by a non-party people's movement which stays away from elections entirely.

In the *movement-electoral party route* to change, we envisage a revolutionary party, controlled and supported by a nonviolent people's movement, which wins elections and eventually gains a majority in Congress and control of the presidency. Using education and legislation, it sets about the transformation of the political and economic system, creating public corporations, setting up cooperatives and worker-controlled enterprises, passing a maximum income and assets law, organizing a comprehensive planning system, dismantling the military forces, setting up child-care facilities and social and medical services, working out equitable relationships with the Third World, transnationalizing some functions fomerly filled by federal government, and so on. When it meets resistance from entrenched wealth, privilege, and power, it cooperates with the people's movement, using nonviolent protest, noncooperation, and intervention to support its initiatives. If faced by an attempted coup d'etat, it uses the same kind of noncooperation that was so effective in preventing the 1920 coup of Wolfgang Kapp in Germany. (Kapp was established in power by a group of military officers, but was faced immediately with a complete general strike, including even the civil service. This was so effective that the erstwhile head of government found himself wandering up and down the corridors of power looking in vain for someone to issue his proclamations. Despite his efforts to repress the resistance by shooting unarmed demonstrators, Kapp found himself without the means of governing and fled to Sweden.[7])

In the *people's movement-non-electoral route,* the transition comes about after the establishment finds itself unable to make any more concessions. An active and well-organized people's movement has engaged in widespread demonstrations, mass boycotts, and strikes, all aimed at protesting existing inequities and demanding radical change to a new kind of economic and political order. At first, the government and corporate system is able to make concessions in the shape of reforms, but eventually every "outpost" of reform is taken and the "fortress" is reached[8]—the establishment realizes that it cannot give further changes without radical reduction in its privileges and power.

Discredited and confronted on every hand by protesting groups, it tries to defend its privilege, but finds that even the formerly reliable police and military can no longer be counted upon because of movement fraternization and nonviolent tactics. Repression discredits the government still further. Eventually, the government and business establishment find themselves powerless to prevent radical caucuses and workers' cadres from taking over existing institutions and factories, or to stop local action groups from occupying and controlling the organizations of local and national life. These action groups, parallel institutions, radical caucuses, and other people's groups elect representatives to regional "Congresses of Free Americans", to which more and more citizens pay their taxes and which become, in effect, the functioning government. The old, delegitimized structure of government and corporations collapses and is replaced by new structures which grow directly out of people's institutions. The regional Congresses institute much the same kind of eco-democratic socialist system described in the movement-electoral-party route, and then cooperate with revolutionary movements in other countries in creating transnational institutions.

The Need for Further Discussion

The kind of revolution that we are advocating—with its nonviolent methodology, its particular view of a desired future, its emphasis on the ecological imperative, its democratic participation—has never before been achieved. Therefore, although we can learn from history, there are no existing historical models to tell us the best direction when we come to the transition stage. For this reason, we look forward to intense dialogue among those who believe in a living revolution to come to greater clarity concerning the best route to follow.

But there is no need to delay action until such a dialogue is far advanced. We can begin *now* in the tasks of consciousness-raising and organization-building, and can begin *now* to "live the revolution" in our own lives.

[1] For some related figures see Dennis Pirages and Paul R. Ehrlich, "If All Chinese Had Wheels," *The New York Times* (March 16, 1972).

[2] James C. Davies, "The J-Curve of Rising and Declining Satisfactions as a Cause of Some Great Revolutions and a Contained Rebellion", in *Violence in America,* National Commission on the Causes and Prevention of Violence, June 1969.

[3] Thomas S. Kuhn, *The Structure of Scientific Revolutions* (Chicago: University of Chicago Press, 1962).

[4] Peasants in China called this "speaking bitterness".

[5] One effort in this direction is the "macro-analysis seminars" developed by the Macro-analysis Collective of the Movement for a New Society. See Chapter 15 for information on these seminars and the macro-analysis manual.

[6] Frederick Engels, introduction to Karl Marx's essay, "The Class Struggles in France, 1848-50", in *Karl Marx and Frederick Engels: Selected Works, Vol. I* (Moscow: Foreign Languages Publishing House, 1955), p. 129.

[7] George Lakey, *Strategy for a Living Revolution* (NY: Grossman; and San Francisco: W. H. Freeman, 1973), pp. 126-7.

[8] Martin Oppenheimer, *The Urban Guerrilla* (Chicago: Quadrangle Books, 1969), pp. 164-5.

14

Reform or Revolution?

REVOLUTIONARY REFORM:
The Movement in a "Pre-Transition" Society

We are living in a socio-economic-political system which needs to be fundamentally changed. We hope, in the future, to live in a society which is much more supportive of human dignity, world community, and ecological harmony. To move from the present system to a new one involves a "transition" to socio-economic-political institutions which are radically different from those of the present system. Therefore, we are living now in what may be termed a "pre-transition society".

Resistance to Change

But will there be a transition at all? Certainly not, if no effective power is generated to challenge the present system and to build a new one. The present arrangement of institutions exploits many millions of human beings here and abroad, and conveys vast wealth and power to the privileged few. We believe that these privileged few are trapped by a system which undercuts their ability to act according to values such as love, shared power, and world community. This system requires them, in fact, to act in a way directly contrary to such values. They are expected to continue to maximize their privilege. One of

270

the lessons of history is that wealth, power, and privilege will be defended by those who benefit from them; although concessions can be made, there will certainly be strong resistance to any attempt to greatly reduce such wealth and power.

Another source of resistance to transition is rationalizations for the status quo: "Our free enterprise system is the best in the world"; "People who foment radical change are communists"; "The poor, the unemployed, and public assistance recipients are lazy"; etc. These myths sustain many who do *not* share in the system's wealth and power in the belief that, nevertheless, the present system is a desirable one. Those who believe in the desirability of the present system and who do not envisage a better one can be expected to support the resistance to change. So also can the many who, while not sharing *vast* wealth, have been brought to a degree of relative comfort and affluence within the system, and who fear that major change will harm them.

Given this resistance, then, the "pre-transition" phase is a time in which significant preparatory work needs to be done if there is to be a transition at all.

Revolutionary Reform

We have already described several aspects of this preparatory work, e.g., conscientization and mass education, organization-building, nonviolent direct action, the development of nonviolent revolutionary groups, radical caucuses, training centers, and counter-institutions. We have said very little so far, however, about the targets of this preparatory work in the *existing* political and economic system. Should we simply ignore present political and economic institutions? Or are there specific political and economic changes which the movement should advocate in the pre-transition period?

Some advocates of social change believe that it is futile—perhaps even harmful—to work for such changes. They fear that any partial steps forward within the present framework will simply reinforce it and make it more durable. They worry that the movement will become so caught up in "reformism" that it will forget its real mandate of bringing about change toward a new society.

We agree that the main focus of action must be on the development of the movement itself and the building of a new society within the shell of the old. Thus our stress on education, organization-building, and the development of counter-institutions. But we cannot agree that amelioration and limited change in the present political economy is always worthless. There are specific changes which, while limited in scope, would do much to relieve human suffering and ease the burden of fear which hangs over so many millions of people. For example, we support all efforts to change the policies and practices of American government and business so that they will eliminate the hunger and malnutrition which afflict some 20 million destitute Americans, even though the changes required to bring everyone an adequate diet would not necessarily be revolutionary. Our concern is that human life be more full, loving, and joyful, and it would be cynical indeed to sacrifice real present betterment of life in hopes that the continued suffering of the hungry will inspire revolutionary fervor. Similarly, we support the defense of civil liberties, even though this may not raise structural issues. The freedom to speak out, to gather people together, and to publish unpopular points of view—on economic as well as political issues—is vital to our vision of a democratic society. These freedoms may easily be taken away in a period of social upheaval, it is true, but the battle to maintain or restore them can be a consciousness-raising one for many people. People expect civil liberties, and will be radicalized in the fight to maintain them.

Secondly, we agree with French theoretician Andre Gorz that it is necessary to work for *revolutionary reforms,* i.e., "reforms which advance toward a radical transformation of society".[1] That is, there are changes in the present political economy which, while not immediately ushering in the new society in toto, nevertheless advance us toward it. Such "non-reformist reforms" bring the future into the present and strengthen the movement's power to bring about a more fundamental change.

Criteria for Revolutionary Reform

Although it is not always possible to distinguish in advance between a reformist and a revolutionary reform, the latter is always characterized by (A) *a shift in power* from established political, economic, and cultural elites and toward oppressed or powerless people such as workers, minority groups, women, and people in their own local neighborhoods; (B) *objectives* consistent with long-range goals for a new society, based on a thorough-going analysis of present society; and (C) *a heightened consciousness* among people as to the need for a radically new society. This suggests that a revolutionary reform may be judged by the following criteria:

(A) A revolutionary reform involves *an extension of people's control,* by which people are enabled to exercise a greater degree of power, either directly or by making those with decision-making power directly responsible to them. Usually, this will involve:

(1) An erosion of power, privilege, wealth, and legitimacy from institutions and groups in whose hands these have been concentrated: e.g., the nation-state; private, profit-oriented capital; technological elites; men; whites; etc.

(2) Decentralization of decision-making power to workers and community people, and equalization of such power among them (e.g., between men and women, between racial groups, etc.).

(3) An increase in movement resources which builds the movement's strength by such means as enhancing the mechanisms of transformation to a new society (e.g., more NRG's, counter-institutions, etc.); increasing the numbers, understanding, and commitment of people involved in social change; and strengthening the internal democracy, effectiveness, and commitment to non-

   violence of social change groups.

(B) A revolutionary reform is based on and effectively communicates to others a *goal for a new society* that reflects a radical analysis of the existing society. Goals for revolutionary reform grow out of an understanding of the links between oppressive conditions and their causes in social structures, of the consequences of an issue for other parts of the world and for future generations, of viable alternatives that could replace present institutions, and of a strategy for change of which the given revolutionary reform is a part.

(c) A revolutionary reform involves a *heightening of people's consciousness,* by which more and more people grow in understanding that present problems are caused by the failure of the present political economy, that a new and better society is possible, and that means are available to move toward it. This will usually involve:

  (1) A more critical view, on the part of the public or sections of it, of establishment perspectives and solutions and a heightened sense of the inadequacies of the present system and the need for a better one.

  (2) Greater public sympathy for revolutionary perspectives and approaches.

  (3) A deeper analysis by the social change movement itself and an increased ability to communicate to others its analysis, vision, and strategy for social change.

Perhaps an example will illustrate how these criteria may be used to choose an action:

  The goal of the proposed campaign is examined in light of the group's analysis of the societal causes of the problem it is seeking to address. A number of generative themes for action have been suggested in the course of the analysis presented in the preceding chapters: ending U.S. support of foreign dictatorships, ending poverty through providing universal services, "de-developing" the

U.S. to reduce its level of consumption, sharing equitably the wealth and power that are denied to many groups in society, etc. With a goal that reflects a searching analysis, a project is devised that seeks to meet the other criteria.

Take, for example, the tenants' rights movement, led nationally by the Washington-based National Tenants' Organization (NTO) and supported locally by innumerable tenants' councils, rent-strike groups, tenants' unions, etc., across the country. A major objective of NTO is that tenants, in both public and private housing have real control over the decisions affecting them in their housing situations.

Let us assume that the achievement of this objective requires a vast extension of cooperative, tenant-controlled housing throughout the private housing market, and the establishment of a high degree of tenant control in public housing planning, management, and budget allocation. Both cooperative ownership and tenant control would reduce the power of landlords, housing speculators, banks, real estate interests, and public housing authorities—whose boards of directors are usually drawn from the local power structure (criterion A. 1.)—and shift this power considerably to millions of tenants and tenants' organizations in cities and towns across the country (A.2.). To the extent that NTO and like organizations at the local level participate in the process of demanding changes and then implementing and controlling them, resources will also shift to the social change movement (A.3.). Since our vision of a better economic system includes a situation in which "practically all housing could be constructed by housing cooperatives and could be owned cooperatively," a decisive move toward co-ops in this field would also meet the criterion (B.) of being consistent with our goals for a new society. To the extent that initiatives for tenant control are interpreted as part of a move toward greater economic democracy and expose the concentration of wealth and power in the real estate industry, the tenant union movement also meets criterion (C.).

What a Revolutionary Reform Is Not

It should be clear from the foregoing discussion of the nature of revolutionary reform that programs aimed at gaining *individual advancement,* and programs that seek improvements for disadvantaged groups *without reducing the power and privilege of the established groups* will never help more than a small number of people. Because such reforms are not directed at redistributing the wealth and power concentrated at the pinnacle of society, they can only benefit those they do by disbenefiting others who are not much better off. Whether adding to the tax burden of others, threatening their small measure of security, or even costing others their jobs, this reshuffling of the scant resources of the powerless creates animosities and divisions among them rather than unifying them around a common goal. Furthermore, because much publicity can be made of a few people being helped, many more people can be bought off thereby from joining a movement for broader change.

For the most part, we would also include efforts to organize people under the auspices of *federal government programs* as reformist reforms. As long as the government, operating hand-in-glove with the multi-national corporate hierarchy, sets a policy of leaving millions unemployed, and so forth, federal programs in community organizing smack of creating a company union. These programs are controlled at the top or are used as political leverage for mayors instead of being genuine moves toward decentralization or shared power. Furthermore, they are thoroughly vulnerable to budget cuts (or, as with President Nixon, impoundments).

A reformist reform aims for what seems *politically realistic,* while a revolutionary reform strives for a chosen goal no matter how immediately unlikely it may seem. In fact, radical demands, even if not met in full, are likely at the very least to bring about as a compromise the same result as reformist reforms—meanwhile raising public consciousness about the need for sweeping change.

The chart below lists some possible reforms, with a checklist showing to what extent they meet the criteria we have suggested. Some of them clearly do not meet enough of the criteria to be considered revolutionary reforms. Others fulfill many or most of the criteria. (A "+" indicates that the reform meets the criterion; a "p" indicates that it may *possibly* meet the criterion, depending on how the reform is implemented; a "−" indicates that the criterion is not met.

REFORM	People's Control			Revolutionary Goal	Heightened Consciousness		
	Erosion Establishment	Decentralization	Augment Movement		Critical	Sympathetic	Analysis
Spread of tenant control	+	+	p	+	p	p	p
National system of free child-care, locally controlled	p	+	+	+	p	p	p
Campaign to end U.S. support for dictators	+	p	p	+	+	p	+
Spread of worker-community control in industry	+	+	p	+	+	p	p
Real tax reform	+	p	p	+	+	p	p
Job training for the unemployed	−	−	−	−	−	−	−
Campaign for corporate responsibility	−	−	p	−	p	p	−

Choosing Actions

We need to propagate our message through action. In the previous chapter we discussed the importance of education and organization-building. In this chapter, we outlined some considerations in selecting an area for action. The nonviolent campaign is the process whereby the Nonviolent Revolutionary Groups, radical caucuses, and other vehicles of change test out their understanding and their strategies in the real world of struggle; it is a many-step process which respects the dignity of the opponent in the movement's pursuit of the truth. Each step is important: defining the issue, carefully researching it, spelling out demands for change, and negotiating for these. A campaign then moves up to public education, building organizational strength, and winning allies. If its goals have not yet been reached, it moves into direct bodily confrontation with injustice and oppression.

The best kind of action is that which puts the guardians of the status quo in a *dilemma*—whichever response they make helps the movement. If they allow the demonstration to proceed, we gain that opportunity to educate the people. If they repress the demonstration, the people are awakened further to the underlying nature of the regime. If the movement is prepared, it will maintain a nonviolent spirit which even more strongly contrasts with the violence of the repression.

For example, in 1971, demonstrators in canoes attempted to block cargo ships in the ports of Philadelphia, Baltimore, Boston, and New York from leaving those harbors with U.S. military or economic aid bound for Pakistan, at the time of Pakistan's cruel slaughter of thousands of then East Pakistanis. Because of the publicity the demonstrators created, some of the ships bound for Pakistan were not able to pick up cargoes. Those that did attempt to leave the harbors with cargoes provided the demonstrators with an opportunity to educate many TV viewers about the American role in the civil strife in Pakistan.

In deciding whether to initiate or join a campaign to press for a particular reform, a group can make use of the criteria outlined in this chapter or some similar evaluation system. The important thing is to define *problems* in terms of the failures of the present political economy and *solutions* in terms of a vision of a new society and the strength needed to move toward it. Thus the campaign itself will be an education in the nature of the present system and the need for a better one.

TRANSITION TO A NEW POLITICAL ECONOMY

It is extremely difficult to try to peer into the murky future and to speculate about how a completely new society might come into being. Here is an area in which judgement, prophecy, utopianism, unanticipated historical events, and human fallibility are inextricably mixed. How much easier it would be to content ourselves with the years immediately ahead, to see ourselves as confronting immediate injustices and struggling for short-range humanizing reforms, forgetting about visions of a possible future with a radically different political and economic system.

Yet we are committed to the view that the present political economy must be replaced by a better one. Therefore, we must ask ourselves, not just how the present system can be reformed, but how its replacement can come about.

Revolutionary Transformation

We are clear that, at some point, we must move from a "pre-transition society" to a transition—a revolutionary transformation in which truly fundamental change in power relationships takes place. Our view is illustrated in the following chart:

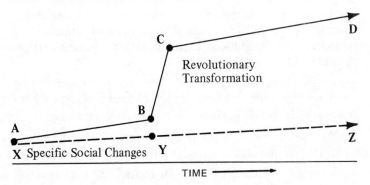

Many persons and groups working for social change view each specific reform as a step along the road toward the "good society". They work for incremental change, or what Andre Gorz calls "reformist reform". On our chart, they follow the dotted line, XYZ. We, on the other hand, see ourselves working along the line ABCD. During the time period AB, the pre-transition period, we are working for revolutionary reforms. The purpose of such reforms is not only to relieve human suffering and to reduce injustice, but also to heighten social consciousness as to the need for more far-reaching changes and to strengthen the vehicles whose nonviolent power can actually bring about the revolutionary transformation of society.

As we have said previously, we're not clear whether the shift of power will come about through an electoral or a non-electoral route, but when it occurs we can expect to see, for example:

—not only the *reform* of guaranteed minimum incomes, but the revolutionary step of setting maximum limits on income and assets, a step which eliminates wealth as well as poverty;

—not just the spread of tenant control of housing, but an entire housing industry controlled by consumer cooperatives;

—not just experiments with listener-supported radio and TV, but an entire system of popularly controlled mass media which are no longer run by big business;

—not just the extension of worker and community influence on industry, but the *control* of industry by workers and consumers through socially owned corporations and cooperatives;

—not just laws which "allow" women increased rights, but a basic shift in power which creates a system where women claim full participation in decision making;

—not only a redistribution of income, but an *end* to private incomes from rents, interest, and dividends;

—not simply limits on the profit motive, but its *replace-*

ment by cooperative enterprises and by comprehensive, decentralized planning;

—not only attacks on growth and consumerism, but the planned "de-development" of this grossly over-developed nation—thereby reducing the need for military defenses;

—not only reduction of military influence, but the dismantling of the military machine and its replacement by a nonviolent civilian defense system;

—not only an end to hot wars such as in Indochina, but an end to U.S. political and economic exploitation of other nations.

---

[1] André Gorz, *Strategy for Labor* (Boston: Beacon Press, 1967), p. 6 ff.

15

Living the Revolution

We have written a great deal in this book about the vision of a better society and the need to generate a powerful movement in the direction of that vision. There is a danger, however, of becoming too fascinated with the goal, the vision, the ends of our action. We cannot be sure that our ends will be attained, whereas we can be sure that the revolutionary means we use are in keeping with the world which we envision for our selves and our children.

> "If the great virtues and teachings of the martyrs, resisters and saints are relegated to a utopian or future-oriented condition, then indeed, they have little value for us at all. But the great heritage that this 'community of liberation' has left us is not some unreal, impossible dream. It is this: Love can, and must be lived today, despite the pain and difficulty of such life. Tomorrow will carry the tenderness and peace which we live now. Do not compromise today. It is all, dear brothers and sisters, that we have." [1]

We are convinced that the American political economy must be radically transformed. We want to build a new society whose institutions will carry out the necessary work and will encourage the development of full, loving persons. But we are clear that such a new society will not evolve unless the agents of social change are doing all they can to become full, loving persons themselves. That kind of new society will not be sustained unless it is thoroughly infiltrated by loving and joyous people whose commitment is to such values as justice, community, cooperation, simplicity, world equality, shared power, mutual well-being, and harmony with nature.

Economic and political structures can do much to enhance human dignity or to crush it, to enable love to find expression or to subvert it, but no system can automatically assure that humans will behave toward one another in a spirit of caring and justice. Ultimately, such behavior depends upon choices made deep within each person, and such choices are crucial if a real revolution for life is to come about. Inward and outward revolution, therefore, must go together. The revolution must be lived in personal and interpersonal relations, as well as struggled for in social, economic and political structures.

This is why we choose to live in the kind of community that we do. Realizing inherent dangers of a life style that would "retreat to the woods" or deal only with personal growth, the Philadelphia Life Center of the Movement for a New Society puts a great deal of effort into combining simple living, personal growth, and responsible relationships, with political and economic activism. That is, we see ourselves living in an evolving model for what we hope the new society might be.

It is our hope that in reading about the model, the readers of this book will think about ways that this and other communities may improve and flourish, new support systems might form and we might find new and better ways of living the revolution.

We do not offer the Life Center as *the* model of how to live the revolution, but one model which we hope people will seriously consider, evaluate, modify, and improve upon. We focus on the Life Center because it represents our most immediate experience.

We realize that what we write is limited by our own experience and background. At this writing, the Life Center is only four years old and we are mostly middle class, white, college-educated people with experiences in

the peace and civil rights movements. Because of these
limitations, we have found it necessary and valuable to be
in dialogue with persons who are starting from other
places and who experience limitations of their own. It is
out of this experience and dialogue that we share our
insights in the belief that anyone seriously committed to
changing our sick society must consider changes in
personal life-style and interpersonal relations so that they
can "live the revolution" in the present society.

THE PHILADELPHIA LIFE CENTER
OF THE
MOVEMENT FOR A NEW SOCIETY

The Philadelphia Life Center is a multi-generational
support community for persons involved in fundamental
social change training and activity. Beginning in 1971 as a
group of about 35 persons, the Life Center has grown to
about 125 persons living in seventeen houses located in
West Philadelphia and all within easy walking distance
of each other. We tie in with a network of other
communities, work collectives, and training centers across
the United States and in other parts of the world. The
U.S. part of the network is called *Movement for a New
Society*.

Our community is enriched by the participation of
activists from other countries. Japan, New Zealand,
England, West Germany, Australia, India, Norway,
France, have been some of the places from which Life
Center participants have come. Usually the activists return to their own countries and provide living links to
international movements. The travel is facilitated by the
MNS Exchange Committee and contacts are maintained
by the Committee of Correspondence, both located at
the Life Center.

SOME ASPECTS OF THE PHILADELPHIA LIFE CENTER/MNS

Households. The living arrangements are by households, autonomous units of 6-10 people with diverse

interests and collective commitments. Houses are responsible for their own management and policies and are tied together only by an informal information network and support system.

Alternative Institutions. We have limited experience in alternative institutions here at the LC/MNS. However, one institution which we use a great deal and have put a lot of thought into its operation is the Community Associates, the print shop which printed this book. A five person collective, CA does commercial printing as well as the publishing of social change manuals, brochures, and books.

A food co-op has been in existance for about 3½ years. LC members as well as people in the neighborhood can order produce and dry goods at more reasonable rates than is possible in stores.

Collectives. The Collectives are the working groups of the MNS. In Philadelphia we have 13 collectives working on a variety of concerns. Each collective, while in constant communication with other work groups in the network, is responsible for its own life and concerns. A collective will usually meet at least once a week to make decisions, develop strategy, discuss work to be done, and do personal sharing of what is happening with each of the members of the group.

The collectives in the Philadelphia area meet together regularly in a Regional MNS meeting where ideas and projects are discussed. It is here that support as well as questioning can take place. Philadelphia MNS collectives are:

Outreach Collective - takes responsibility for putting people in touch with each other in various parts of the country, and for distributing literature. 4722 Baltimore Ave., Philadelphia, PA 19143

Feminist Collective - a collective of women who are working to clarify the role that sexism has in creating and perpetrating oppressions of many kinds. 4811 Springfield Ave., Philadelphia, PA 19143

Training/Action Affinity Group - a nonviolence training team who work in conflict resolution, educational processes, direct action training as well as other kinds of social change empowerment. 4811 Springfield Ave., Philadelphia, PA 19143

Churchmouse Collective - a group that directs its energies toward issues of global justice that challenge the church. One focus has been Simple Living. 4719 Cedar, Philadelphia, PA 19143

Orientation Week-End Coordinating Committee - The first full week end of every month is a time for visiting the Life Center and getting an abreviated view of training here. OWCC coordinates. 4722 Baltimore, Philadelphia, PA 19143

Fatted Sprout - An alternative food service to provide inexpensive, nutritious, and interesting food for groups in the city. 803 S. 49th, Philadelphia, PA 19143

Philadelphia Namibia Action Group - Part of an international campaign to end oppression in South Africa dominated Namibia. 4811 Springfield Ave., Philadelphia, PA 19143

Community Associates - a printing enterprise that does low cost printing for MNS as well as other groups. 4722 Baltimore Ave., Philadelphia, PA 19143

Philadelphia Macro-Analysis Collective - One of the Macro collectives that researches materials, serves as a resource for groups interested in Macro-Analysis seminars. 4719 Cedar, Philadelphia, PA 19143

Medium Term Organizing Collective - Coordinator for the short term training for organizers held at the Life Center. 4722 Baltimore Ave., Philadelphia, PA 19143

B-1 Bomber Peace Conversion Collective - Organizers of the "Fair Shake Festival" to raise consciousness about the government's spending of tax dollars. Compiles information and serves as resource to

groups questioning military/industrial appropria-
tions. 4719 Springfield Ave., Philadelphia, PA
19143

Committee of Correspondence - A group that continues
communications with individuals and groups in
other countries that have MNS related concerns.
4722 Baltimore Ave., Philadelphia, PA 19143

Training Organizing Collective - coordinators of the
two-year training program. 4713 Windsor Ave.,
Philadelphia, PA 19143

Other groups and individuals in the MNS network
develop their own styles and tasks, yet are committed as
we are to nonviolent revolution. In Seattle, people are
struggling against the institutions of sexism (contact
Bruce Kokopeli, 811 33rd Ave. E., Seattle 98112). At the
Eugene, Oregon, Life Center, emphasis is on tax resistance
and opposition to nuclear power (1059 Hilyard St.,
Eugene, OR 97401). A San Francisco Life Center is
under way, evolving a new model (contact Jan and Dave
Hartsough, 723 Shrader St., San Francisco, CA 94117).

A group exploring social change in the rural Southwest is the San Juan Collective (P.O. Drawer 1429,
Durango, CO 81301). In DeKalb, a group encourages the
growth of macro-analysis seminars (c/o DeKalb Learning
Exchange, 157½ E. Lincoln Highway, DeKalb, IL
60115).

In several parts of the country there are regional
associations of MNS groups which get together for celebration and growth. To find out what the various MNS
groups are doing, people subscribe to the MNS newsletter
Dandelion, which appears about four times a year.

To get the *Dandelion* or find the nearest MNS group
in your area, write to the Outreach Collective, 4722
Baltimore Ave., Philadelphia, PA 19143

Training. By training, we mean preparing people for
long term social change organizing and struggle. We have

found it is important for social change people to have skills ranging from group dynamics to planning for and doing direct action.

There is a two-year program for social change organizers which is located in Philadelphia. Evolving out of a need to understand how we can systematically approach the developing of organizers and provide the support and challenging needed, the Philadelphia Training Program began in 1973 and is now working with its third group.

Another mode of training is the Medium Term Training Program, coordinated by the Medium Term Training Collective. This program is set up for persons living outside the Philadelphia area who come for a three day, one week, or two week training session. General skills shared are group dynamics, strategy skills, street speaking, direct action and campaign planning, conflict resolution, and others that the group defines.

Orientation week-ends provide an opportunity for people to visit the Life Center and have a somewhat abreviated look at how training takes place. Included are short information sessions on the Life Center/MNS, a Macro-Analysis seminar, a nonviolence training session which provides an opportunity for the group to examine how we can learn to deal with personal as well as societal violence.

Other training takes place as collectives and individuals feel a need to get or share skills or insights. Much training also takes place in an informal manner as we develop new ways of interrelating and working.

Action. An important part of training/organizing is nonviolent direct action. From the beginning of PLC/MNS we have been training people for action. United Farmworkers demonstrations, Assembly to Save the Peace Agreement, and B-1 Bomber rallies are just some examples of actions that have been participated in or organized out of the community. Increasingly, Life Center folks have been working in our neighborhood and finding the need for local action such as a candlelight walk by neighbors through the surrounding area to show community solidarity and fight fear after a brutal crime in the neighborhood.

Connections to Other Groups. Many LC/MNS folks either work with other social change groups or have strong connections with them. We feel it is important to not only be in communication with but in an active process of learning from other people. Groups such as Wages for Housework (602 S. 48th St., Philadelphia, PA 19143) whose focus is the raising of consciousness about the exploitation of women's labor, provide constant input into our thinking about the effect of sex roles on our society. Other important relationships for our developing strategy are Children and Nonviolence (of the Friends Peace Committee), National Coalition for Social Change, American Friends Service Committee, War Tax Resistance, Friends Peace Committee, War Resister's League, and others.

Manuals. The last way that we will mention in which we hope to share our model is the growing body of writing available. Aritcles, pamphlets, and manuals are playing an important role in helping others to think about possible alternatives for themselves.

Most of the manuals, kind of "do-it-yourself" pieces, are available from the Outreach Collective of the MNS.

Macro-Analysis Manual - a complete listing of readings and description of processes and exercises for the 22 week group self-education course. Macro is designed to help pull together the many aspects of social concern, economics, military, environmental concerns, third world relationships, into one "big picture". ($1.00 plus 18¢ postage)

A Manual for a Living Revolution or the "Monster Manual" - A manual for organizers which includes tools of analysis, vision, strategy. There is also much about the role of trainer and many helpful suggestions about how to develop workshops suited to the needs of groups. (available soon)

How to Work Collectively Manual - A manual describing the workings of one collective and processes that they developed in order to function more effectively and humanly. (Pamela Haines, 254 S. Farragut, Philadelphia, PA 19143)

In process is a Direct Action Manual which will spell out step-by-step the components of a direct action campaign. Covers strategy design, dealing with press, police, and how to develop a collective working spirit that will sustain the campaign.

SOME COMMON ASSUMPTIONS

Within the Life Center/MNS there is a great diversity of interests, styles, and foci. Because the houses and work collectives all are autonomous there is an exciting and sometimes confusing variety of approaches to dealing with the problems and joys of everyday life. But we all share common assumptions and beliefs which allow and enhance the freedoms which exist and serve as guidelines for our growth.

Simplicity. Members of the PLC for the most part work only part time at income producing employment, so as to leave larger blocks of time for social change work. Freed from the 9 to 5 treadmill and from the trap of "working your way up the ladder" in jobs, community members can then consider their social change work their primary focus.

Simplification is aided by buying inexpensive clothing, getting food through our own co-op and garden, more efficient use of bicycles and public transportation whenever possible for travel, repairing our own homes, and sharing of household furniture and appliances.

Involved in the simplification of life style is a healthy respect for the needs of the individuals. Most community members have a room of their own and people learn that privacy is something that is easily attained in a sensitive household.

Skill Sharing. Since it is our vision that in the new

society we will have much less of the compartmentalizing of knowledge and skills that is so pervasive now, we act out our vision by skill sharing as much as possible. Everyone learns to plan and prepare meals, and in most houses to bake bread. Men learn the skills of household cleaning as well as women. Women of the community more and more are learning home repair.

The skills of working with groups, of public speaking, of folk dancing, of community organizing are shared also. No more, an elitist society of super-charged specialists who lay claim to a body of knowledge that is unavailable to many capable other people!

Anti-Sexism. It is imperative in a society that is built upon the power and economically motivated tracking into sex roles that we must break this pattern in our daily lives. Women are strong, competent, and intelligent human beings. Men are gentle, feeling, affectionate, and playful. We all have all of those traits usually only attributed to the other sex. By giving each other emotional support as well as challenging sexist behavior we can grow to be more full human beings.

Elimination of sexist language is one small step in consciousness raising. Awareness of use of power in relationships is a critical step in the advancement toward a non-sexist society.

Children raised in the environment of a community in which men and women share equal work and responsibility and who are sensitive to needed changes in ways men and women perceive themselves, are growing up with a broader, freer vision of what it is to be a man or a woman.

Sexism is by no means eliminated in our community. Years of societal training have ingrained many destructive subleties in all of us, but we are seeing the results of confrontation and challenging as well as loving support.

Egalitarianism. In the Life Center, we see that all community members share equally in responsibility for the life of the community. No one is the "head of the group". No one decides for all.

This does not, however, mean that no one ever takes specific responsibility for anything. Quite the contrary. This was one of the hard lessons of the Life Center. Just saying "everyone is in charge" in reality often means "no one is in charge", and little gets accomplished. What needs to happen for an effecient egalitarian process to function is honest assessment of skills, talents, interests, then specific decisions, agreed upon by all concerned, about which persons will for a given *period of time* be responsible for a specific activity. This must be evaluated and carefully examined at intervals to see what adjustments or changes need to be made.

Cooperation and Non-Competition. In a community working at egalitarian processes, one of the most important elements is that of cooperation. Our society teaches us to compete, to be best, to win out over someone else. It is our hope at the Life Center that eventually this will disappear in our culture and we will see only cooperation and encouragement and we build that hope into our style of living.

"What can we do to help?" is a common question. Often the help is in the form of encouragement, specific affirmation that acknowledges appreciation of a person or of their ideas. Sometimes it is the loan of a typewriter from one collective to another. A group of folks will just show up to help a household which is moving or doing repairs. Sometimes the help is in the form of feedback.

A common form of assistance is the use of "outside facilitators" for groups. A person who is not a member of the house (or collective) will come into a group for one or several sessions to facilitate discussions on difficult matters or to help with conflict resolution.

Affirmation. Support best comes about through recognizing all of those good things about people that exist in abundance. There is no such thing as too much affirmation. All of us need and thrive on real appreciation of ourselves.

We have learned that specific affirmative feedback is

a powerful social change catalyst. Weekly house meetings incorporate time for hearing good things that are happening and most groups provide time for each individual to hear those things about her/himself that others really appreciate.

In an atmosphere of trusting affirmation, people then feel good enough about themselves, their work, and the people around them that they can hear feedback on needed changes as well as to surface problems they are having so that work might begin on those problems.

Feelings. Feelings are important and it is our experience that any social change community dealing with the complexity of issues such as social justice, communal living, and responsible relationships must devise ways of helping folks to express their feelings in healthy ways. One method used in the LC/MNS is Re-evaluation counseling, a form of peer counseling which helps people sort out old hurts from current realities. By identifying those old experiences that have angered, frightened, or hurt us and working on them in a counseling context, we are more able to see each situation in a new fresh light.

Certainly not all of the members of LC/MNS are in co-counseling, but insights and practices of "RC" have permeated the thinking and processes of our groups. We have learned that it is important to affirm people's feelings, and to find appropriate outlets for negative feelings.

Querying. Groups and individuals seeking to make decisions, evaluating directions, or struggling with problems might ask for help in the form of clearness or querying. Other people can come together with them and raise questions that would open up new ways of thinking.

It is assumed also, that as loving individuals, we have the responsibility to raise questions at any time with members of the community.

Study. For the person truly interested in fundamental change, there is no substitute for careful thought and study. All of us must become involved in the most searching kind of study until we can begin to answer the basic questions of social change: "How do you analyze what's wrong with the present society? What's your vision of a better society? What is your strategy for moving toward that better society? What should we be doing right now?"

We have already mentioned the national movement of study/action groups called "Macro-Analysis Seminars". The seminars are designed to help people develop social change actions out of a deep understanding of how the U.S. political economy works and how it needs to be transformed. One of our first such seminars led directly into a nonviolent action campaign directed against U.S. military and economic support of the Pakistani dictatorship of Yahya Kahn. Using a "nonviolent fleet" of canoes and kayaks, we blockaded the ports of Boston, New York City, Philadelphia, and Baltimore against Pakistani ships, gaining the support of longshoremen who refused to load such ships. Because of the dramatic nature of these actions there was world-wide mass media coverage, giving us an opportunity to educate about an economic system which finds it necessary to give support to brutal dictatorships around the world.

Group Dynamics. We have been working for the last four years to develop processes for groups which allow for healthy discussion without exclusion, and maximize the creative energy of any collection of people. We use concensus for making decisions, believing that in order for people to put whole hearted effort into anything over a long period of time, they must feel themselves to be in a decision-making process where they are not going to be losers. Consensus is an exciting, egalitarian, method of working toward a commonly accepted decision that can be acted on by all, not just a majority.

Other processes, carefully examine how women and men participate in groups, how we deal with feelings, and how goals and visions can be agreed upon.

Celebration. Celebration for us means many things. It means the basic attitude and appreciation for life which we hope would move all of us to meet the

challenges of every new day. It means the festival atmosphere that surrounds holidays and calls us together as
family. Christmas finds thirty or so people in a neighborhood park singing and dancing while decorating a
"peoples" tree with homemade ornaments. Celebration
can mean one house having a New Year's party for the
children and adults on their block. It means the frequent
"get-togethers" for making music, playing soccer in the
park, or for making applesauce. There are people for
whom celebration means worship and the honoring of
religious holidays.

Celebration has meant the calling together of the
whole community when in deep sorrow over the loss of
two beautiful and vibrant members, and rejoicing that we
had known them.

It takes many forms, but basically it is affirming
that life brings joy and hope. It is saying "yes" to today
so that we can move to tomorrow with the assurance that
it deserves.

These are some of the elements that have been
important here in the political community that we call
our home. We are in a growing, changing, process. Much
needs to be improved. We look forward to the time when
our in-community communication is more efficient. We
are moving now to be more in touch with other social
change groups and their struggles. We are hoping to feel
more rooted in and responsible for the geographic area in
which we live. Our mistakes are part of our learning
process and careful evaluation of what we have done well,
not done well, or not done at all will yield more exciting
change.

The common assumptions and the basic elements
are only part of the story, however. The real sustaining
force of revolutionary change is the spirit and vitality of
those people involved in that change. Personal commitment, courage, love, discipline will be the backbone of
the reshaping of our society.

More and more in social change organizations and
networks throughout the United States and other countries, people are blossoming with new energy ahd hope.

People are coming alive with the realization that by engaging in thoughtful, courageous, and ongoing struggle, we *are* the revolution!

"Come alive, we are the revolution

Come alive, we are the revolution

And everything is coming

Yes everything is going all right.

We're gonna plant some seeds
We are the seeds

We need some sunshine
We are the sunshine . . .

We need some spirit
We are the spirit . . .

We need some changes
We are the changes . . .

We are the revolution!

---

[1] Edward Guinan, editor, *Peace and Nonviolence* (N.Y.: Paulist Press, 1973)